Mike Holt's

UNDERSTANDING THE
NATIONAL ELECTRICAL CODE®

WORKBOOK

[Articles 90 - 480]

BASED ON THE
2020 NEC®

Mike Holt Enterprises
MikeHolt.com • 888.NEC.CODE (632.2633)

NOTICE TO THE READER

Mike Holt's Understanding the National Electrical Code® Workbook (Articles 90-480), based on the 2020 NEC®
Second Printing: February 2022

Author: Mike Holt
Technical Illustrator: Mike Culbreath
Cover Design: Bryan Burch
Layout Design and Typesetting: Cathleen Kwas

COPYRIGHT © 2020 Charles Michael Holt
ISBN 978-1-950431-06-9

Produced and Printed in the USA

If you are an instructor and would like to request an examination copy of this or other Mike Holt Publications:

Call: 888.NEC.CODE (632.2633) • Fax: 352.360.0983

E-mail: Info@MikeHolt.com • Visit: www.MikeHolt.com/Instructors

You can download a sample PDF of all our publications by visiting www.MikeHolt.com/products.

I dedicate this book to the
Lord Jesus Christ, *my mentor and teacher.*
Proverbs 16:3

We Care...

Since the day I started my business over 40 years ago, my team and I have been working hard to produce products that get results and to help individuals learn how to be successful. I have built my business on the idea that customers come first and everyone on my team will do everything they possibly can to help you succeed. I want you to know that we value you, and are honored that you have chosen us to be your partner in training.

I believe that you are the future of this industry and that it is you who will make the difference in years to come. My goal is to share with you everything that I know and to encourage you to pursue your education on a continuous basis. I hope that not only will you learn theory, Code, calculations, or how to pass an exam, but that in the process, you will become the expert in the field and the person others know to trust.

We genuinely care about you and are dedicated to providing quality electrical training that will help you take your skills to the next level. Thanks for choosing us for electrical training.

God bless and much success,

TABLE OF CONTENTS

ABOUT THIS WORKBOOK

Mike Holt's Understanding the National Electrical Code® Workbook (Articles 90-480), based on the 2020 NEC®

The *National Electrical Code®* establishes the general requirements for safe electrical installations in Article 90 and Chapters 1 through 4 which apply to all installations, unless modified in Chapters 5 through 7 of the *Code*. The scope of Chapters 1 through 4 cover definitions and general requirements, wiring methods and materials, and equipment for general use. Rules for service and feeder calculations are also covered.

This workbook was designed to complement *Mike Holt's Illustrated Guide to Understanding the National Electrical Code, Volume 1*, textbook and contains over 1,500 *NEC®* practice questions that are in *Code* order. It also includes two final exams, one in straight order and one in random order, each with 100 questions. These questions will test your knowledge and comprehension of the *NEC*.

The Scope of This Workbook

The questions in this workbook are drawn from the *NEC*'s Article 90 (Introduction) and the general installation requirements contained in Articles 100 through 480 (Chapters 1 through 4). This program is based on solidly grounded alternating-current systems, 1,000V or less, using 90°C insulated copper conductors sized to 60°C rated terminals for 100A and less rated circuits, and 75°C rated terminals for over 100A rated circuits, unless indicated otherwise.

How to Use This Workbook

You will need to use the *2020 National Electrical Code* as a reference to ensure you answer questions correctly and to improve your ability to navigate the *Code* book. This workbook is meant to be a practice tool to test your knowledge and retention of the *NEC* rules. There is no "pass" or "fail," only practice, review, and learning.

If you find yourself unable to answer the questions, or if you are not familiar with the material being reviewed, we recommend that you get a copy of *Mike Holt's Illustrated Guide to Understanding the National Electrical Code, Volume 1, based on the 2020 NEC* textbook and its video program.

Visit www.MikeHolt.com/Code.

Technical Questions

As you progress through this workbook, you might find yourself feeling confused by the questions. Don't become frustrated, and don't get down on yourself. Remember, this is the *National Electrical Code*. Review the explanations and examples in *Mike's Understanding the National Electrical Code, Volume 1* textbook, or refer to the Code book. If you're still confused, visit www.MikeHolt.com/forum, and post your question on our free Code Forum. The forum is a moderated community of electrical professionals.

Workbook Corrections

We're committed to providing you with the finest product with the fewest errors and take great care to ensure our textbooks are correct. But we're realistic and know that errors might be found after printing.

If you believe that there's an error of any kind (typographical, grammatical, technical, etc.) in this textbook or in the Answer Key, send an e-mail that includes the textbook title, page number, and any other pertinent information to corrections@MikeHolt.com.

ADDITIONAL PRODUCTS TO HELP YOU LEARN

Understanding the National Electrical Code, based on the 2020 NEC®, Volume 1 and 2 textbooks

This product is a combination of Mike's best-selling illustrated textbooks in one great package. Mike's ability to clarify the meaning of the *Code* with his straightforward, concise writing style, along with his full-color detailed instructional graphics, is the reason that these books continue to grow in popularity. This bundle includes:

Understanding the NEC Volume 1 textbook [Articles 90–480]
Understanding the NEC Volume 2 textbook [Articles 500–820]

To order, visit www.MikeHolt.com/Code.

Electrical Calculations Video Library

Whether you're preparing for an exam, or already work in the field, it's essential to understand how to perform electrical calculations in accordance with the *NEC*. This program will teach you step-by-step how to properly set up and solve electrical calculations.

Electrical Exam Preparation textbook

▸ *Raceway and Box Calculations* videos
▸ *Conductor Sizing and Protection Calculations* videos
▸ *Motor, Air-Conditioning, and Transformer Calculations* videos
▸ *Voltage-Drop Calculations* videos
▸ *Dwelling Unit Calculations* videos
▸ *Multifamily Dwelling Calculations* videos
▸ *Commercial Calculations* videos

Understanding the *NEC* Complete Training Library

Do you want a comprehensive understanding of the *Code*? Then you need Mike's Understanding the *NEC* Complete Training Library. This program takes you step-by-step through the *NEC*, in *Code* order with detailed illustrations, great practice questions, and in-depth video analysis. This library is perfect for engineers, electricians, contractors, and electrical inspectors.

Understanding the National Electrical Code—Volume 1 textbook
Understanding the National Electrical Code—Volume 2 textbook
Bonding and Grounding textbook
Understanding the National Electrical Code (Articles 90–480) workbook

▸ *General Requirements* videos
▸ *Wiring and Protection* videos
▸ *Bonding and Grounding* videos
▸ *Wiring Methods and Materials* videos
▸ *Equipment for General Use* videos
▸ *Special Occupancies* videos
▸ *Special Equipment* videos
▸ *Special Conditions and Communications Systems* videos

To order, visit www.MikeHolt.com/Code.

To order visit www.MikeHolt.com/products or call 888.632.2633.

Mike Holt's Business Success Program

It's time to take your business skills to the next level. Whether you have recently passed an exam, recently opened a business or are just looking to understand the electrical business from a different vantage point, Mike's Business Success Program can help you in the following areas:

Estimating. You will understand estimating and make sure that all your jobs are profitable, with this step-by-step Estimating training program.

Business Management. Part Motivation, part Business Wisdom, this module will help you get where you want to go faster.

Leadership. This program distills Mike's knowledge of running a successful business for over 40 years into the primary building blocks of being a leader.

This program includes:

Leadership Skills textbook

Business Management workbook and videos

Estimating textbook and videos

Mike Holt's Life Skills Program

This program explores the core skills needed to build a successful life. As Mike shares the ups and downs of life while building a world-class business, he explores the key ideas and values that have allowed him to keep moving forward. In the process he has built a business that has endured for over 40 years, while also finding extreme success in sports. You will learn how Mike became a nationally recognized expert in his field, along with how he became a world-class athlete.

The workbook style questions will help you apply the lessons learned and also discover areas that you need to develop to improve your own professional and personal life. As you work through the content you will slowly build your own blueprint for the next steps needed and gain insight into what can help you get to the next level. Invest in yourself and this program to discover what areas may be holding you back and new ways to see success that can have a profound effect on how you approach your own life. This product includes:

Life Skills workbook

▸ *Life Skills* videos

▸ *Life Skills* MP3

Order your copy today and get started on your own custom plan. Visit www.MikeHolt.com/life.

To order visit www.MikeHolt.com/products or call 888.632.2633.

HOW TO USE THE *NATIONAL ELECTRICAL CODE*

The original *NEC* document was developed in 1897 as a result of the united efforts of various insurance, electrical, architectural, and other cooperative interests. The National Fire Protection Association (NFPA) has sponsored the *National Electrical Code* since 1911.

The purpose of the *Code* is the practical safeguarding of persons and property from hazards arising from the use of electricity. It isn't intended as a design specification or an instruction manual for untrained persons. It is, in fact, a standard that contains the minimum requirements for an electrical installation that's essentially free from hazard. Learning to understand and use the *Code* is critical to you working safely; whether you're training to become an electrician, or are already an electrician, electrical contractor, inspector, engineer, designer, or instructor.

The *NEC* was written for qualified persons; those who understand electrical terms, theory, safety procedures, and electrical trade practices. Learning to use the *Code* is a lengthy process and can be frustrating if you don't approach it the right way. First, you'll need to understand electrical theory and if you don't have theory as a background when you get into the *NEC*, you're going to struggle. Take one step back if necessary and learn electrical theory. You must also understand the concepts and terms in the *Code* and know grammar and punctuation in order to understand the complex structure of the rules and their intended purpose(s). The *NEC* is written in a formal outline which many of us haven't seen or used since high school or college so it's important for you to pay particular attention to this format. Our goal for the next few pages is to give you some guidelines and suggestions on using your *Code* book to help you understand that standard, and assist you in what you're trying to accomplish and, ultimately, your personal success as an electrical professional!

Language Considerations for the *NEC*

Terms and Concepts

The *NEC* contains many technical terms, and it's crucial for *Code* users to understand their meanings and applications. If you don't understand a term used in a rule, it will be impossible to properly apply the *NEC* requirement. Article 100 defines those that are used generally in two or more articles throughout the *Code*; for example, the term "Dwelling Unit" is found in many articles. If you don't know the *NEC* definition for a "dwelling unit" you can't properly identify its *Code* requirements. Another example worth mentioning is the term "Outlet." For many people it has always meant a receptacle—not so in the *NEC*!

Many *Code* articles use terms unique to that specific article, and the definitions of those terms only apply to that given article. Definitions for them are usually found in the beginning of the article. For example, Section 250.2 contains the definitions of terms that only apply to Article 250—Grounding and Bonding. Whether definitions are unique to a specific article, or apply throughout the *NEC*, is indicated at the beginning of the definitions (xxx.2) section of the article. For example,

Article 690 contains definitions (in 690.2) that apply ONLY to that article while Article 705 introduces definitions (in 705.2) that apply throughout the entire *Code*.

Small Words, Grammar, and Punctuation

Technical words aren't the only ones that require close attention. Even simple words can make a big difference to the application of a rule. Is there a comma? Does it use "or," "and," "other than," "greater than," or "smaller than"? The word "or" can imply alternate choices for wiring methods. A word like "or" gives us choices while the word "and" can mean an additional requirement must be met.

An example of the important role small words play in the *NEC* is found in 110.26(C)(2), where it says equipment containing overcurrent, switching, "or" control devices that are 1,200A or more "and" over 6 ft wide require a means of egress at each end of the working space. In this section, the word "or" clarifies that equipment containing any of the three types of devices listed must follow this rule. The word "and" clarifies that 110.26(C)(2) only applies if the equipment is both 1,200A or more and over 6 ft wide.

Grammar and punctuation play an important role in establishing the meaning of a rule. The location of a comma can dramatically change the requirement of a rule such as in 250.28(A), where it says a main bonding jumper shall be a wire, bus, screw, or similar suitable conductor. If the comma between "bus" and "screw" was removed, only a "bus screw" could be used. That comma makes a big change in the requirements of the rule.

Slang Terms or Technical Jargon

Trade-related professionals in different areas of the country often use local "slang" terms that aren't shared by all. This can make it difficult to communicate if it isn't clear what the meaning of those slang terms are. Use the proper terms by finding out what their definitions and applications are before you use them. For example, the term "pigtail" is often used to describe the short piece of conductor used to connect a device to a splice, but a "pigtail" is also used for a rubberized light socket with pre-terminated conductors. Although the term is the same, the meaning is very different and could cause confusion. The words "splice" and "tap" are examples of terms often interchanged in the field but are two entirely different things! The uniformity and consistency of the terminology used in the *Code*, makes it so everyone says and means the same thing regardless of geographical location.

NEC Style and Layout

It's important to understand the structure and writing style of the *Code* if you want to use it effectively. The *National Electrical Code* is organized using twelve major components.

1. Table of Contents
2. Chapters—Chapters 1 through 9 (major categories)
3. Articles—Chapter subdivisions that cover specific subjects
4. Parts—Divisions used to organize article subject matter
5. Sections—Divisions used to further organize article subject matter
6. Tables and Figures—Represent the mandatory requirements of a rule
7. Exceptions—Alternatives to the main *Code* rule
8. Informational Notes—Explanatory material for a specific rule (not a requirement)
9. Tables—Applicable as referenced in the *NEC*
10. Annexes—Additional explanatory information such as tables and references (not a requirement)
11. Index
12. Changes to the *Code* from the previous edition

1. Table of Contents. The Table of Contents displays the layout of the chapters, articles, and parts as well as the page numbers. It's an excellent resource and should be referred to periodically to observe the interrelationship of the various *NEC* components. When attempting to locate the rules for a specific situation, knowledgeable *Code* users often go first to the Table of Contents to quickly find the specific *NEC* rule that applies.

2. Chapters. There are nine chapters, each of which is divided into articles. The articles fall into one of four groupings: General Requirements (Chapters 1 through 4), Specific Requirements (Chapters 5 through 7), Communications Systems (Chapter 8), and Tables (Chapter 9).

Chapter 1—General
Chapter 2—Wiring and Protection
Chapter 3—Wiring Methods and Materials
Chapter 4—Equipment for General Use
Chapter 5—Special Occupancies
Chapter 6—Special Equipment
Chapter 7—Special Conditions
Chapter 8—Communications Systems (Telephone, Data, Satellite, Cable TV, and Broadband)
Chapter 9—Tables–Conductor and Raceway Specifications

3. Articles. The *NEC* contains approximately 140 articles, each of which covers a specific subject. It begins with Article 90, the introduction to the *Code* which contains the purpose of the *NEC*, what is covered and isn't covered, along with how the *Code* is arranged. It also gives information on enforcement, how mandatory and permissive rules are written, and how explanatory material is included. Article 90 also includes information on formal interpretations, examination of equipment for safety, wiring planning, and information about formatting units of measurement. Here are some other examples of articles you'll find in the *NEC*:

Article 110—Requirements for Electrical Installations
Article 250—Grounding and Bonding
Article 300—General Requirements for Wiring Methods and Materials
Article 430—Motors, Motor Circuits, and Motor Controllers
Article 500—Hazardous (Classified) Locations
Article 680—Swimming Pools, Fountains, and Similar Installations
Article 725—Remote-Control, Signaling, and Power-Limited Circuits
Article 800—General Requirements for Communications Systems

4. Parts. Larger articles are subdivided into parts. Because the parts of a *Code* article aren't included in the section numbers, we tend to forget to what "part" an *NEC* rule is relating. For example, Table 110.34(A) contains working space clearances for electrical equipment. If we aren't careful, we might think this table applies to all electrical installations, but Table 110.34(A) is in Part III, which only contains requirements for "Over 1,000 Volts, Nominal" installations. The rules for working clearances for electrical equipment for systems 1,000V, nominal, or less are contained in Table 110.26(A)(1), which is in Part II—1,000 Volts, Nominal, or Less.

5. Sections. Each *NEC* rule is called a "*Code* Section." A *Code* section may be broken down into subdivisions; first level subdivision will be in parentheses like (A), (B),..., the next will be second level subdivisions in parentheses like (1), (2),..., and third level subdivisions in lowercase letters such as (a), (b), and so on.

For example, the rule requiring all receptacles in a dwelling unit bathroom to be GFCI protected is contained in Section 210.8(A)(1) which is in Chapter 2, Article 210, Section 8, first level subdivision (A), and second level subdivision (1).

Note: According to the *NEC Style Manual*, first and second level subdivisions are required to have titles. A title for a third level subdivision is permitted but not required.

Many in the industry incorrectly use the term "Article" when referring to a *Code* section. For example, they say "Article 210.8," when they should say "Section 210.8." Section numbers in this workbook are shown without the word "Section," unless they're at the beginning of a sentence. For example, Section 210.8(A) is shown as simply 210.8(A).

6. Tables and Figures. Many *NEC* requirements are contained within tables, which are lists of *Code* rules placed in a systematic arrangement. The titles of the tables are extremely important; you must read them carefully in order to understand the contents, applications, and limitations of each one. Notes are often provided in or below a table; be sure to read them as well since they're also part of the requirement. For example, Note 1 for Table 300.5 explains how to measure the cover when burying cables and raceways and Note 5 explains what to do if solid rock is encountered.

7. Exceptions. Exceptions are *NEC* requirements or permissions that provide an alternative method to a specific rule. There are two types of exceptions—mandatory and permissive. When a rule has several exceptions, those exceptions with mandatory requirements are listed before the permissive exceptions.

Mandatory Exceptions. A mandatory exception uses the words "shall" or "shall not." The word "shall" in an exception means that if you're using the exception, you're required to do it in a specific way. The phrase "shall not" means it isn't permitted.

Permissive Exceptions. A permissive exception uses words such as "shall be permitted," which means it's acceptable (but not mandatory) to do it in this way.

8. Informational Notes. An Informational Note contains explanatory material intended to clarify a rule or give assistance, but it isn't a *Code* requirement.

9. Tables. Chapter 9 consists of tables applicable as referenced in the *NEC*. They're used to calculate raceway sizing, conductor fill, the radius of raceway bends, and conductor voltage drop.

10. Informative Annexes. Annexes aren't a part of the *Code* requirements and are included for informational purposes only.

Annex A. Product Safety Standards
Annex B. Application Information for Ampacity Calculation
Annex C. Raceway Fill Tables for Conductors and Fixture Wires of the Same Size
Annex D. Examples
Annex E. Types of Construction
Annex F. Critical Operations Power Systems (COPS)
Annex G. Supervisory Control and Data Acquisition (SCADA)
Annex H. Administration and Enforcement
Annex I. Recommended Tightening Torques
Annex J. ADA Standards for Accessible Design

11. Index. The Index at the back of the *NEC* is helpful in locating a specific rule using pertinent keywords to assist in your search.

12. Changes to the *Code*. Changes in the *NEC* are indicated as follows:

▸ Rules that were changed since the previous edition are identified by shading the revised text.

▸ New rules aren't shaded like a change, instead they have a shaded "N" in the margin to the left of the section number.

▸ Relocated rules are treated like new rules with a shaded "N" in the left margin by the section number.

▸ Deleted rules are indicated by a bullet symbol " • " located in the left margin where the rule was in the previous edition. Unlike older editions the bullet symbol is only used where one or more complete paragraphs have been deleted. There's no indication used where a word, group of words, or a sentence was deleted.

▸ A △ represents text deletions and figure/table revisions.

How to Locate a Specific Requirement

How to go about finding what you're looking for in the *Code* book depends, to some degree, on your experience with the *NEC*. Experts typically know the requirements so well that they just go to the correct rule. Very experienced people might only need the Table of Contents to locate the requirement for which they're looking. On the other hand, average users should use all the tools at their disposal, including the Table of Contents, the Index, and the search feature on electronic versions of the *Code* book.

Let's work through a simple example: What *NEC* rule specifies the maximum number of disconnects permitted for a service?

Using the Table of Contents. If you're an experienced *Code* user, you might use the Table of Contents. You'll know Article 230 applies to "Services," and because this article is so large, it's divided up into multiple parts (eight parts to be exact). With this knowledge, you can quickly go to the Table of Contents and see it lists the Service Equipment Disconnecting Means requirements in Part VI.

> **Author's Comment:**
>
> ▸ The number "70" precedes all page numbers in this standard because the *NEC* is NFPA Standard Number 70.

Using the Index. If you use the Index (which lists subjects in alphabetical order) to look up the term "service disconnect," you'll see there's no listing. If you try "disconnecting means," then "services," you'll find that the Index indicates the rule is in Article 230, Part VI. Because the *NEC* doesn't give a page number in the Index, you'll need to use the Table of Contents to find it, or flip through the *Code* book to Article 230, then continue to flip through pages until you find Part VI.

Many people complain that the *NEC* only confuses them by taking them in circles. Once you gain experience in using the *Code* and deepen your understanding of words, terms, principles, and practices, you'll find it much easier to understand and use than you originally thought.

With enough exposure in the use of the *NEC*, you'll discover that some words and terms are often specific to certain articles. The word "solar" for example will immediately send experienced *Code* book users to Article 690—Solar Photovoltaic (PV) Systems. The word "marina" suggests what you seek might be in Article 555. There are times when a main article will send you to a specific requirement in another one in which compliance is required in which case it will say (for example), "in accordance with 230.xx." Don't think of these situations as a "circle," but rather a map directing you to exactly where you need to be.

Customizing Your *Code* Book

One way to increase your comfort level with your *Code* book is to customize it to meet your needs. You can do this by highlighting and underlining important *NEC* requirements. Preprinted adhesive tabs are also an excellent aid to quickly find important articles and sections that are regularly referenced. However, understand that if you're using your *Code* book to prepare to take an exam, some exam centers don't allow markings of any type. For more information about tabs for your *Code* book, visit www.MikeHolt.com/tabs.

Highlighting. As you read through or find answers to your questions, be sure you highlight those requirements in the *NEC* that are the most important or relevant to you. Use one color, like yellow, for general interest and a different one for important requirements you want to find quickly. Be sure to highlight terms in the Index and the Table of Contents as you use them.

Underlining. Underline or circle key words and phrases in the *Code* with a red or blue pen (not a lead pencil) using a short ruler or other straightedge to keep lines straight and neat. This is a very handy way to make important requirements stand out. A short ruler or other straightedge also comes in handy for locating the correct information in a table.

Interpretations

Industry professionals often enjoy the challenge of discussing, and at times debating, the *Code* requirements. These types of discussions are important to the process of better understanding the *NEC* requirements and applications. However, if you decide you're going to participate in one of these discussions, don't spout out what you think without having the actual *Code* book in your hand. The professional way of discussing a requirement is by referring to a specific section rather than talking in vague generalities. This will help everyone involved clearly understand the point and become better educated. In fact, you may become so well educated about the *NEC* that you might even decide to participate in the change process and help to make it even better!

Become Involved in the *NEC* Process

The actual process of changing the *Code* takes about two years and involves hundreds of individuals trying to make the *NEC* as current and accurate as possible. As you advance in your studies and understanding of the *Code*, you might begin to find it very interesting, enjoy it more, and realize that you can also be a part of the process. Rather than sitting back and allowing others to take the lead, you can participate by making proposals and being a part of its development. For the 2020 cycle, there were 3,730 Public Inputs and 1,930 comments. Hundreds of updates and five new articles were added to keep the *NEC* up to date with new technologies and pave the way to a safer and more efficient electrical future.

Here's how the process works:

STEP 1—Public Input Stage

Public Input. The revision cycle begins with the acceptance of Public Input (PI) which is the public notice asking for anyone interested to submit input on an existing standard or a committee-approved new draft standard. Following the closing date, the committee conducts a First Draft Meeting to respond to all Public Inputs.

First Draft Meeting. At the First Draft (FD) Meeting, the Technical Committee considers and provides a response to all Public Input. The Technical Committee may use the input to develop First Revisions to the standard. The First Draft documents consist of the initial meeting consensus of the committee by simple majority. However, the final position of the Technical Committee must be established by a ballot which follows.

Committee Ballot on First Draft. The First Draft developed at the First Draft Meeting is balloted. In order to appear in the First Draft, a revision must be approved by at least two-thirds of the Technical Committee.

First Draft Report Posted. First revisions which pass ballot are ultimately compiled and published as the First Draft Report on the document's NFPA web page. This report serves as documentation for the Input Stage and is published for review and comment. The public may review the First Draft Report to determine whether to submit Public Comments on the First Draft.

STEP 2—Public Comment Stage

Public Comment. Once the First Draft Report becomes available, there's a Public Comment period during which anyone can submit a Public Comment on the First Draft. After the Public Comment closing date, the Technical Committee conducts/holds their Second Draft Meeting.

Second Draft Meeting. After the Public Comment closing date, if Public Comments are received or the committee has additional proposed revisions, a Second Draft Meeting is held. At the Second Draft Meeting, the Technical Committee reviews the First Draft and may make additional revisions to the draft Standard. All Public Comments are considered, and the Technical Committee provides an action and response to each Public Comment. These actions result in the Second Draft.

Committee Ballot on Second Draft. The Second Revisions developed at the Second Draft Meeting are balloted. To appear in the Second Draft, a revision must be approved by at least two-thirds of the Technical Committee.

Second Draft Report Posted. Second Revisions which pass ballot are ultimately compiled and published as the Second Draft Report on the document's NFPA website. This report serves as documentation of the Comment Stage and is published for public review.

Once published, the public can review the Second Draft Report to decide whether to submit a Notice of Intent to Make a Motion (NITMAM) for further consideration.

STEP 3—NFPA Technical Meeting (Tech Session)

Following completion of the Public Input and Public Comment stages, there's further opportunity for debate and discussion of issues through the NFPA Technical Meeting that takes place at the NFPA Conference & Expo®. These motions are attempts to change the resulting final Standard from the committee's recommendations published as the Second Draft.

STEP 4—Council Appeals and Issuance of Standard

Issuance of Standards. When the Standards Council convenes to issue an NFPA standard, it also hears any related appeals. Appeals are an important part of assuring that all NFPA rules have been followed and that due process and fairness have continued throughout the standards development process. The Standards Council considers appeals based on the written record and by conducting live hearings during which all interested parties can participate. Appeals are decided on the entire record of the process, as well as all submissions and statements presented.

After deciding all appeals related to a standard, the Standards Council, if appropriate, proceeds to issue the Standard as an official NFPA Standard. The decision of the Standards Council is final subject only to limited review by the NFPA Board of Directors. The new NFPA standard becomes effective twenty days following the Standards Council's action of issuance.

Temporary Interim Amendment—(TIA)

Sometimes, a change to the *NEC* is of an emergency nature. Perhaps an editing mistake was made that can affect an electrical installation to the extent it may create a hazard. Maybe an occurrence in the field created a condition that needs to be addressed immediately and can't wait for the normal *Code* cycle and next edition of the standard. When these circumstances warrant it, a TIA or "Temporary Interim Amendment" can be submitted for consideration.

The NFPA defines a TIA as, "tentative because it has not been processed through the entire standards-making procedures. It is interim because it is effective only between editions of the standard. A TIA automatically becomes a Public Input of the proponent for the next edition of the standard; as such, it then is subject to all of the procedures of the standards-making process."

Author's Comment:

▶ Proposals, comments, and TIAs can be submitted for consideration online at the NFPA website, www.nfpa.org. From the homepage, look for "Codes & Standards," then find "Standards Development," and click on "How the Process Works." If you'd like to see something changed in the *Code*, you're encouraged to participate in the process.

ARTICLE 90

INTRODUCTION TO THE *NATIONAL ELECTRICAL CODE*

Introduction to Article 90—Introduction to the *National Electrical Code*

Article 90 opens by saying the *National Electrical Code (NEC/Code)* is not intended as a design specification or instruction manual. It has one purpose only, and that is the "practical safeguarding of persons and property from hazards arising from the use of electricity." That does not necessarily mean the installation will be efficient, convenient, or able to accommodate future expansion; just safe. The necessity of carefully studying the *Code* rules cannot be overemphasized. Understanding where to find the requirements in the *NEC* that apply to the installation is invaluable. Rules in several different articles often apply to even a simple installation. Article 90 then goes on to describe the scope and arrangement of the *NEC*. The balance of it provides the reader with information essential to understanding the *Code* rules.

You are not going to remember every section of every article of the *Code* but, hopefully, you will come away with knowing where to look after studying Mike Holt's Understanding the *National Electrical Code, Volume 1* textbook, and practicing with this workbook.

 Please use the 2020 *Code* book to answer the following questions.

1. The *NEC* is _____.

   (a) intended to be a design manual
   (b) meant to be used as an instruction guide for untrained persons
   (c) for the practical safeguarding of persons and property
   (d) published by the Bureau of Standards

2. Compliance with the *Code* and proper maintenance result in an installation that is _____.

   (a) essentially free from hazards
   (b) not necessarily efficient or convenient
   (c) not necessarily adequate for good service or future expansion
   (d) all of these

3. Compliance with the provisions of the *NEC* will result in _____.

   (a) good electrical service
   (b) an efficient electrical system
   (c) an electrical system essentially free from hazard
   (d) all of these

4. The *Code* contains provisions considered necessary for safety, which will not necessarily result in _____.

   (a) efficient use
   (b) convenience
   (c) good service or future expansion of electrical use
   (d) all of these

5. Electrical hazards often occur because the initial _____ did not provide for increases in the use of electricity and therefore wiring systems become overloaded.

    (a) inspection
    (b) owner
    (c) wiring
    (d) builder

6. Hazards often occur because of _____.

    (a) overloading of wiring systems by methods or usage not in conformity with the *NEC*
    (b) initial wiring not providing for increases in the use of electricity
    (c) manufacturing defects
    (d) overloading of wiring systems by methods or usage not in conformity with the *NEC* and initial wiring not providing for increases in the use of electricity

7. Which of the following systems shall be installed and removed in accordance with the *NEC* requirements?

    (a) Signaling conductors, equipment, and raceways
    (b) Communications conductors, equipment, and raceways
    (c) Electrical conductors, equipment, and raceways
    (d) all of these

8. The *NEC* applies to the installation of _____.

    (a) electrical conductors and equipment within or on public and private buildings
    (b) signaling and communication conductors
    (c) optical fiber cables
    (d) all of these

9. This *Code* covers the installation of _____ for public and private premises, including buildings, structures, mobile homes, recreational vehicles, and floating buildings.

    (a) optical fiber cables
    (b) electrical equipment
    (c) raceways
    (d) all of these

10. Installations supplying _____ power to ships and watercraft in marinas and boatyards are covered by the *NEC*.

    (a) shore
    (b) primary
    (c) secondary
    (d) auxiliary

11. Installations used to export electric power from vehicles to premises wiring or for _____ current flow are covered by the *NEC*.

    (a) emergency
    (b) primary
    (c) bidirectional
    (d) secondary

12. The *NEC* does apply to installations in _____.

    (a) floating buildings
    (b) mobile homes
    (c) recreational vehicles
    (d) all of these

13. The *NEC* does not cover electrical installations in ships, watercraft, railway rolling stock, aircraft, or automotive vehicles.

    (a) True
    (b) False

14. The *Code* covers underground mine installations and self-propelled mobile surface mining machinery and its attendant electrical trailing cable.

    (a) True
    (b) False

15. The *Code* does not cover installations under the exclusive control of an electrical utility such as _____.

    (a) service drops and laterals
    (b) electric utility office buildings
    (c) electric utility warehouses
    (d) electric utility garages

16. Installations of communications equipment that are under the exclusive control of communications utilities and located outdoors or in building spaces used exclusively for such installations _____ covered by the *NEC*.

    (a) are
    (b) are sometimes
    (c) are not
    (d) may be

17. Chapters 1 through 4 of the *NEC* apply _____.

    (a) generally to all electrical installations
    (b) only to special occupancies and conditions
    (c) only to special equipment and material
    (d) all of these

18. Chapters 5, 6, and 7 apply to special occupancies, special equipment, or other special conditions and may supplement or modify the requirements in Chapters 1 through 7.

    (a) True
    (b) False

19. Chapters 5, 6, and 7 of the *NEC* apply to _____.

    (a) special occupancies
    (b) special equipment
    (c) special conditions
    (d) all of these

20. Communications wiring such as telephone, antenna, and CATV wiring within a building shall not be required to comply with the installation requirements of Chapters 1 through 7, except where specifically referenced in Chapter 8.

    (a) True
    (b) False

21. Installations shall comply with the material located in the *NEC* Annexes because they are part of the requirements of the *Code*.

    (a) True
    (b) False

22. The _____ has the responsibility for deciding on the approval of equipment and materials.

    (a) manufacturer
    (b) authority having jurisdiction
    (c) testing agency
    (d) the owner of the premises

23. The authority having jurisdiction has the responsibility for _____.

    (a) making interpretations of rules
    (b) deciding upon the approval of equipment and materials
    (c) waiving specific requirements in the *Code* and permitting alternate methods and material if safety is maintained
    (d) all of these

24. If the *NEC* requires new products that are not yet available at the time a new edition is adopted, the _____ may permit the use of the products that comply with the most recent previous edition of the *Code* adopted by that jurisdiction.

    (a) electrical engineer
    (b) master electrician
    (c) authority having jurisdiction
    (d) permit holder

25. In the *NEC*, the word(s) "_____" indicate a mandatory requirement.

    (a) shall
    (b) shall not
    (c) shall be permitted
    (d) shall or shall not

26. When the *Code* uses "_____," it means the identified actions are allowed but not required, and they may be options or alternative methods.

    (a) shall
    (b) shall not
    (c) shall be permitted
    (d) shall or shall not

27. Explanatory material, such as references to other standards, references to related sections of the *NEC*, or information related to a *Code* rule, are included in the form of Informational Notes.

    (a) True
    (b) False

28. Nonmandatory Informative Annexes contained in the back of the *Code* book are _____.

    (a) for information only
    (b) not enforceable as a requirement of the *Code*
    (c) enforceable as a requirement of the *Code*
    (d) for information only and not enforceable as a requirement of the *Code*

29. It is the intent of the *NEC* that factory-installed _____ wiring of listed equipment need not be inspected at the time of installation of the equipment, except to detect alterations or damage.

    (a) external
    (b) associated
    (c) internal
    (d) all of these

30. Factory-installed _____ wiring of listed equipment need not be inspected at the time of installation of the equipment, except to detect alterations or damage.

    (a) external
    (b) associated
    (c) internal
    (d) all of these

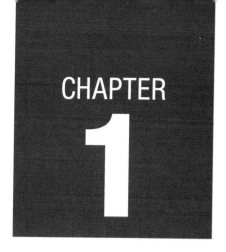

CHAPTER 1

GENERAL RULES

Introduction to Chapter 1—General Rules

Before you can make sense of the *NEC*, you must become familiar with its general rules, concepts, definitions, and requirements. Chapter 1 consists of two topics; Article 100 which provides definitions that help ensure consistency when *Code*-related matters are the topic of discussion, and Article 110 which supplies the general requirements needed to correctly apply the *NEC*.

After gaining an understanding of Chapter 1, some of the *Code* requirements that might be confusing to many, will become increasingly clear to you. *NEC* requirements will make more sense to you because you will have the foundation from which to build upon your understanding and application of the rules.

▶ **Article 100—Definitions.** Article 100 is organized into three parts. Part I contains the definitions of terms used throughout the *Code* for systems that operate at 1,000V, nominal, or less. The definitions of terms in Part II apply to systems that operate at over 1,000V, nominal, are not within the scope of Mike Holt books. Part III contains definitions applicable to "Hazardous (Classified) Locations" found in Chapter 5 of the *NEC*.

This article overall, only contains terms used in more than one article. Definitions of standard terms, such as volt, voltage drop, ampere, impedance, and resistance, are not contained in Article 100. If the *NEC* does not define a term, then a dictionary or building code acceptable to the authority having jurisdiction should be consulted.

Definitions are sometimes located at the beginning of an article. When this occurs, those terms only apply to that given article. There is uniformity in the location of the definitions specific to an article in that the article number will be followed by ".2." For example, definitions specific to solar photovoltaic (PV) systems are found in 690.2.

▶ **Article 110—Requirements for Electrical Installations.** This article contains general requirements applicable to all electrical installations.

ARTICLE
100 DEFINITIONS

Introduction to Article 100—Definitions

Have you ever had a conversation with someone only to discover that what you said and what he or she heard were completely different? This often happens when people have different definitions or interpretations of the words being used, and that is why the definitions of key *NEC* terms are located at the beginning of the *Code* (Article 100), or at the beginning of each article. If we can all agree on important definitions, then we speak the same language and avoid misunderstandings. Words taken out of context have created more than their fair share of problems. Because the *NEC* exists to protect people and property, it is very important for you to be able to convey and comprehend the language used. Review and study Article 100 until you are confident you know the definitions presented.

Please use the 2020 *Code* book to answer the following questions.

1. Article 100 contains definitions essential to the application of the *Code*. Definitions are also found in _____.

   (a) the index
   (b) the annex
   (c) XXX.2 of other articles
   (d) article scope(s)

2. Part III of Article 100 contains definitions which are applicable to _____.

   (a) Solar (PV) Systems
   (b) Hazardous (Classified) Locations
   (c) Electrical Systems Over 1,000V
   (d) Healthcare Facilities

3. Part I of Article 100 contains definitions intended to apply wherever the terms are used throughout this *Code*. Part III of Article100 contains definitions for _____.

   (a) Hazardous (Classified) Locations
   (b) Solar (PV) Systems
   (c) Communications Systems
   (d) Grounding and Bonding

4. Equipment that is capable of being reached for operation, renewal, and inspection defines _____.

   (a) accessible (as applied to equipment)
   (b) accessible (as applied to wiring methods)
   (c) accessible, readily
   (d) all of these

5. Capable of being reached quickly for operation, renewal, or inspections without resorting to portable ladders or the use of tools (other than keys) is known as "_____."

   (a) accessible (as applied to equipment)
   (b) accessible (as applied to wiring methods)
   (c) accessible, readily
   (d) all of these

6. An appliance is utilization equipment, generally other than industrial, that is normally built in standardized sizes or types and is installed or connected as a unit to perform one or more functions such as food mixing, deep frying.

   (a) True
   (b) False

7. The maximum current, in amperes, that a conductor can carry continuously under the conditions of use, where the temperature will not be raised in excess of the conductor's insulation temperature rating is called its "_____."

    (a) short-circuit rating
    (b) ground-fault rating
    (c) ampacity
    (d) all of these

8. "_____" means acceptable to the authority having jurisdiction.

    (a) Identified
    (b) Listed
    (c) Approved
    (d) Labeled

9. An arc-fault circuit interrupter is a device intended to de-energize the circuit when a(n) _____ is detected.

    (a) overcurrent condition
    (b) arc fault
    (c) ground fault
    (d) harmonic fundamental

10. A device that, when inserted in a receptacle, establishes a connection between the conductors of the attached flexible cord and the conductors connected permanently to the receptacle is called a(n) "_____."

    (a) attachment plug
    (b) plug cap
    (c) plug
    (d) any of these

11. A device that, by insertion into a locking support and mounting receptacle, establishes a connection between the conductors of the attached utilization equipment and the branch-circuit conductors connected to the locking support and mounting receptacle is otherwise known as a(an) _____.

    (a) Cord Cap Attachment
    (b) Attachment Fitting
    (c) End Cap Fitting
    (d) Attachment Plug

12. By definition, an attachment fitting is different from an attachment plug because no _____ is associated with the fitting.

    (a) cable
    (b) fixture wire
    (c) cord
    (d) wiring compartment

13. In many circumstances, the authority having jurisdiction can be a property owner or his/her designated agent.

    (a) True
    (b) False

14. According to the *Code*, "automatic" is performing a function without the necessity of _____.

    (a) protection from damage
    (b) human intervention
    (c) mechanical linkage
    (d) all of these

15. A "_____" is an area that includes a sink (basin) with a toilet, urinal, tub, shower, bidet, or similar plumbing fixtures.

    (a) bath area
    (b) bathroom
    (c) rest area
    (d) master suite

16. A battery system includes storage batteries and battery chargers, and can include inverters, converters, and associated electrical equipment.

    (a) True
    (b) False

17. "Bonded" is defined as _____ to establish electrical continuity and conductivity.

    (a) isolated
    (b) guarded
    (c) connected
    (d) separated

18. The connection between two or more portions of the equipment grounding conductor is the definition of a(n) _____.

    (a) system bonding jumper
    (b) main bonding jumper
    (c) equipment ground-fault jumper
    (d) equipment bonding jumper

19. The connection between the grounded circuit conductor and the equipment grounding conductor, or the supply-side bonding jumper, or both, at the service is the _____ bonding jumper.

    (a) main
    (b) system
    (c) equipment
    (d) circuit

20. A conductor installed on the supply side of a service or within a service equipment enclosure, or for a separately derived system, to ensure the required electrical conductivity between metal parts required to be electrically connected is known as the "_____."

    (a) supply-side bonding jumper
    (b) ungrounded conductor
    (c) electrical supply source
    (d) grounding electrode conductor

21. The connection between the grounded circuit conductor and the supply-side bonding jumper or equipment grounding conductor, or both, at a _____ is called a "system bonding jumper."

    (a) service disconnect
    (b) separately derived system
    (c) motor control center
    (d) separate building or structure disconnect

22. The circuit conductors between the final overcurrent device protecting the circuit and the outlet(s) are known as "_____ conductors."

    (a) feeder
    (b) branch-circuit
    (c) home run
    (d) main circuit

23. A branch circuit that supplies only one utilization equipment is a(n) _____ branch circuit.

    (a) individual
    (b) general-purpose
    (c) isolated
    (d) special-purpose

24. A multiwire branch circuit consists of _____.

    (a) two or more ungrounded conductors that have a voltage between them
    (b) a grounded conductor that has equal voltage between it and each ungrounded conductor of the circuit
    (c) a grounded conductor connected to the neutral or grounded conductor of the system
    (d) all of these

25. The *NEC* defines a(n) "_____" as a structure that stands alone or that is separated from adjoining structures by fire walls.

    (a) unit
    (b) apartment
    (c) building
    (d) utility

26. An enclosure designed for either surface mounting or flush mounting provided with a frame in which a door(s) can be hung is called a(n) "_____."

    (a) enclosure
    (b) outlet box
    (c) cutout box
    (d) cabinet

27. Coaxial cable is a cylindrical assembly composed of a conductor centered inside a metallic tube or shield, separated by a(n) _____ material and usually covered by an insulating jacket.

    (a) insulating
    (b) conductive
    (c) isolating
    (d) dielectric

28. An "optical fiber cable" is a factory assembly or field assembly of one or more optical fibers having a(n) _____ covering.

    (a) conductive
    (b) nonconductive
    (c) overall
    (d) metallic

29. Composite optical fiber cables contain optical fibers and _____.

    (a) strength members
    (b) vapor barriers
    (c) current-carrying electrical conductors
    (d) recycled plastic

30. Conductive optical fiber cables contain noncurrent-carrying conductive members such as metallic _____.

    (a) strength members
    (b) vapor barriers
    (c) armor or sheath
    (d) any of these

31. Nonconductive optical fiber cable contains no metallic members and no other _____ materials.

    (a) electrically conductive
    (b) inductive
    (c) synthetic
    (d) insulating

32. A charge controller is equipment that controls _____, or both, and that is used to charge a battery or other energy storage device.

    (a) maximum voltage or current
    (b) dc voltage or dc current
    (c) peak load voltage or current
    (d) ac voltage or ac current

33. A cable routing assembly is composed of single or connected multiple channels as well as associated fittings, forming a structural system to _____ communications wires and cables, optical fiber and data cables; and Class 2, Class 3, and Type PLTC cables; and power-limited fire alarm cables in plenum, riser, and general-purpose applications.

    (a) support
    (b) route
    (c) protect
    (d) support and route

34. A device designed to open and close a circuit by nonautomatic means and to _____ the circuit automatically on a predetermined overcurrent without damage to itself when properly applied within its rating.

    (a) energize
    (b) reset
    (c) connect
    (d) open

35. "_____" is a term indicating that there is purposely introduced delay in the tripping action of the circuit breaker, which decreases as the magnitude of the current increases.

    (a) Adverse time
    (b) Inverse time
    (c) Time delay
    (d) Timed unit

36. Due to its power limitations, a Class 2 circuit considers safety from a fire initiation standpoint and provides acceptable protection from electric shock.

    (a) True
    (b) False

37. Since Class 3 control circuits permit higher allowable levels of voltage and current than Class 2 circuits, additional _____ are specified to provide protection against the electric shock hazard.

    (a) circuits
    (b) safeguards
    (c) conditions
    (d) requirements

38. A "clothes closet" is defined as a _____ room or space intended primarily for storage of garments and apparel.

    (a) habitable
    (b) nonhabitable
    (c) conditioned
    (d) finished

39. "Communications equipment" is the electronic equipment that performs the telecommunications operations for the transmission of _____, and includes power equipment, technical support equipment, and conductors dedicated solely to the operation of the equipment.

    (a) audio
    (b) video
    (c) data
    (d) all of these

40. Wires are considered _____ if rendered inaccessible by the structure or finish of the building.

    (a) inaccessible
    (b) concealed
    (c) hidden
    (d) enclosed

41. A separate portion of a conduit or tubing system that provides access through a removable cover(s) to the interior of the system at a junction of two or more sections of the system or at a terminal point of the system defines the term "_____."

    (a) junction box
    (b) accessible raceway
    (c) conduit body
    (d) cutout box

42. The circuit of a control apparatus or system that carries the electric signals directing the performance of the controller but does not carry the main power current defines a _____ circuit.

    (a) control
    (b) low-voltage
    (c) function
    (d) performance

43. A load is considered to be continuous if the maximum current is expected to continue for _____ hour(s) or more.

    (a) ½
    (b) 1
    (c) 2
    (d) 3

44. A "_____" is a device or group of devices that govern, in some predetermined manner, the electric power delivered to the apparatus to which it is connected.

    (a) relay
    (b) breaker
    (c) transformer
    (d) controller

45. A "dc-to-dc converter" is a device that can provide an output _____ voltage and current at a higher or lower value than the input _____ voltage and current.

    (a) ac, dc
    (b) ac, ac
    (c) dc, dc
    (d) dc, ac

46. The selection and installation of overcurrent protective devices so that an overcurrent condition will be localized to restrict outages to the circuit or equipment affected, is called "_____."

    (a) overcurrent protection
    (b) interrupting capacity
    (c) selective coordination
    (d) overload protection

47. The _____ of any system is the ratio of the maximum demand of a system, or part of a system, to the total connected load of a system.

    (a) load
    (b) demand factor
    (c) minimum load
    (d) calculated factor

48. A unit of an electrical system, other than a conductor, that carries or controls electric energy as its principal function is a(n) "_____."

    (a) raceway
    (b) fitting
    (c) device
    (d) enclosure

49. A(An) "_____" is a device, or group of devices, by which the conductors of a circuit can be disconnected from their source of supply.

    (a) feeder
    (b) enclosure
    (c) disconnecting means
    (d) conductor interrupter

50. A dormitory unit is a building or a space in a building in which group sleeping accommodations are provided for more than _____ persons who are not members of the same family in one room, or a series of closely associated rooms, under joint occupancy and single management, with or without meals, but without individual cooking facilities.

    (a) six
    (b) ten
    (c) twelve
    (d) sixteen

51. "Continuous duty" is defined as _____.

    (a) when the load is expected to continue for five hours or more
    (b) operation at a substantially constant load for an indefinitely long time
    (c) operation at loads and for intervals of time, both of which may be subject to wide variations
    (d) operation at which the load may be subject to maximum current for six hours or more

52. "Varying duty" is defined as _____.

    (a) intermittent operation in which the load conditions are regularly recurrent
    (b) operation at a substantially constant load for an indefinite length of time
    (c) operation for alternate intervals of load and rest, or load, no load, and rest
    (d) operation at loads, and for intervals of time, both of which may be subject to wide variation

53. A building that contains three or more dwelling units is called a "_____."

    (a) one-family dwelling
    (b) two-family dwelling
    (c) dwelling unit
    (d) multifamily dwelling

54. A _____ is a single unit that provides complete and independent living facilities for one or more persons, including permanent provisions for living, sleeping, cooking, and sanitation.

    (a) one-family dwelling
    (b) two-family dwelling
    (c) dwelling unit
    (d) multifamily dwelling

55. Systems of illumination utilizing fluorescent lamps, high-intensity discharge (HID) lamps, or neon tubing are all types of _____.

    (a) Area Lighting
    (b) Flood Lighting
    (c) Security Lighting
    (d) Electric Discharge Lighting

56. An effective ground-fault current path is an intentionally constructed, low-impedance electrically conductive path designed and intended to carry current during a ground-fault condition from the point of a ground fault on a wiring system to _____.

    (a) ground
    (b) earth
    (c) the electrical supply source
    (d) the grounding electrode

57. A specified distance above a water level above which electrical equipment can be installed and electrical _____ can be made is referred to as the electrical datum plane.

    (a) installations
    (b) connections
    (c) inspections
    (d) maintenance

58. Power production, distribution, and utilization equipment and facilities, such as _____ systems that are connected to premises wiring and are external to and not controlled by an interactive system defines an "electric power production and distribution network."

    (a) electric utility
    (b) parallel power production
    (c) interactive power
    (d) microgrid

59. A fixed, stationary, or portable self-contained, electrically operated and/or electrically illuminated utilization equipment with words or symbols designed to convey information or attract attention describes _____.

    (a) an electric sign
    (b) equipment
    (c) appliances
    (d) exit lighting

60. An automotive-type vehicle for on-road use, such as _____ primarily powered by an electric motor is known as an electric vehicle.

    (a) passenger automobiles
    (b) buses, trucks, and vans
    (c) neighborhood electric vehicles, and electric motorcycles
    (d) all of these

61. Off-road, self-propelled electric vehicles, such as _____ are not considered electric vehicles.

    (a) industrial trucks, hoists, and lifts
    (b) golf carts and airline ground support equipment
    (c) tractors and boats
    (d) all of these

62. Surrounded by a case, housing, fence, or wall(s) that prevents persons from accidentally contacting energized parts is called "_____."

    (a) guarded
    (b) covered
    (c) protection
    (d) enclosed

63. As used in the *NEC*, equipment includes _____.

    (a) fittings
    (b) appliances
    (c) machinery
    (d) all of these

64. When the term "exposed," as it applies to live parts, is used in the *Code*, it refers to _____.

    (a) being capable of being inadvertently touched or approached nearer than a safe distance by a person
    (b) parts that are not suitably guarded, isolated, or insulated
    (c) wiring on, or attached to, the surface or behind panels designed to allow access
    (d) being exposed to outdoor elements such as rain

65. As applied to wiring methods, "on or attached to the surface, or behind access panels designed to allow access" is known as _____.

    (a) open
    (b) uncovered
    (c) exposed
    (d) bare

66. The largest amount of current capable of being delivered at a point on the system during a short-circuit condition is defined as "_____ current."

    (a) objectionable
    (b) excessive
    (c) induced
    (d) avilable fault

67. The *NEC* defines a "_____" as all circuit conductors between the service equipment, the source of a separately derived system, or other power supply source, and the final branch-circuit overcurrent device.

    (a) service
    (b) feeder
    (c) branch circuit
    (d) all of these

68. A(An) _____ that performs field evaluations of electrical or other equipment is known as a "Field Evaluation Body (FEB)."

    (a) home inspector
    (b) field installer
    (c) organization or part of an organization
    (d) insurance underwriter

69. Equipment or materials to which has been attached a(an) _____ of an FEB indicating the equipment or materials were evaluated and found to comply with requirements as described in an accompanying field evaluation report is known as "field labeled (as applied to evaluated products)."

    (a) symbol
    (b) label
    (c) other identifying mark
    (d) any of these

70. An accessory, such as a locknut, intended primarily to perform a mechanical function rather than an electrical function best describes _____.

    (a) a part
    (b) equipment
    (c) a device
    (d) a fitting

71. A fitting is defined as an accessory such as a locknut, bushing, or other part of a wiring system that is intended primarily to perform a(an) _____ rather than an electrical function.

    (a) mechanical
    (b) supplemental
    (c) auxiliary
    (d) physical

72. A(An) _____ or ventilated environment that allows heat dissipation and air flow around an installed conductor describes a conductor that is installed in free air.

    (a) open
    (b) low ambient temperature
    (c) air-conditioned
    (d) cable tray

73. A "_____" is a building or portion of a building in which one or more self-propelled vehicles can be kept for use, sale, storage, rental, repair, exhibition, or demonstration purposes.

    (a) garage
    (b) residential garage
    (c) service garage
    (d) commercial garage

74. "Generating capacity, inverter" is defined as the sum of parallel-connected inverter maximum continuous output power at 40°C in _____.

    (a) amps or kVA
    (b) volts or kV
    (c) watts or kW
    (d) a 24-hour period

75. The word "Earth" best describes what *NEC* term?

    (a) Bonded
    (b) Ground
    (c) Effective ground-fault current path
    (d) Guarded

76. A(An) _____ is an unintentional, electrically conductive connection between an ungrounded conductor of an electrical circuit, and the normally noncurrent-carrying conductors, metallic enclosures, metallic raceways, metallic equipment, or earth.

    (a) grounded conductor
    (b) ground fault
    (c) equipment ground
    (d) bonding jumper

77. A system or circuit conductor that is intentionally grounded is called a(n) "_____."

    (a) grounding conductor
    (b) unidentified conductor
    (c) grounded conductor
    (d) grounding electrode conductor

78. By definition, an equipment grounding conductor is considered to be a grounded conductor.

    (a) True
    (b) False

79. A device intended for the protection of personnel that functions to de-energize a circuit or portion thereof within an established period of time when the current to ground exceeds the values established for a Class A device, is a(n) "_____."

    (a) dual-element fuse
    (b) inverse time breaker
    (c) ground-fault circuit interrupter
    (d) safety switch

80. A Class A GFCI trips when the ground-fault current is _____ or higher.

    (a) 4 mA
    (b) 5 mA
    (c) 6 mA
    (d) 7 mA

81. A ground-fault current path is an electrically conductive path from the point of a ground fault through normally noncurrent-carrying conductors, equipment, or the earth to the _____.

    (a) ground
    (b) enclosure
    (c) electrical supply source
    (d) grounding electrode

82. Examples of ground-fault current paths include any combination of conductive materials including _____.

    (a) equipment grounding conductors
    (b) metallic raceways
    (c) metal water and gas piping
    (d) all of these

83. A system intended to provide protection of equipment from damaging line-to-ground fault currents by causing a disconnecting means to open all ungrounded conductors of the faulted circuit at current levels less than the supply circuit overcurrent device defines "_____."

    (a) ground-fault protection of equipment
    (b) guarded
    (c) personal protection
    (d) automatic protection

84. Connected (connecting) to ground or to a conductive body that extends the ground connection is called "_____."

    (a) equipment grounding
    (b) bonded
    (c) grounded
    (d) all of these

85. Connected to ground without the insertion of any resistor or impedance device is referred to as "_____."

    (a) grounded
    (b) solidly grounded
    (c) effectively grounded
    (d) a grounding conductor

86. The installed conductive path(s) that is part of a ground-fault current path and connects normally noncurrent-carrying metal parts of equipment together and to the system grounded conductor or to the grounding electrode conductor, or both, is known as a(n) "_____ conductor."

    (a) grounding electrode
    (b) grounding
    (c) equipment grounding
    (d) neutral

87. A conducting object through which a direct connection to earth is established is a "_____."

    (a) bonding conductor
    (b) grounding conductor
    (c) grounding electrode
    (d) grounded conductor

88. A(n) _____ is a conductive path(s) that is part of an effective ground-fault current path and connects normally non–current-carrying metal parts of equipment together and to the system grounded conductor or to the grounding electrode conductor, or both.

    (a) grounding electrode conductor
    (b) main bonding jumper
    (c) system bonding jumper
    (d) equipment grounding conductor

89. A conductor used to connect the system grounded conductor, or the equipment to a grounding electrode or to a point on the grounding electrode system, is called the "_____ conductor."

    (a) main grounding
    (b) common main
    (c) equipment grounding
    (d) grounding electrode

90. A "_____" is an accommodation that combines living, sleeping, sanitary, and storage facilities within a compartment.

    (a) guest room
    (b) guest suite
    (c) dwelling unit
    (d) single-family dwelling

91. A "_____" is an accommodation with two or more contiguous rooms comprising a compartment that provides living, sleeping, sanitary, and storage facilities.

    (a) guest room
    (b) guest suite
    (c) dwelling unit
    (d) single-family dwelling

92. A habitable room in a building is a room for _____, but excluding bathrooms, toilet rooms, closets, hallways, storage or utility spaces, and similar areas.

    (a) living
    (b) sleeping
    (c) eating or cooking
    (d) all of these

93. A handhole enclosure is an enclosure for use in underground systems, provided with an open or closed bottom, and sized to allow personnel to _____.

    (a) enter and exit freely
    (b) reach into but not enter
    (c) have full working space
    (d) visually examine the interior

94. A hoistway is any _____ in which an elevator or dumbwaiter is designed to operate.

    (a) hatchway or well hole
    (b) vertical opening or space
    (c) shaftway
    (d) all of these

95. A hybrid system is comprised of multiple power sources, such as _____, but not the utility power system.

    (a) photovoltaic
    (b) wind
    (c) micro-hydro generators
    (d) all of these

96. A system comprised of multiple power sources that could include photovoltaic, wind, micro-hydro generators, engine-driven generators, and others, is the definition of a(n) _____.

    (a) Hybrid System
    (b) Micro-grid System
    (c) Combination System
    (d) Off-grid System

97. Recognized as suitable for the specific purpose, function, use, environment, and application is the definition of "_____."

    (a) labeled
    (b) identified (as applied to equipment)
    (c) listed
    (d) approved

98. Information and technology equipment and systems are used for creation and manipulation of _____.

    (a) data
    (b) voice
    (c) video
    (d) all of these

99. "Within sight from" means visible and not more than _____ ft distant from the equipment.

    (a) 10
    (b) 20
    (c) 25
    (d) 50

100. An interactive inverter is an inverter intended for use in parallel with a(n) _____ to supply common loads that may deliver power to the utility.

    (a) electric utility
    (b) photovoltaic (PV) system
    (c) battery
    (d) generator

101. An electric power production system that is operating in parallel with and capable of delivering energy to an electric primary source supply system defines a(an) _____ system.

    (a) hybrid
    (b) inverted
    (c) interactive
    (d) internal

102. The highest current at rated voltage that a device is identified to interrupt under standard test conditions is the "_____."

    (a) interrupting rating
    (b) manufacturer's rating
    (c) interrupting capacity
    (d) withstand rating

103. A device that provides a means to connect intersystem bonding conductors for _____ systems to the grounding electrode system is an "intersystem bonding termination."

    (a) limited-energy
    (b) low-voltage
    (c) communications
    (d) power and lighting

104. A(An) _____ is a device that changes direct-current input to an alternating-current output.

    (a) diode
    (b) rectifier
    (c) transistor
    (d) inverter

105. The conductors connected to the direct-current input of an inverter are known as the _____.

    (a) branch circuit
    (b) feeder
    (c) inverter input circuit
    (d) inverter output circuit

106. The conductors connected to the alternating-current output of an inverter are known as the _____.

    (a) bipolar photovoltaic array
    (b) monopole subarray
    (c) emergency standby power
    (d) inverter output circuit

107. The operational mode for stand-alone power production equipment defines the term _____.

    (a) Island Mode
    (b) Isolation Mode
    (c) Isolated Mode
    (d) Stand-by Mode

108. When defining different levels of accessibility, _____ means not readily accessible to persons unless special means for access are used.

    (a) readily accessible
    (b) not readily accessible
    (c) isolated
    (d) accessible to qualified persons only

109. A "kitchen" is defined as an area with a sink and _____ provisions for food preparation and cooking.

    (a) listed
    (b) labeled
    (c) temporary
    (d) permanent

110. Equipment or materials to which a label, symbol, or other identifying mark of a product evaluation organization that is acceptable to the authority having jurisdiction has been attached is known as "_____."

    (a) listed
    (b) labeled
    (c) approved
    (d) identified

111. A laundry area is an area containing or designed to contain a _____.

    (a) laundry tray
    (b) clothes washer
    (c) clothes dryer
    (d) any of these

112. An outlet intended for the direct connection of a lampholder or a luminaire is a(n) "_____."

    (a) outlet
    (b) receptacle outlet
    (c) lighting outlet
    (d) general-purpose outlet

113. Lighting track is a manufactured assembly designed to support and _____ luminaires that are capable of being readily repositioned on the track.

    (a) connect
    (b) protect
    (c) energize
    (d) all of these

114. Equipment, materials, or services included in a list published by an organization that is acceptable to the authority having jurisdiction are said to be "_____."

    (a) booked
    (b) a digest
    (c) a manifest
    (d) listed

115. A _____ location is protected from weather and not subject to saturation with water or other liquids.

    (a) dry
    (b) damp
    (c) wet
    (d) moist

116. A _____ location may be temporarily subject to dampness and wetness.

    (a) dry
    (b) damp
    (c) moist
    (d) wet

117. Conduit installed underground or encased in concrete slabs that are in direct contact with the earth is considered a _____ location.

    (a) dry
    (b) damp
    (c) wet
    (d) moist

118. The term "Luminaire" means a single individual lampholder by itself.

    (a) True
    (b) False

119. A wire that is run along with or integral with a cable or conductor to provide mechanical support for the cable or conductor is a _____.

    (a) tension wire
    (b) messenger wire
    (c) guy wire
    (d) strain relief wire

120. A "neutral conductor" is the conductor connected to the _____ of a system, which is intended to carry current under normal conditions.

    (a) grounding electrode
    (b) neutral point
    (c) intersystem bonding termination
    (d) electrical grid

121. The common point on a wye-connection in a polyphase system is a "neutral point."

    (a) True
    (b) False

122. "Nonautomatic" is defined as requiring _____ to perform a function.

    (a) protection from damage
    (b) human intervention
    (c) mechanical linkage
    (d) all of these

123. A(n) "_____" is a point on the wiring system at which current is taken to supply utilization equipment.

    (a) box
    (b) receptacle
    (c) outlet
    (d) device

124. "Outline lighting" is an arrangement of _____ to outline or call attention to the shape of a building.

    (a) incandescent lamps
    (b) electric-discharge lighting
    (c) electrically powered light sources
    (d) any of these

125. Any current in excess of the rated current of equipment or the ampacity of a conductor is called "_____."

    (a) trip current
    (b) fault current
    (c) overcurrent
    (d) a short circuit

126. A(n) "_____" is intended to provide limited overcurrent protection for specific applications and utilization equipment such as luminaires and appliances. This limited protection is in addition to the protection provided by the required branch-circuit overcurrent protective device.

    (a) supplementary overcurrent device
    (b) surge protection device
    (c) arc-fault circuit interrupter
    (d) Class A GFCI

127. An overload is the same as a short circuit or ground fault.

    (a) True
    (b) False

128. A panel, including buses and automatic overcurrent devices, designed to be placed in a cabinet or cutout box and accessible only from the front is known as a "_____."

    (a) switchboard
    (b) disconnect
    (c) panelboard
    (d) switch

129. A "_____" is the total components and subsystem that, in combination, converts solar energy into electric energy for connection to a utilization load.

    (a) photovoltaic system
    (b) solar array
    (c) secondary source
    (d) standby source

130. Electrical generating equipment supplied by any source other than a(an) _____, up to the source system disconnecting means is the definition of power production equipment.

    (a) utility service
    (b) PV system
    (c) parallel power production system
    (d) emergency standby system

131. Electrical generating equipment supplied by any source other than a utility service, up to the source system disconnecting means defines _____.

    (a) a service drop
    (b) power production equipment
    (c) the service point
    (d) utilization equipment

132. Premises wiring includes _____ wiring from the service point or power source to the outlets.

    (a) interior
    (b) exterior
    (c) underground
    (d) interior and exterior

133. According to Article 100, a _____ is the machine that supplies the mechanical horsepower to a generator.

    (a) prime mover
    (b) motor
    (c) capacitor
    (d) starter

134. The *NEC* defines a(n) "_____" as one who has skills and knowledge related to the construction and operation of the electrical equipment and installations and has received safety training to recognize and avoid the hazards involved.

    (a) inspector
    (b) master electrician
    (c) journeyman electrician
    (d) qualified person

135. NFPA 70E, *Standard for Electrical Safety in the Workplace*, provides information to help determine the electrical safety training requirements expected of a qualified person.

    (a) True
    (b) False

136. A "raceway" is an enclosed channel designed expressly for the holding of wires, cables, or busbars, with additional functions as permitted in the *Code*.

    (a) True
    (b) False

137. A communications raceway is an enclosed channel of nonmetallic materials designed for holding communications wires and cables; optical fiber cables; data cables associated with information technology and communications equipment; Class 2, Class 3, and Type PLTC cables; and power-limited fire alarm cables in _____ applications.

    (a) plenum
    (b) riser
    (c) general-purpose
    (d) all of these

138. Constructed, protected, or treated so as to prevent rain from interfering with the successful operation of the apparatus under specified test conditions defines the term "_____."

    (a) raintight
    (b) waterproof
    (c) weathertight
    (d) rainproof

139. A raintight enclosure is constructed or protected so that exposure to a beating rain will not result in the entrance of water under specified test conditions.

    (a) True
    (b) False

140. A contact device installed at an outlet for the connection of an attachment plug, or for the direct connection of electrical utilization equipment designed to mate with the corresponding contact device, is known as a(n) "_____."

    (a) attachment point
    (b) tap
    (c) receptacle
    (d) wall plug

141. A single receptacle is a single contact device with no other contact device on the same _____.

    (a) circuit
    (b) yoke
    (c) run
    (d) equipment

142. An outlet where one or more receptacles are installed is called "_____."

    (a) a device
    (b) equipment
    (c) a receptacle
    (d) a receptacle outlet

143. A duplex receptacle is an example of a multiple receptacle that has two receptacles on the same _____.

    (a) yoke or strap
    (b) strap
    (c) device
    (d) cover plate

144. Electromechanical systems, equipment, apparatus, or components that are restored to operating conditions defines equipment that is or has been _____.

    (a) redeployed
    (b) redesigned
    (c) reconditioned
    (d) reassigned

145. As defined, the term "reconditioned" is frequently referred to as _____.

    (a) redeployed
    (b) redesigned
    (c) re-purposed
    (d) refurbished

146. Any electrical circuit that controls any other circuit through a relay or an equivalent device is called a "_____."

    (a) primary circuit
    (b) remote-control circuit
    (c) signal circuit
    (d) controller

147. Equipment enclosed in a case or cabinet with a means of sealing or locking so that live parts cannot be made accessible without opening the enclosure is said to be "_____."

    (a) guarded
    (b) protected
    (c) sealable
    (d) lockable

148. A(n) "_____ system" is an electrical source, other than a service, having no direct connection(s) to circuit conductors of any other electrical source other than those established by grounding and bonding connections.

    (a) separately derived
    (b) classified
    (c) direct
    (d) emergency

149. The conductors and equipment for delivering electric energy from the serving utility to the wiring system of the premises served is called a "_____."

    (a) branch circuit
    (b) feeder
    (c) service
    (d) service attachment

150. Service conductors originate at the service point and terminate at the service disconnecting means.

    (a) True
    (b) False

151. "Overhead service conductors" are the conductors between the _____ and the first point of connection to the service-entrance conductors at the building or other structure.

    (a) service disconnect
    (b) service point
    (c) grounding electrode
    (d) equipment grounding conductor

152. "Underground service conductors" are the underground conductors between the service point and the first point of connection to the service-entrance conductors in a terminal box, meter, or other enclosure, _____ the building wall.

    (a) inside or outside
    (b) concealed within
    (c) above
    (d) below

153. A "service drop" is defined as the overhead conductors between the utility electric supply system and the _____.

    (a) service equipment
    (b) service point
    (c) grounding electrode
    (d) equipment grounding conductor

154. "Overhead system service-entrance conductors" are the service conductors between the terminals of the _____ and a point where they are joined by a tap or splice to the service drop or overhead service conductors.

    (a) service equipment
    (b) service point
    (c) grounding electrode
    (d) equipment grounding conductor

155. "Underground system service-entrance conductors" are the service conductors between the terminals of the _____ and the point of connection to the service lateral or underground service conductors.

    (a) service equipment
    (b) service point
    (c) grounding electrode
    (d) equipment grounding conductor

156. The "_____" is the necessary equipment, usually consisting of a circuit breaker(s) or switch(es) and fuse(s) and their accessories, connected to the load end of service conductors, and intended to constitute the main control and cutoff of the supply.

    (a) service equipment
    (b) service
    (c) service disconnect
    (d) service overcurrent device

157. "Service Equipment" includes the necessary equipment connected to the utility electric system and intended to constitute the _____ of the utility electric system.

    (a) main control
    (b) disconnect
    (c) main control and disconnect
    (d) main control or disconnect

158. The underground conductors between the utility electric supply system and the service point are known as the "_____."

    (a) utility service
    (b) service lateral
    (c) service drop
    (d) main service conductors

159. The "_____" is the point of connection between the facilities of the serving utility and the premises wiring.

    (a) service entrance
    (b) service point
    (c) overcurrent protection
    (d) beginning of the wiring system

160. The prospective symmetrical fault current at a nominal voltage to which an apparatus or system is able to be connected without sustaining damage exceeding defined acceptance criteria is known as the "_____."

    (a) short-circuit current rating
    (b) arc-flash rating
    (c) overcurrent rating
    (d) available fault current

161. A "signaling circuit" is any electrical circuit that energizes signaling equipment.

    (a) True
    (b) False

162. "Special permission" is the written consent from the _____.

    (a) testing laboratory
    (b) manufacturer
    (c) owner
    (d) authority having jurisdiction

163. A "stand-alone system" supplies power independently of an electrical production and distribution network.

    (a) True
    (b) False

164. A "structure" is that which is built or constructed, other than equipment.

    (a) True
    (b) False

165. A permanently connected surge-protective device (SPD) intended for installation on the load side of the service disconnect overcurrent device, including SPDs located at the branch panel, is a Type _____ SPD.

    (a) 1
    (b) 2
    (c) 3
    (d) 4

166. A switch constructed so that it can be installed in device boxes or on box covers, or otherwise used in conjunction with wiring systems recognized by the *NEC* is called a "_____ switch."

    (a) transfer
    (b) motor-circuit
    (c) general-use snap
    (d) bypass isolation

167. "Ungrounded" means not connected to ground or to a conductive body that extends the ground connection.

    (a) True
    (b) False

168. "Utilization equipment" is equipment that utilizes electricity for _____ purposes.

    (a) electromechanical
    (b) heating
    (c) lighting
    (d) any of these

169. The "voltage of a circuit" is defined by the *Code* as the _____ root-mean-square (effective) difference of potential between any two conductors of the circuit concerned.

    (a) lowest
    (b) greatest
    (c) average
    (d) nominal

170. A nominal value assigned to a circuit or system for the purpose of conveniently designating its voltage class, such as 120/240V, is called "_____ voltage."

    (a) root-mean-square
    (b) circuit
    (c) nominal
    (d) source

171. An enclosure constructed so that moisture will not enter the enclosure under specific test conditions is called "_____."

    (a) watertight
    (b) moistureproof
    (c) waterproof
    (d) rainproof

172. A(n) "_____" enclosure is constructed or protected so that exposure to the weather will not interfere with successful operation.

    (a) weatherproof
    (b) weathertight
    (c) weather-resistant
    (d) all weather

ARTICLE
110

REQUIREMENTS FOR ELECTRICAL INSTALLATIONS

Introduction to Article 110—Requirements for Electrical Installations

Article 110 sets the stage for how the rest of the *NEC* is implemented. It is critical for you to completely understand all aspects of this article since it is the foundation for much of the *Code*. As you read and master Article 110, you are building your foundation for correctly applying the *NEC*. While the purpose of the *National Electrical Code* is to provide a safe installation, this article is perhaps focused a little more on providing an installation that is safe for the installer and maintenance electrician, so time spent here is a good investment.

 Please use the 2020 *Code* book to answer the following questions.

1. General requirements for the examination and approval, installation and use, access to and spaces about electrical conductors and equipment; enclosures intended for personnel entry; and tunnel installations are within the scope of _____.

   (a) Article 800
   (b) Article 300
   (c) Article 110
   (d) Annex J

2. The conductors and equipment required or permitted by this *Code* shall be acceptable only if _____.

   (a) labeled
   (b) listed
   (c) approved
   (d) identified

3. In judging equipment for approval, considerations such as _____ shall be evaluated.

   (a) mechanical strength
   (b) wire-bending space
   (c) arcing effects
   (d) all of these

4. Listed or labeled equipment shall be installed and used in accordance with any instructions included in the listing or labeling.

   (a) True
   (b) False

5. Product testing, evaluation, and listing (product certification) shall be performed by _____.

   (a) recognized qualified electrical testing laboratories
   (b) the manufacturer
   (c) qualified person
   (d) electrical engineer

6. Where electrical conductor material is not specified, the sizes given in the *NEC* shall apply to _____ conductors.

   (a) aluminum
   (b) copper-clad aluminum
   (c) copper
   (d) all of these

7. Conductors used to carry current shall be _____ unless otherwise provided in this *Code*.

(a) copper
(b) aluminum
(c) copper-clad aluminum
(d) any of these

8. Conductor sizes are expressed in American Wire Gage (AWG) or in _____.

(a) inches
(b) circular mils
(c) square inches
(d) cubic inches

9. Wiring shall be installed so that the completed system will be free from _____, other than as required or permitted elsewhere in the *Code*.

(a) short circuits
(b) ground faults
(c) connections to the earth
(d) all of these

10. Only wiring methods recognized as _____ are included in this *Code*.

(a) expensive
(b) efficient
(c) suitable
(d) cost effective

11. Equipment intended to interrupt current at fault levels shall have an interrupting rating at nominal circuit voltage at least equal to the current that is available at the line terminals of the equipment.

(a) True
(b) False

12. The _____, and other characteristics of the circuit to be protected shall be selected and coordinated to permit the circuit protective devices used to clear a fault to do so without extensive damage to the electrical equipment of the circuit.

(a) overcurrent protective devices
(b) total impedance
(c) equipment short-circuit current ratings
(d) all of these

13. Unless identified for use in the operating environment, no conductors or equipment shall be _____ having a deteriorating effect on the conductors or equipment.

(a) located in damp or wet locations
(b) exposed to fumes, vapors, liquids, or gases
(c) exposed to excessive temperatures
(d) all of these

14. Some cleaning and lubricating compounds can cause severe deterioration of many plastic materials used for insulating and structural applications in equipment.

(a) True
(b) False

15. Equipment not _____ for outdoor use or identified for indoor use such as "dry locations" or "indoor use only", shall be protected against damage from the weather during construction.

(a) listed
(b) identified
(c) suitable
(d) marked

16. The *NEC* requires that electrical equipment be _____.

(a) installed in a neat and workmanlike manner
(b) installed under the supervision of a licensed person
(c) completed before being inspected
(d) all of these

17. Unused openings other than those intended for the operation of equipment, intended for mounting purposes, or permitted as part of the design for listed equipment shall be _____.

(a) filled with cable clamps or connectors only
(b) taped over with electrical tape
(c) repaired only by welding or brazing in a metal slug
(d) closed to afford protection substantially equivalent to the wall of the equipment

18. Internal parts of electrical equipment, including busbars, wiring terminals, insulators, and other surfaces, shall not be damaged or contaminated by foreign materials such as _____, or corrosive residues.

(a) paint and plaster
(b) cleaners
(c) abrasives
(d) any of these

19. Cables and conductors installed _____ on the surfaces of ceilings and sidewalls shall be supported by the building structure in such a manner that the cables and conductors will not be damaged by normal building use.

    (a) exposed
    (b) concealed
    (c) floating
    (d) bundled

20. Fiber optic cables installed exposed to _____, or other contaminants may result in an undetermined alteration of optical fiber cable properties.

    (a) paint or plaster
    (b) cleaners or abrasives
    (c) corrosive residues
    (d) any of these

21. Cables and conductors installed exposed on the surfaces of ceilings and sidewalls shall be secured by hardware including straps, staples, cable ties, hangers, or _____ designed and installed so as not to damage the cable.

    (a) approved fittings
    (b) identified fittings
    (c) listed fittings
    (d) similar fittings

22. Conductor terminal and splicing devices shall be _____ for the conductor material and they shall be properly installed and used.

    (a) listed
    (b) approved
    (c) identified
    (d) all of these

23. Connectors and terminals for conductors more finely stranded than Class B and Class C, as shown in Table 10 of Chapter 9, shall be _____ for the specific conductor class or classes.

    (a) listed
    (b) approved
    (c) identified
    (d) all of these

24. Conductors of dissimilar metals shall not be intermixed in a terminal or splicing connector where physical contact occurs between dissimilar conductors (such as _____ or aluminum and copper-clad aluminum), unless the device is identified for the purpose and conditions of use.

    (a) copper
    (b) steel
    (c) aluminum
    (d) zinc

25. Connection of conductors to terminal parts shall ensure a thoroughly good connection without damaging the conductors and shall be made by means of _____.

    (a) solder lugs
    (b) pressure connectors
    (c) splices to flexible leads
    (d) any of these

26. All _____ shall be covered with an insulation equivalent to that of the conductors or with an identified insulating device.

    (a) splices
    (b) joints
    (c) free ends of conductors
    (d) All of these

27. The temperature rating associated with the ampacity of a _____ shall be selected and coordinated so as not to exceed the lowest temperature rating of any connected termination, conductor, or device.

    (a) terminal
    (b) conductor
    (c) device
    (d) all of these

28. For circuits rated 100A or less, when the equipment terminals are listed for use with 75°C conductors, the _____ column of Table 310.16 shall be used to determine the ampacity of THHN conductors.

    (a) 30°C
    (b) 60°C
    (c) 75°C
    (d) 90°C

29. Conductors shall have their ampacity determined using the _____ column of Table 310.16 for circuits rated over 100A, or marked for conductors larger than 1 AWG, unless the equipment terminals are listed for use with higher temperature-rated conductors.

    (a) 30°C
    (b) 60°C
    (c) 75°C
    (d) 90°C

30. Separately installed pressure connectors shall be used with conductors at the _____ not exceeding the ampacity at the listed and identified temperature rating of the connector.

    (a) voltages
    (b) temperatures
    (c) listings
    (d) ampacities

31. Tightening torque values for terminal connections shall be as indicated on equipment or in installation instructions provide by the manufacturer. An approved means shall be used to _____ the indicated torque value.

    (a) maximize
    (b) adjust
    (c) optimize
    (d) achieve

32. Tightening torque values for terminal connections shall be as indicated on equipment or in installation instructions provided by the manufacturer. An approved means shall be used to achieve the_____ torque value.

    (a) indicated
    (b) identified
    (c) maximum
    (d) minimum

33. Examples of approved means of achieving terminal connection torque values include torque tools or an experienced qualified person that can demonstrate that the proper torque has been applied.

    (a) True
    (b) False

34. On a 4-wire, delta-connected system where the midpoint of one phase winding is grounded, only the conductor or busbar having the higher phase voltage-to-ground shall be durably and permanently marked by an outer finish that is _____ in color.

    (a) black
    (b) red
    (c) blue
    (d) orange

35. Electrical equipment such as switchboards, switchgear, panelboards, industrial control panels, meter socket enclosures, and motor control centers, that are in other than dwelling units, and are likely to require _____ while energized, shall be field or factory marked to warn qualified persons of potential electric arc-flash hazards.

    (a) examination
    (b) adjustment
    (c) servicing or maintenance
    (d) any of these

36. In other than dwelling units, in addition to requirements for field or factory marking of equipment to warn qualified persons of potential electric arc-flash hazards, a permanent label shall be field or factory applied to service equipment rated _____ or more.

    (a) 600A
    (b) 1,000A
    (c) 1,200A
    (d) 1,600A

37. Service equipment labeling in other than dwelling units shall not be required if an arc-flash label is applied in accordance with _____ industry practice.

    (a) routine
    (b) acceptable
    (c) documented
    (d) manufacturing

38. NFPA 70E, *Standard for Electrical Safety in the Workplace*, provides guidance, such as determining severity of potential exposure, planning safe work practices, arc-flash labeling, and selecting _____.

    (a) personal protective equipment
    (b) coordinated overcurrent protective devices
    (c) emergency egress plans
    (d) fire suppression systems

39. Acceptable industry practices for equipment labeling are described in NFPA 70E, *Standard for Electrical Safety in the Workplace*. This standard provides specific criteria for developing arc-flash labels for equipment that provides _____, and so forth.

    (a) nominal system voltage and incident energy levels
    (b) arc-flash boundaries
    (c) minimum required levels of personal protective equipment
    (d) all of these

40. The manufacturer's name, trademark, or other descriptive marking by which the organization responsible for the product can be identified shall be _____.

    (a) approved
    (b) documented
    (c) placed on all electrical equipment
    (d) listed

41. Reconditioned equipment shall be marked with the _____ by which the organization responsible for reconditioning the electrical equipment can be identified, along with the date of the reconditioning.

    (a) name
    (b) trademark
    (c) descriptive marking
    (d) any of these

42. Reconditioned equipment shall be identified as "reconditioned" and the original listing mark _____.

    (a) removed
    (b) updated
    (c) modified
    (d) preserved

43. As applied to electrical equipment, the term reconditioned may be interchangeable with the term(s) "_____."

    (a) rebuilt
    (b) refurbished
    (c) remanufactured
    (d) any of these

44. Reconditioned equipment original listing mark may include the mark of the certifying body and not the entire equipment label.

    (a) True
    (b) False

45. Where caution, warning, or danger signs or labels are required by this *Code*, the label marking shall warn of the hazards using effective _____.

    (a) words
    (b) colors
    (c) symbols
    (d) any combination of words, colors, or symbols

46. Each disconnecting means shall be legibly marked to indicate its purpose unless located and arranged so _____.

    (a) that it can be locked out and tagged
    (b) it is not readily accessible
    (c) the purpose is evident
    (d) that it operates at less than 300 volts-to-ground

47. The *NEC* requires tested series-rated installations of circuit breakers or fuses to be legibly marked in the field to indicate the equipment has been applied with a series combination rating.

    (a) True
    (b) False

48. _____ at other than dwelling units shall be legibly field marked with the available fault current, include the date the fault-current calculation was performed, and be of sufficient durability to withstand the environment involved.

    (a) Service equipment
    (b) Sub panels
    (c) Motor control centers
    (d) all of these

49. When service equipment is required to be field marked with the available fault current the value of available fault current for use in determining appropriate minimum short-circuit current ratings of service equipment is available from _____ in published or other forms.

    (a) the architect
    (b) the engineer
    (c) electric utilities
    (d) all of these

50. When modifications to the electrical installation occur that affect the maximum available fault current at the service, the maximum available fault current shall be verified or _____ as necessary to ensure the service equipment ratings are sufficient for the maximum available fault current at the line terminals of the equipment.

    (a) recalculated
    (b) increased
    (c) decreased
    (d) adjusted

51. Field markings of maximum available fault current at a service are not required in industrial installations where conditions of maintenance and supervision ensure that only qualified persons service the equipment.

    (a) True
    (b) False

52. If a disconnecting means is required to be locked in the open position by the *NEC*, the disconnect shall be capable of being locked in the open or closed position.

    (a) True
    (b) False

53. Access and _____ shall be provided and maintained about all electrical equipment to permit ready and safe operation and maintenance of such equipment.

    (a) ventilation
    (b) cleanliness
    (c) circulation
    (d) working space

54. Working space is required for equipment operating at 1,000V, nominal, or less to ground and likely to require _____ while energized.

    (a) examination
    (b) adjustment
    (c) servicing or maintenance
    (d) all of these

55. NFPA 70E, *Standard for Electrical Safety in the Workplace*, provides guidance, such as determining severity of potential exposure, planning safe work practices including establishing an electrically _____ work condition, arc flash labeling, and selecting personal protective equipment.

    (a) safe
    (b) efficient
    (c) cost effective
    (d) all of these

56. Working space distances for enclosed live parts shall be measured from the _____ of equipment or apparatus, if the live parts are enclosed.

    (a) enclosure front or opening
    (b) front or back
    (c) mounting pad
    (d) footprint

57. A minimum working space depth of _____ to live parts of equipment operating at 277 volts-to-ground is required where there are exposed live parts on one side and no live or grounded parts on the other side.

    (a) 2 ft
    (b) 3 ft
    (c) 4 ft
    (d) 6 ft

58. The minimum working space on a circuit for equipment operating at 120 volts-to-ground, with exposed live parts on one side and no live or grounded parts on the other side of the working space, is _____ .

    (a) 1 ft
    (b) 3 ft
    (c) 4 ft
    (d) 6 ft

59. Concrete, brick, or tile walls are considered _____, as applied to working space requirements.

    (a) inconsequential
    (b) in the way
    (c) grounded
    (d) free from hazards

60. The required working space for access to live parts of equipment operating at 300 volts-to-ground, where there are exposed live parts on one side and grounded parts on the other side, is _____.

(a) 3 ft
(b) 3½ ft
(c) 4 ft
(d) 4½ ft

61. The minimum working space on a circuit for equipment operating at 750 volts-to-ground, with exposed live parts on one side and grounded parts on the other side of the working space, is _____.

(a) 1 ft
(b) 3 ft
(c) 4 ft
(d) 6 ft

62. The required working space for access to live parts of equipment operating at 300 volts-to-ground, where there are exposed live parts on both sides of the workspace is _____.

(a) 3 ft
(b) 3½ ft
(c) 4 ft
(d) 4½ ft

63. The working space in front of the electric equipment shall not be less than _____ wide, or the width of the equipment, whichever is greater.

(a) 15 in.
(b) 30 in.
(c) 40 in.
(d) 60 in.

64. Equipment associated with the electrical installation can be located above or below other electrical equipment within their working space when the associated equipment does not extend more than _____ from the front of the electrical equipment.

(a) 3 in.
(b) 6 in.
(c) 12 in.
(d) 30 in.

65. The minimum height of working spaces about electrical equipment, switchboards, panelboards, or motor control centers operating at 1,000V, nominal, or less and likely to require examination, adjustment, servicing, or maintenance while energized shall be 6 1/2 ft or the height of the equipment, whichever is greater, except for service equipment or panelboards in existing dwelling units that do not exceed 200A.

(a) True
(b) False

66. Where equipment operating at 1,000 volts, nominal, or less to ground and likely to require examination, adjustment, servicing, or maintenance while energized is required by installation instructions or function to be located in a space with limited access, and where equipment is installed above a lay-in ceiling, there shall be an opening not smaller than _____.

(a) 6 in. x 6 in.
(b) 12 in. x 12 in.
(c) 22 in. x 22 in.
(d) 22 in. x 30 in.

67. Where equipment operating at 1,000 volts, nominal, or less to ground and likely to require examination, adjustment, servicing, or maintenance while energized is required by installation instructions or function to be located in a space with limited access, the width of the working space shall be the width of the equipment enclosure or a minimum of _____, whichever is greater.

(a) 12 in.
(b) 22 in.
(c) 26 in.
(d) 30 in.

68. Where equipment operating at 1,000 volts, nominal, or less to ground and likely to require examination, adjustment, servicing, or maintenance while energized is required by installation instructions or function to be located in a space with limited access, all enclosure doors or hinged panels shall be capable of opening a minimum of _____.

(a) 60 degrees
(b) 90 degrees
(c) 120 degrees
(d) 180 degrees

69. Where equipment operating at 1,000 volts, nominal, or less to ground and likely to require examination, adjustment, servicing, or maintenance while energized is required by installation instructions or function to be located in a space with limited access, the space in front of the enclosure shall comply with the depth requirements of Table 110.26(A)(1).

    (a) True
    (b) False

70. Working space shall not be used for _____.

    (a) storage
    (b) raceways
    (c) lighting
    (d) accessibility

71. When normally enclosed live parts are exposed for inspection or servicing, the working space, if in a passageway or general open space, shall be suitably _____.

    (a) accessible
    (b) guarded
    (c) open
    (d) enclosed

72. For large equipment that contains overcurrent devices, switching devices, there shall be one entrance to and egress from the required working space not less than _____ wide.

    (a) 24 in.
    (b) 30 in.
    (c) 36 in.
    (d) 42 in.

73. For large equipment that contains overcurrent devices, switching devices, there shall be one entrance to and egress from the required working space not less than 24 in. wide and _____ high at each end of the working space.

    (a) 5½ ft
    (b) 6 ft
    (c) 6½ ft
    (d) 7 ft

74. For large equipment that contains service disconnecting means installed in accordance with 230.71 where the combined ampere rating is _____ amperes or more and over 6 ft wide, there shall be one entrance to and egress from the required working space not less than 24 in. wide and 6 1/2 ft high at each end of the working space

    (a) 800A
    (b) 1000A
    (c) 1200A
    (d) 2000A

75. For equipment rated 800A or more that contains overcurrent devices, switching devices, or control devices; and where the entrance to the working space has a personnel door(s) less than 25 ft from the nearest edge of the working space, the door shall _____.

    (a) open either in or out with simple pressure and shall not have any lock
    (b) open in the direction of egress and be equipped with listed panic hardware
    (c) be equipped with a locking means
    (d) be equipped with an electronic opener

76. Illumination shall be provided for all working spaces about service equipment, switchboards, switchgear, panelboards, or motor control centers _____.

    (a) over 600V
    (b) installed indoors
    (c) rated 1,200A or more
    (d) using automatic means of control

77. All switchboards, panelboards, and motor control centers shall be _____.

    (a) located in dedicated spaces
    (b) protected from damage
    (c) in weatherproof enclosures
    (d) located in dedicated spaces and protected from damage

78. The minimum height of dedicated equipment space for motor control centers installed indoors is _____ above the enclosure, or to the structural ceiling, whichever is lower.

    (a) 3 ft
    (b) 5 ft
    (c) 6 ft
    (d) 6½ ft

79. The area above the dedicated space required by 110.26(E)(1)(a) is permitted to contain foreign systems, provided protection is installed to avoid damage to the electrical equipment from condensation, leaks, or breaks in such foreign systems.

    (a) True
    (b) False

80. The dedicated space above a panelboard extends to a dropped or suspended ceiling, which is considered a structural ceiling.

    (a) True
    (b) False

81. All switchboards, switchgear, panelboards, and motor control centers shall be located in dedicated spaces and protected from damage, and outdoor installations shall be _____.

    (a) installed in identified enclosures
    (b) protected from accidental contact by unauthorized personnel or by vehicular traffic
    (c) protected from accidental spillage or leakage from piping systems
    (d) all of these

82. All switchboards, switchgear, panelboards, and motor control centers shall be located in dedicated spaces and protected from damage and the working clearance space for outdoor installations shall include the zone described in _____.

    (a) 110.26(A)
    (b) 110.26(B)
    (c) 110.26(C)
    (d) 110.26(D)

83. All switchboards, switchgear, panelboards, and motor control centers shall be located in dedicated spaces and protected from damage and, for outdoor installations, the space equal to the width and depth of the equipment and extending from grade to a height of _____ above the equipment, shall be dedicated to the electrical installation.

    (a) 2 ft
    (b) 4 ft
    (c) 6 ft
    (d) 8 ft

84. Electrical equipment rooms or enclosures housing electrical apparatus that are controlled by a lock(s) shall be considered _____ to qualified persons.

    (a) readily accessible
    (b) accessible
    (c) available
    (d) secured

85. The term "rainproof" is typically used in conjunction with enclosure type(s) _____.

    (a) 3
    (b) 3R and 3RX
    (c) 4
    (d) 4R and 4RX

CHAPTER 2

WIRING AND PROTECTION

Introduction to Chapter 2—Wiring and Protection

Chapter 2 provides the general rules for wiring and sizing services, feeders, and branch circuits; and for the overcurrent protection of conductors as well as the proper grounding and bonding of electrical circuits and systems. The rules in this chapter apply to all electrical installations covered by the *NEC*—except as modified in Chapters 5, 6, and 7 [90.3].

Communications Systems [Chapter 8] (twisted-pair conductors, antennas, and coaxial cable) are not subject to the general requirements of Chapters 1 through 4, or the special requirements of Chapters 5 through 7, unless there is a specific reference in Chapter 8 to a rule in Chapters 1 through 7 [90.3].

As you go through Chapter 2, remember that it is primarily focused on correctly sizing and protecting circuits. Every article in this chapter deals with a different aspect of providing a safe installation.

▶ **Article 200—Use and Identification of Neutral and Grounded-Phase Conductors.** This article contains the requirements for the use and identification, of the grounded conductor, which (in most cases) is the neutral conductor.

▶ **Article 210—Branch Circuits.** Article 210 contains the requirements for branch circuits, such as conductor sizing, identification, AFCI and GFCI protection, as well as receptacle and lighting outlet requirements.

▶ **Article 215—Feeders.** This article covers the requirements for the installation and ampacity of feeders.

▶ **Article 220—Branch-Circuit, Feeder, and Service Calculations.** Article 220 provides the requirements for calculating the sizes required for branch circuits, feeders, and services. It also provides guidance in determining such things as the mandatory number of branch circuits and the number of receptacles on each.

▶ **Article 225—Outside Feeders.** This article covers the requirements for wiring methods located outside (both overhead and underground). It includes feeders that run on or between buildings, poles, and other structures which may be present on the premises and used to feed equipment.

▶ **Article 230—Services.** Article 230 covers the installation requirements for service conductors and equipment. It is very important to know where the service begins and ends when applying Article 230.

▶ **Article 240—Overcurrent Protection.** This article provides the requirements for overcurrent protection and overcurrent protective devices. Overcurrent protection for conductors and equipment is provided to open the circuit if the current reaches a value that will cause an excessive or dangerous temperature on the conductors or conductor insulation.

▶ **Article 242—Overvoltage Protection.** Part I of this article covers the general installation and connection requirements for surge-protective devices (SPDs) permanently installed on both the line side and load side of service disconnects. Part II covers SPDs permanently installed on wiring systems 1,000V and less. Part III covers surge arresters for systems over 1,000V which are beyond the scope of this book.

• • •

▶ **Article 250—Grounding and Bonding.** Article 250 covers the grounding requirements for providing a path to the Earth to reduce overvoltage from lightning, and the bonding requirements for the low-impedance fault current path necessary to facilitate the operation of overcurrent protective devices in the event of a ground fault.

ARTICLE 200
USE AND IDENTIFICATION OF GROUNDED CONDUCTORS

Introduction to Article 200—Use and Identification of Grounded Conductors

This article contains the requirements for the identification of grounded conductors and their terminals. There are two types of grounded conductors; neutral conductors and grounded-phase conductors. A system where the transformer secondary is wye-connected with the neutral point grounded will have a grounded conductor that is identified as a neutral conductor. ▶Figure 200–1

A system where the transformer secondary is delta-connected with one point of the transformer winding grounded will have a grounded-phase conductor ▶Figure 200–2

A system where the transformer secondary is delta-connected with one winding or coil grounded at its midpoint will have a neutral but will also produce one phase with a higher voltage-to-ground known as a "high-leg." ▶Figure 200–3

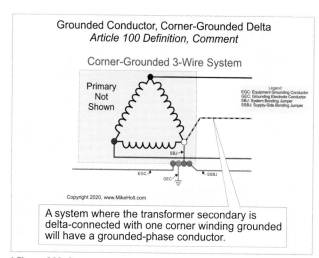

▶Figure 200–2

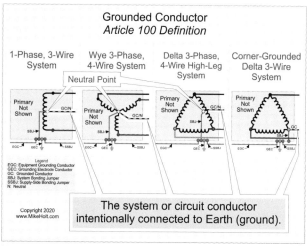

▶Figure 200–1

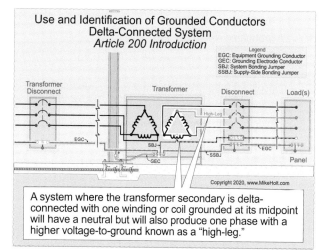

▶Figure 200–3

Please use the 2020 *Code* book to answer the following questions.

1. Article 200 provides the requirements for _____.

   (a) identification of terminals
   (b) grounded conductors in premises wiring systems
   (c) identification of grounded conductors
   (d) all of these

2. The continuity of a grounded conductor shall not depend on a connection to _____.

   (a) a metallic enclosure
   (b) a raceway
   (c) cable armor
   (d) any of these

3. _____ conductors shall not be used for more than one branch circuit, one multiwire branch circuit, or more than one set of ungrounded feeder conductors except as allowed elsewhere in the *Code*.

   (a) Equipment grounding
   (b) Neutral
   (c) Grounding electrode
   (d) Bonding

4. An insulated grounded conductor _____ or smaller shall be identified by a continuous white or gray outer finish, or by three continuous white or gray stripes along its entire length on other than green insulation.

   (a) 8 AWG
   (b) 6 AWG
   (c) 4 AWG
   (d) 3 AWG

5. At the time of installation, grounded conductors _____ or larger can be identified by distinctive white or gray markings at their terminations.

   (a) 10 AWG
   (b) 8 AWG
   (c) 6 AWG
   (d) 4 AWG

6. Where grounded conductors of different systems are installed in the same raceway, cable, or enclosure, each neutral conductor shall be identified to distinguish the systems by _____.

   (a) a continuous white or gray outer finish for one system
   (b) a neutral conductor with a different continuous white or gray outer finish or white or gray with a stripe for one system
   (c) other identification allowed by 200.6(A) or (B) that distinguishes each system from other systems
   (d) any of these

7. The insulated grounded conductor(s) in a multiconductor cable _____ or larger, shall be permitted to be re-identified at the time of installation at its terminations.

   (a) 8 AWG
   (b) 6 AWG
   (c) 4 AWG
   (d) 2 AWG

8. The white conductor within a cable can be used for a(n) _____ conductor where permanently reidentified to indicate its use as an ungrounded conductor at each location where the conductor is visible and accessible.

   (a) grounded
   (b) ungrounded
   (c) equipment grounding
   (d) grounding electrode

9. In devices or utilization equipment with polarized connections, identification of terminals to which a neutral conductor is to be connected shall be substantially _____ or silver in color.

   (a) white
   (b) green
   (c) gold
   (d) bronze

10. The identification of terminals to which a neutral conductor is to be connected shall be substantially white or _____ in color.

    (a) clear
    (b) grey
    (c) silver
    (d) gold

11. Receptacles shall have the terminal intended for connection to the grounded conductor identified by a metal or metal coating that is substantially white or silver in color or by the word "_____".

    (a) green
    (b) white
    (c) silver
    (d) neutral

12. The screw shell of a luminaire or lampholder shall be connected to the _____.

    (a) grounded conductor
    (b) ungrounded conductor
    (c) equipment grounding conductor
    (d) forming shell terminal

ARTICLE 210

BRANCH CIRCUITS

Introduction to Article 210—Branch Circuits

This article contains branch-circuit requirements such as those for conductor sizing and identification, GFCI and AFCI protection, and receptacle and lighting outlet requirements. It consists of three parts:

▸ Part I. General Provisions

▸ Part II. Branch-Circuit Ratings

▸ Part III. Required Outlets

Table 210.3 in this article identifies specific-purpose branch circuits. Its provisions for those that supply the equipment listed amend or supplement the requirements in Article 210 for branch circuits, so it is important to be aware of the contents of this table.

Please use the 2020 *Code* book to answer the following questions.

1. Article 210 provides the general requirements for _____.

   (a) outside branch circuits
   (b) branch circuits
   (c) ungrounded conductors
   (d) feeder calculations

2. Each multiwire branch circuit shall be provided with a means that will simultaneously disconnect all _____ conductors at the point where the branch circuit originates.

   (a) circuit
   (b) grounded
   (c) grounding
   (d) ungrounded

3. Multiwire branch circuits shall supply only _____.

   (a) line-to-neutral loads
   (b) branch circuits in dwelling units
   (c) conductors originating from different panelboards
   (d) three-phase loads

4. Where more than one nominal voltage system supplies branch circuits in a building, each _____ conductor of a branch circuit shall be identified by phase or line and system voltage class at all termination, connection, and splice points in compliance with 210.5(C)(1)(a) and (b).

   (a) neutral
   (b) ungrounded
   (c) grounding
   (d) all of these

5. In existing installations where a voltage system(s) already exists and a different voltage system is being added, it shall be permissible to mark only the old system voltage.

   (a) True
   (b) False

6. Where two or more branch circuits supply devices or equipment on the same yoke or mounting strap, a means to disconnect simultaneously the ungrounded supply conductors shall be provided _____.

(a) at the point where the branch circuits originate
(b) at the location of the device or equipment
(c) at the point where the feeder originates
(d) within sight of the device or equipment

7. The GFCI protection required by 210.8(A) through (F) shall be _____.

(a) the circuit breaker type only
(b) accessible
(c) readily accessible
(d) concealed

8. Requirements for branch-circuit GFCI protection for personnel are contained in 210.8 and requirements for _____ are contained in 422.5(A).

(a) feeders
(b) appliances
(c) motors
(d) all of these

9. Ground-fault circuit-interrupter protection for personnel shall be provided as required in 210.8(A) through (F). Additional GFCI requirements for specific circuits and equipment are contained in Chapters 4, 5, and 6.

(a) True
(b) False

10. For the application of GFCI protection for personnel, when determining the distance from receptacles for sinks [210.8(A)(7) and 210.8(B)(5)] and bathtubs or shower stalls [210.8(A)(9)], the distance shall be measured as the _____ path the cord of an appliance connected to the receptacle would follow without piercing a floor, wall, ceiling, or fixed barrier, or the shortest path without passing through a window.

(a) longest
(b) shortest
(c) most direct
(d) straight-line

11. All 15A and 20A, 125V, single-phase receptacles installed in bathrooms of _____ shall have ground-fault circuit-interrupter (GFCI) protection for personnel.

(a) guest rooms in hotels/motels
(b) dwelling units
(c) office buildings
(d) all occupancies

12. GFCI protection shall be provided for all 15A and 20A, 125V, single-phase receptacles installed in a dwelling unit _____.

(a) attic
(b) garage and laundry area
(c) utility room
(d) den

13. All 15A and 20A, 125V, single-phase receptacles located outdoors of dwelling units, including receptacles installed under the eaves of roofs, shall be GFCI protected except for a receptacle that is supplied by a branch circuit dedicated to _____ if the receptacle is not readily accessible and the equipment or receptacle has ground-fault protection of equipment (GFPE) [426.28 or 427.22].

(a) electric snow-melting or deicing equipment
(b) pipeline and vessel heating equipment
(c) holiday decorative lighting
(d) a or b

14. All 15A and 20A, 125V, single-phase receptacles installed in crawl spaces at or below grade level of dwelling units shall have GFCI protection.

(a) True
(b) False

15. All 15A and 20A, 125V, single-phase receptacles installed in _____ of dwelling units shall have GFCI protection.

(a) laundry areas
(b) finished basements
(c) unfinished basements
(d) all of these

16. GFCI protection shall be provided for all 15A and 20A, 125V, single-phase receptacles in dwelling unit finished portions of basements intended as habitable space.

(a) True
(b) False

17. GFCI protection shall be provided for all 15A and 20A, 125V, single-phase receptacles _____ in dwelling unit kitchens.

(a) installed to serve the countertop surfaces
(b) within 6 ft from the top inside edge of the bowl of the sink
(c) for all receptacles
(d) installed to serve the countertop surfaces and within 6 ft from the top inside edge of the bowl of the sink

18. In dwelling units, GFCI protection shall be provided for all 125V through 250V receptacles supplied by single-phase branch circuits rated 150V or less to ground where receptacles are installed within _____ ft from the top inside edge of the bowl of a sink.

(a) 3
(b) 4
(c) 5
(d) 6

19. All 125V through 250V single-phase receptacles supplied by single-phase branch circuits rated 150V or less to ground installed in dwelling unit boathouses shall have _____ protection for personnel.

(a) GFCI
(b) AFCI
(c) AFCI and GFCI
(d) no

20. In other than dwelling units, all single-phase receptacles rated 150 volts-to-ground or less, 50A or less and three-phase receptacles rated 150 volts-to-ground or less, 100A or less installed in(on) _____ shall have GFCI protection for personnel.

(a) rooftops
(b) kitchens
(c) bathrooms
(d) all of these

21. All single-phase receptacles rated 150V to ground or less, 50A or less and three-phase receptacles rated 150V to ground or less, 100A or less installed _____ of commercial occupancies shall have GFCI protection.

(a) in bathrooms
(b) on rooftops
(c) in kitchens
(d) all of these

22. In other than dwelling units, GFCI protection is required for receptacles installed in _____.

(a) kitchens
(b) unfinished areas of basements
(c) laundry areas
(d) all of these

23. In other than dwelling units, GFCI protection shall be provided for all outdoor single-phase receptacles rated 150V to ground or less, 50A or less and three-phase receptacles rated 150V to ground or less, 100A or less.

(a) True
(b) False

24. In other than dwelling units, GFCI protection shall be provided for all 125V through 250V receptacles supplied by single-phase branch circuits rated 150V or less to ground, 50A or less, where receptacles are installed within _____ ft from the top inside edge of the bowl of a sink.

(a) 3
(b) 4
(c) 5
(d) 6

25. All single-phase receptacles rated 150V to ground or less, 50A or less and three-phase receptacles rated 150V to ground or less, 100A or less installed indoors, in other than dwelling units, in damp and wet locations shall be GFCI protected.

(a) True
(b) False

26. All single-phase receptacles rated 150V to ground or less, 50A or less and three-phase receptacles rated 150V to ground or less, 100A or less installed in locker rooms with associated showering facilities shall be GFCI protected.

(a) True
(b) False

27. All single-phase receptacles rated 150V to ground or less, 50A or less and three-phase receptacles rated 150V to ground or less, 100A or less installed in other than dwelling unit garages, service bays, and similar areas shall be GFCI protected, unless located in _____.

(a) showrooms
(b) vehicle exhibition halls
(c) paint booths
(d) showrooms and vehicle exhibition halls

28. In other than dwelling locations, GFCI protection is required for all single-phase receptacles rated 150V to ground or less, 50A or less and three-phase receptacles rated 150V to ground or less, 100A or less in _____.

    (a) indoor damp and wet locations
    (b) locker rooms with associated showering facilities
    (c) garages, service bays, and similar areas other than vehicle exhibition halls and showrooms
    (d) all of these

29. In other than dwelling locations, GFCI protection is required for all single-phase receptacles rated 150V to ground or less, 50A or less and three-phase receptacles rated 150V to ground or less, 100A or less in unfinished portions or areas of the basement.

    (a) True
    (b) False

30. Receptacles installed in bathrooms within six feet of the outside edge of a _____ shall have GFCI protection.

    (a) bathtub or shower stall
    (b) bidet
    (c) toilet
    (d) window opening

31. Receptacles installed within _____ of the outside edge of a bathtub or shower stall shall have GFCI protection.

    (a) 2 ft
    (b) 3 ft
    (c) 4 ft
    (d) 6 ft

32. GFCI protection shall be provided for lighting outlets not exceeding 120 volts installed in _____.

    (a) crawl spaces
    (b) unfinished basements
    (c) attic spaces
    (d) bathrooms

33. For equipment requiring servicing, GFCI protection shall be provided for the receptacles required by _____.

    (a) 210.10
    (b) 210.25(B)
    (c) 210.62
    (d) 210.63

34. All outdoor outlets for dwellings, other than those covered in 210.8(A)(3), Ex to (3), that are supplied by single-phase branch circuits rated 150 volts-to-ground or less, _____ shall have ground-fault circuit- interrupter protection for personnel.

    (a) 15A or more
    (b) 20A or less
    (c) 30A or less
    (d) 50A or less

35. Two or more _____ small-appliance branch circuits shall be provided to supply power for receptacle outlets in the dwelling unit kitchen, dining room, breakfast room, pantry, or similar dining areas.

    (a) 15A
    (b) 20A
    (c) auxiliary
    (d) supplemental

36. There shall be a minimum of one _____ branch circuit for the laundry outlet(s) required by 210.52(F).

    (a) 15A
    (b) 20A
    (c) auxiliary
    (d) supplemental

37. In addition to the number of branch circuits required by other parts of 210.11, at least _____ 120V, 20A branch circuit shall be provided to supply the bathroom(s) receptacle outlet(s).

    (a) one
    (b) two
    (c) three
    (d) four

38. One or more 120V, 15A branch circuit shall be provided to supply bathroom(s) receptacle outlet(s) required by 210.52(D).

    (a) True
    (b) False

39. An individual 20A branch circuit can supply a single dwelling unit bathroom for receptacle outlet(s) and other equipment within the same bathroom.

    (a) True
    (b) False

40. In addition to the number of branch circuits required by other parts of 210.11, at least one 120V, 20A branch circuit shall be installed to supply receptacle outlets in _____ garages with electric power.

    (a) attached
    (b) detached
    (c) unfinished
    (d) attached and detached

41. The 120V, 20A branch circuit required for a garage is not permitted to supply readily accessible outdoor receptacle outlets.

    (a) True
    (b) False

42. All 15A or 20A, 120V branch circuits that supply outlets or devices in dwelling unit kitchens, family rooms, dining rooms, living rooms, parlors, libraries, dens, bedrooms, sunrooms, recreation rooms, closets, hallways, laundry areas, or similar rooms or areas shall be AFCI protected by a listed arc-fault circuit interrupter.

    (a) True
    (b) False

43. 120V, single-phase, 15A and 20A branch circuits supplying _____ installed in dormitory unit bedrooms, living rooms, hallways, closets, bathrooms, and similar rooms shall be protected by any of the means described in 210.12(A)(1) through (6).

    (a) outlets
    (b) devices
    (c) luminaires
    (d) outlets and devices

44. 120V, single-phase, 15A and 20A branch circuits supplying outlets and devices installed in _____ of hotels and motels shall be protected by any of the means described in 210.12(A)(1) through (6).

    (a) guest rooms
    (b) conference rooms
    (c) lobbies and common hallways
    (d) game rooms

45. Where branch-circuit wiring in a dwelling unit is modified, replaced, or extended in any of the areas specified in 210.12(A), the branch circuit shall be protected by a _____.

    (a) listed outlet branch-circuit type AFCI located at the first receptacle outlet of the existing branch circuit
    (b) listed combination AFCI circuit breaker only
    (c) GFCI circuit breaker
    (d) GFCI at first receptacle in the circuit

46. Branch circuits shall be rated in accordance with the maximum permitted ampere rating of the _____.

    (a) overcurrent device
    (b) circuit conductors
    (c) load to be served
    (d) equipment in use

47. Conductors for feeders sized to prevent a voltage drop where the maximum total voltage drop on both feeders and branch circuits to the farthest outlet does not exceed _____ percent, will provide reasonable efficiency of operation.

    (a) 2%
    (b) 3%
    (c) 4%
    (d) 5%

48. The recommended maximum total voltage drop on branch-circuit conductors is _____ percent.

    (a) 2
    (b) 3
    (c) 4
    (d) 6

49. Where a branch circuit supplies continuous loads, or any combination of continuous and noncontinuous loads, the rating of the overcurrent device shall not be less than the noncontinuous load plus 125 percent of the continuous load.

    (a) True
    (b) False

50. A single receptacle installed on an individual branch circuit shall have an ampere rating not less than that of the branch circuit.

    (a) True
    (b) False

51. If a 20A branch circuit supplies multiple receptacles, the receptacles shall have an ampere rating of no less than _____.

    (a) 10A
    (b) 15A
    (c) 20A
    (d) 30A

52. The total rating of utilization equipment fastened in place, other than luminaires, shall not exceed _____ of a multiple outlet branch circuit rating.

    (a) 25%
    (b) 50%
    (c) 80%
    (d) 100%

53. The maximum rating of a single fixed in place utilization equipment supplied by a 20 ampere multiple outlet branch circuit shall be no greater than _____ amperes.

    (a) 7.5A
    (b) 10A
    (c) 16A
    (d) 20A

54. Appliance receptacle outlets installed for a specific appliance in a dwelling unit, such as laundry equipment, shall be located within _____ of the intended location of the appliance.

    (a) sight
    (b) 3 ft
    (c) 6 ft
    (d) the length of the cord

55. The *Code* provides rules for the minimum number of receptacle outlets required in a dwelling unit. The minimum required receptacle outlets shall be in addition to receptacle outlets that are located within _____.

    (a) closets
    (b) bathrooms
    (c) 6 ft of the floor
    (d) cabinets or cupboards

56. When applying the general provisions for receptacle spacing to the rooms of a dwelling unit which require receptacles in the wall space, no point measured horizontally along the floor line of any wall space may be more than _____ ft from an outlet.

    (a) 6
    (b) 8
    (c) 10
    (d) 12

57. In a dwelling unit, a receptacle is required in any space _____ ft or more in width (including space measured around corners) and unbroken along the floor line by doorways and similar openings, fireplaces, and fixed cabinets that do not have countertops or similar work surfaces.

    (a) 2
    (b) 3
    (c) 4
    (d) 5

58. In dwelling units, when determining the spacing of receptacle outlets, _____ on exterior walls shall not be considered wall space.

    (a) fixed panels
    (b) fixed glass
    (c) sliding panels
    (d) all of these

59. Receptacle outlets in or on floors shall not be counted as part of the required number of receptacle outlets for dwelling unit wall spaces, unless they are located within _____ in. of the wall.

    (a) 6
    (b) 12
    (c) 18
    (d) 24

60. Receptacles installed for countertop and similar work surfaces as specified in 210.52(C) shall not be considered as the receptacle outlets required by 210.52(A).

    (a) True
    (b) False

61. In dwelling units, outdoor receptacles can be connected to one of the 20A small-appliance branch circuits.

    (a) True
    (b) False

62. Receptacles installed in a dwelling unit kitchen to serve countertop surfaces shall be supplied by not fewer than _____ small-appliance branch circuits.

    (a) one
    (b) two
    (c) three
    (d) four

63. Receptacles outlets are required for kitchen countertops and work surfaces _____ in. and wider

    (a) 12 in.
    (b) 15 in.
    (c) 18 in.
    (d) 24 in.

64. Where using multioutlet assemblies for kitchen countertops and work surfaces, each _____ of multioutlet assembly containing two or more receptacles installed in individual or continuous lengths shall be considered to be one receptacle outlet.

    (a) 12 in.
    (b) 18 in.
    (c) 24 in.
    (d) 36 in.

65. A receptacle outlet shall be installed at each dwelling unit kitchen wall countertop and work surface space that is 12 in. or wider and receptacle outlets shall be installed so that no point along the wall line is more than _____ in., measured horizontally from a receptacle outlet in that space.

    (a) 10
    (b) 12
    (c) 16
    (d) 24

66. For an island or peninsular countertop, at least one receptacle outlet shall be provided for the first _____ sq ft or fraction thereof, of the countertop or work surface.

    (a) 9 sq ft
    (b) 10 sq ft
    (c) 12 sq ft
    (d) 15 sq ft

67. An island or peninsular countertop measuring 12 sq ft requires _____ receptacle outlet(s).

    (a) 1
    (b) 2
    (c) 3
    (d) 4

68. At least one receptacle outlet shall be located within _____ of the outer end of a peninsular countertop or work surface.

    (a) 1 ft
    (b) 2 ft
    (c) 3 ft
    (d) 4 ft

69. Kitchen and dining room countertop receptacle outlets in dwelling units shall be installed on or above the countertop or work surface, but not more than _____ in. above the countertop or work surface.

    (a) 12
    (b) 18
    (c) 20
    (d) 24

70. Receptacle outlets installed on or above countertop or work surfaces shall be located not more than _____ in. above the countertop or work surface.

    (a) 6
    (b) 12
    (c) 20
    (d) 36

71. Receptacle outlets installed below the countertop or work surface in dwelling units, shall be located not more than _____ in. below the countertop or work surface.

    (a) 6
    (b) 12
    (c) 20
    (d) 36

72. Receptacle outlet assemblies _____ for use in countertops or work surfaces are permitted to be installed in countertops or work surfaces.

    (a) listed
    (b) labeled
    (c) identified
    (d) all of these

73. Receptacles installed below a countertop or work surface shall not be located where the countertop or work surface extends more than _____ in. beyond its support base.

    (a) 3
    (b) 6
    (c) 9
    (d) 12

74. Receptacle outlets rendered not readily accessible by _____ or appliances occupying assigned spaces shall not be considered as the required countertop or work surface outlets.

    (a) appliances fastened in place
    (b) appliance garages
    (c) sinks or range tops
    (d) all of these

75. Additional requirements for installing receptacles in dwelling unit countertops and work surfaces can be found in Article _____.

    (a) 402
    (b) 404
    (c) 406
    (d) 410

76. In dwelling units, the required bathroom receptacle outlet can be installed on the side or face of the basin cabinet if not more than _____ in. below the top of the basin or basin countertop.

    (a) 12
    (b) 18
    (c) 24
    (d) 36

77. In dwelling unit bathrooms, not less than one 15A or 20A, 125V receptacle outlet shall be installed within _____ ft of the outside edge of each bathroom basin.

    (a) 2
    (b) 3
    (c) 4
    (d) 6

78. The receptacle outlet for a dwelling unit bathroom shall be located on a(n) _____ adjacent to the basin or basin countertop, on the countertop, or on the side or face of the basin cabinet, and never more than 12 in. below the top of the basin or basin countertop.

    (a) wall or partition
    (b) base cabinet
    (c) light fixture
    (d) interior wall

79. Receptacle outlet assemblies listed for use in countertops shall be permitted to be installed in countertops of dwelling unit bathrooms.

    (a) True
    (b) False

80. There shall be a minimum of _____ receptacle(s) installed outdoors at a one-family dwelling and each unit of a two-family dwelling unit that is at grade level.

    (a) zero
    (b) two
    (c) three
    (d) four

81. At least one receptacle outlet not more than _____ ft above a balcony, deck, or porch shall be installed at each balcony, deck, or porch that is attached to and accessible from a dwelling unit.

    (a) 2
    (b) 3
    (c) 6½
    (d) 8

82. A laundry receptacle outlet shall not be required in each dwelling unit of a multifamily building, if laundry facilities are provided on the premises for all building occupants.

    (a) True
    (b) False

83. For one- and two-family dwellings, at least one receptacle outlet shall be installed in each _____.

    (a) separate unfinished portion of a basement
    (b) attached or detached garage with electric power
    (c) accessory building with electric power
    (d) all of these

84. Where a portion of the dwelling unit basement is finished into one or more habitable rooms, each separate unfinished portion shall have a receptacle outlet installed.

    (a) True
    (b) False

85. Hallways in dwelling units that are _____ ft long or longer require a receptacle outlet.

    (a) 6
    (b) 8
    (c) 10
    (d) 12

86. Foyers with an area greater than _____ sq ft shall have a receptacle located in each wall space 3 ft or more in width unbroken by doorways, windows next to doors that extend to the floor, and similar openings.

    (a) 40
    (b) 60
    (c) 80
    (d) 100

87. Guest rooms or guest suites provided with permanent provisions for _____ shall have receptacle outlets installed in accordance with all of the applicable requirements for a dwelling unit in accordance with 210.52.

    (a) whirlpool tubs
    (b) bathing
    (c) cooking
    (d) Internet access

88. The number of receptacle outlets for guest rooms in hotels and motels shall not be less than that required for a dwelling unit. These receptacles can be located to be convenient for permanent furniture layout, but at least _____ receptacle outlet(s) shall be readily accessible.

    (a) one
    (b) two
    (c) three
    (d) four

89. Receptacles installed behind a bed in the guest rooms in hotels and motels shall be located to prevent the bed from contacting an attachment plug, or the receptacle shall be provided with a suitable guard.

    (a) True
    (b) False

90. The required heating, air-conditioning, and refrigeration equipment receptacle outlet shall be located _____ the equipment.

    (a) 6 ft above
    (b) not over 8 ft from
    (c) on
    (d) on the same level

91. The required receptacle outlet for heating, air-conditioning, and refrigeration equipment shall not be connected to the load side of the equipment's branch-circuit disconnecting means.

    (a) True
    (b) False

92. A 15A or 20A, 125V receptacle outlet shall be located within 25 ft of heating, air-conditioning, and refrigeration equipment for _____ occupancies.

    (a) dwelling
    (b) commercial
    (c) industrial
    (d) all of these

93. "Where equipment, other than service equipment, requires dedicated equipment space as specified in 110.26(E), the required receptacle outlet shall be located within _____ the electrical equipment."

    (a) the same room or area as
    (b) or adjacent to
    (c) sight of
    (d) or below

94. A meeting room with any floor dimension that is _____ ft or greater in any direction and that has a floor area of at least 215 sq ft shall have at least one floor receptacle outlet.

    (a) 8 ft
    (b) 10 ft
    (c) 12 ft
    (d) 15 ft

95. A meeting room measuring 12 ft x 15 ft requires _____ floor receptacle outlet(s).

    (a) 0
    (b) 1
    (c) 2
    (d) 3

96. At least one lighting outlet controlled by a listed wall-mounted control device shall be installed in every habitable room, kitchen, and bathroom of a dwelling unit.

    (a) True
    (b) False

97. In rooms other than kitchens and bathrooms of dwelling units, one or more receptacles controlled by a wall switch shall be permitted in lieu of _____.

    (a) lighting outlets
    (b) luminaires
    (c) the receptacles required by 210.52(B) and (D)
    (d) all of these

98. In dwelling units, lighting outlets can be controlled by occupancy sensors where equipped with a _____ that will allow the sensor to function as a wall switch.

    (a) manual override
    (b) photocell
    (c) sensor
    (d) secondary supply

99. For dwelling units, attached garages, and detached garages with electric power, at least _____ lighting outlet(s) controlled by a listed wall-mounted control device shall be installed to provide illumination on the exterior side of outdoor entrances or exits with grade-level access.

    (a) one
    (b) two
    (c) three
    (d) one or two

100. When locating lighting outlets in dwelling units, a vehicle door in a garage shall be considered an outdoor entrance.

    (a) True
    (b) False

101. Where a lighting outlet(s) is installed for interior stairways, there shall be a listed wall-mounted control device at each floor level and landing level that includes an entryway to control the lighting outlet(s) where the stairway between floor levels has six risers or more unless remote, central, or automatic control is used.

    (a) True
    (b) False

102. In a dwelling unit, illumination for outdoor entrances that have grade-level access can be controlled by _____ control.

    (a) remote
    (b) central
    (c) automatic
    (d) any of these

103. In a dwelling unit, lighting outlets for interior stairways controlled in accordance with 210.70(A)(2)(3) shall not be controlled by the use of dimmer switches unless they provide the full range of _____ at each location.

    (a) illumination
    (b) emergency lighting
    (c) dimming control
    (d) protection

104. In a dwelling unit, at least one lighting outlet _____ shall be located at the point of entry to the attic, underfloor space, utility room, or basement where these spaces are used for storage or contain equipment requiring servicing.

    (a) that is unswitched
    (b) containing or controlled by a switch
    (c) that is GFCI protected
    (d) that is shielded from damage

105. Lighting outlets in guest rooms or guest suites shall be permitted to be controlled by occupancy sensors that are located at a customary wall switch location and equipped with a manual override that allows the sensor to function as a wall switch.

    (a) True
    (b) False

106. At least one wall switch-controlled lighting outlet shall be installed in every habitable room and bathroom of a guest room or guest suite of hotels, motels, and similar occupancies. A receptacle outlet controlled by a wall switch may be used to meet this requirement in other than _____.

    (a) bathrooms
    (b) kitchens
    (c) sleeping areas
    (d) bathrooms and kitchens

107. In all occupancies for attics and underfloor spaces, utility rooms, and basements where a lighting outlet is installed for equipment requiring service, the lighting outlet shall be _____.

    (a) installed at the entrance to such spaces
    (b) installed at or near the equipment
    (c) of the motion sensor type
    (d) GFCI protected

108. For attics and underfloor spaces, utility rooms, and basements in all occupancies, at least _____ lighting outlet(s) containing a switch or controlled by a wall switch shall be installed where these spaces are used for storage or contain equipment requiring servicing.

    (a) one
    (b) two
    (c) three
    (d) four

109. Each meeting room of not more than _____ sq ft in other than dwelling units shall have outlets for nonlocking-type, 125V, 15A or 20A receptacles installed in accordance with 210.71(B).

    (a) 500
    (b) 1,000
    (c) 1,500
    (d) 2,000

110. For the purposes of 210.65, meeting rooms are typically designed or intended for the gathering of seated occupants for such purposes as conferences, deliberations, or similar purposes, where _____ electronic equipment such as computers, projectors, or similar equipment is likely to be used.

    (a) approved
    (b) portable
    (c) listed
    (d) permanently installed

111. For the purposes of 210.71, examples of rooms that are not meeting rooms include _____.

    (a) auditoriums
    (b) schoolrooms
    (c) coffee shops
    (d) all of these

112. The required number of receptacle outlets on fixed walls in meeting rooms shall be determined in accordance with _____.

    (a) 210.52(A)(1)
    (b) 210.52(A)(1) and (A)(2)
    (c) 210.52(A)(1) through (A)(3)
    (d) 210.52(A)(1) through (A)(4)

113. A meeting room that is at least 12 ft wide and that has a floor area of at least 215 sq ft shall have at least one receptacle outlet located in the floor at a distance not less than _____ from any fixed wall for each 215 sq ft or major portion of floor space.

    (a) 6 ft
    (b) 6 ft 6 in.
    (c) 7 ft
    (d) 7 ft 6 in.

ARTICLE
215

FEEDERS

Introduction to Article 215—Feeders

Article 215 covers the rules for the installation and ampacity of feeders. The requirements for feeders have some similarities to those for branch circuits, and in some ways, feeders resemble service conductors. It is important to understand the distinct differences between these three types of circuits in order to correctly apply the *Code* requirements.

Feeders are the conductors between the service disconnect, the separately derived system, or other supply source, and the final branch-circuit overcurrent protective device. Conductors past the final overcurrent protective device protecting the circuit and the outlet are branch-circuit conductors and fall within the scope of Article 210 [Article 100 Definitions]. ▶Figure 215–1

Service conductors are the conductors from the service point to the service disconnect [Article 100 Definitions]. If there is no serving utility, and the electric power is derived from a gener-

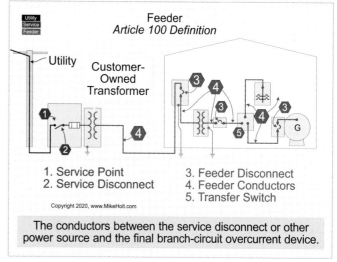

1. Service Point
2. Service Disconnect
3. Feeder Disconnect
4. Feeder Conductors
5. Transfer Switch

Copyright 2020, www.MikeHolt.com

The conductors between the service disconnect or other power source and the final branch-circuit overcurrent device.

▶Figure 215–1

ator or other on-site electric power source, then the conductors from the supply source are defined as feeders and there are no service conductors. It is easy to be confused between feeder, branch-circuit, and service conductors so it is important to evaluate each installation carefully using the Article 100 Definitions to be sure the correct *NEC* rules are followed.

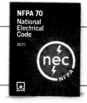

Please use the 2020 *Code* book to answer the following questions.

1. The minimum feeder conductor ampacity shall be no less than the noncontinuous load plus _____ percent of the continuous load, and not less than the maximum load after the application of adjustment and correction factors.

   (a) 80
   (b) 100
   (c) 125
   (d) 150

2. Where a portion of a feeder is connected at both its supply and load ends to separately installed pressure connections in accordance with 110.14(C)(2), it shall be permitted to have an allowable ampacity _____ the sum of the continuous load plus the noncontinuous load.

   (a) not less than
   (b) equal to
   (c) not greater than
   (d) 80% of

3. Feeder conductors shall be permitted to be sized at 100 percent of the continuous and noncontinuous load where a portion of the feeder is connected at both its supply and load ends to separately installed pressure connections.

(a) True
(b) False

4. Feeder grounded conductors that are not connected to an overcurrent device shall be permitted to be sized at _____ percent of the continuous and noncontinuous load.

(a) 80
(b) 100
(c) 115
(d) 125

5. Feeder grounded conductors shall be permitted to be sized at _____ percent of the continuous and noncontinuous load where a portion of the feeder is connected at both its supply and load ends to separately installed pressure connections.

(a) 80
(b) 100
(c) 125
(d) 150

6. Feeder equipment grounding conductors that are insulated or covered _____ and larger, shall be permitted, at the time of installation, to be permanently identified as an equipment grounding conductor at each end and at every point where the conductor is accessible.

(a) 8 AWG
(b) 6 AWG
(c) 4 AWG
(d) 1/0 AWG

7. Each feeder disconnect rated 1,000A or more and installed on solidly grounded wye electrical systems of more than 150V to ground, but not exceeding _____ phase-to-phase, shall be provided with ground-fault protection of equipment in accordance with 230.95.

(a) 50V
(b) 100V
(c) 150V
(d) 600V

8. Where a premises wiring system contains feeders supplied from more than one nominal voltage system, each ungrounded conductor of a feeder shall be identified by phase or line and system by _____, or other approved means.

(a) color coding
(b) marking tape
(c) tagging
(d) any of these

ARTICLE 220

BRANCH-CIRCUIT, FEEDER, AND SERVICE LOAD CALCULATIONS

Introduction to Article 220—Branch-Circuit, Feeder, and Service Load Calculations

This article focuses on the requirements for calculating demand loads (including demand factors) in order to size branch circuits [210.19(A)(1)], feeders [215.2(A)(1)], and service conductors [230.42(A)].

Part I describes the layout of Article 220 and provides a table showing where other types of load calculations can be found in the *NEC*. Part II provides requirements for branch-circuit calculations and for specific types of branch circuits. Part III covers the requirements for feeder and service calculations using what is commonly called the "Standard Method of Calculation." Part IV provides optional calculations that can be used in place of the standard calculations provided in Parts II and III—if your installation meets certain requirements. "Farm Load Calculations" are discussed in Part V of this article.

In some cases, the *Code* provides an optional method (Part IV) for feeder and service calculations in addition to the standard method (Part III); however, they do not yield identical results. In fact, the optional method of calculation will often result in a smaller feeder or service. When taking an exam, read the instructions carefully to be sure which method the test question wants you to use. Be sure to review the examples in Annex D of the *NEC* to gain more practice with these calculations. The *Code* recognizes that not all demand for power will occur at the same time and it is because of this varying demand that certain demand factors are able to be applied.

Please use the 2020 *Code* book to answer the following questions.

1. Article _____ provides requirements for calculating branch-circuit, feeder, and service loads.

   (a) 200
   (b) 210
   (c) 220
   (d) 230

2. Unless otherwise specified, for purposes of calculating branch-circuit and feeder loads, nominal system voltages of 120, 120/240, 208Y/120, 240, 347, 480Y/277, 480, 600Y/347, and 600 volts are to be used.

   (a) True
   (b) False

3. When calculations in Article 220 result in a fraction of an ampere that is less than _____, such fractions can be dropped.

   (a) 0.49
   (b) 0.50
   (c) 0.51
   (d) 0.80

4. The 3 VA per-square-foot general lighting load for dwelling units does not include _____.

   (a) finished basements
   (b) finished attics
   (c) unused or unfinished spaces not adaptable for future use
   (d) utility rooms

5. The 125 percent multiplier for a continuous load as specified in 210.20(A) _____ included when using the unit loads in table 220.12 for calculating the minimum lighting load for a specified occupancy.

    (a) is
    (b) is not
    (c) is permitted to be
    (d) shall not be

6. The 125 percent multiplier for a continuous load as specified in 210.20(A) is included when using the unit loads in table 220.12 for calculating the minimum lighting load for auditoriums, lodge rooms, banks, and stores.

    (a) True
    (b) False

7. Where the lighting load for a nondwelling building is designed and constructed to comply with an energy code adopted by the local authority, the lighting load shall be permitted to be calculated using the unit values specified in the _____.

    (a) energy code
    (b) manufacturer's instructions
    (c) *NEC*
    (d) lighting design manual

8. Where a building is designed and constructed to comply with an energy code adopted by the local authority, the lighting load is permitted to be calculated using the unit values specified in the energy code if _____.

    (a) a continuous power monitoring system is installed
    (b) a power monitoring system is installed with alarm values to alert personnel when the lighting load exceeds the energy code values and can provide to automatically reduce the connected load
    (c) a continuous load multiplier of 125 percent is applied
    (d) all of these

9. Sign and outline lighting outlets are to be calculated at a minimum of _____ VA for each required branch circuit specified in 600.5(A).

    (a) 1,000
    (b) 1,200
    (c) 1,500
    (d) 2,000

10. Show window loads are permitted to be calculated at 180 volt-amperes per linear ft of show window.

    (a) True
    (b) False

11. Where fixed multioutlet assemblies are used in other than dwelling units or the guest rooms of hotels or motels, each _____ ft or fraction thereof of each separate and continuous length shall be considered as one outlet of not less than 180 VA where appliances are unlikely to be used simultaneously.

    (a) 5
    (b) 5½
    (c) 6
    (d) 6½

12. Where appliances are likely to be used simultaneously, each 1ft (or fraction thereof) of fixed multioutlet assembly is considered _____.

    (a) 15A
    (b) 90 VA
    (c) 20A
    (d) 180 VA

13. For other than dwelling occupancies, banks, or office buildings, each receptacle outlet shall be calculated at not less than _____ VA.

    (a) 90
    (b) 180
    (c) 270
    (d) 360

14. For circuits supplying loads consisting of motor-operated utilization equipment that is fastened in place and has a motor larger than _____ in combination with other loads, the total calculated feeder load shall be based on 125 percent of the largest motor load plus the sum of the other loads.

    (a) ½ hp
    (b) ¼ hp
    (c) ⅛ hp
    (d) ¹⁄₁₆ hp

15. The 3 VA per sq ft general lighting load for dwelling units includes general-use receptacles and lighting outlets.

    (a) True
    (b) False

16. Branch circuits that supply lighting units that have ballasts, transformers, autotransformers, or LED drivers shall have the calculated load based on _____ of the units, not to the total wattage of the lamps.

    (a) 50 percent of the rating
    (b) 80 percent of the rating
    (c) the total ampere rating
    (d) 150 percent of the rating

17. The minimum feeder load for show-window lighting is _____ VA per linear foot.

    (a) 180
    (b) 200
    (c) 300
    (d) 400

18. For other than dwelling units or guest rooms of hotels or motels, the feeder and service calculation for track lighting shall be calculated at 150 VA for every _____ ft of lighting track or fraction thereof unless the track is supplied through a device that limits the current to the track.

    (a) 1
    (b) 2
    (c) 3
    (d) 4

19. Feeder and service loads for fixed electric space-heating loads shall be calculated at _____ percent of the total connected load.

    (a) 80
    (b) 100
    (c) 125
    (d) 200

20. A dwelling unit containing three 120V small-appliance branch circuits has a calculated load of _____ VA for the small-appliance circuits.

    (a) 1,500
    (b) 3,000
    (c) 4,500
    (d) 6,000

21. A dwelling unit containing two 120V laundry branch circuits has a calculated load of _____ VA for the laundry circuits.

    (a) 1,500
    (b) 3,000
    (c) 4,500
    (d) 6,000

22. When sizing a feeder for the fixed appliance loads in dwelling units, a demand factor of 75 percent of the total nameplate ratings can be applied if there are _____ or more appliances fastened in place on the same feeder.

    (a) two
    (b) three
    (c) four
    (d) five

23. The dwelling unit appliance load demand factor of 75% for four or more appliances shall not apply to _____.

    (a) electric cooking equipment
    (b) clothes dryers
    (c) space heating equipment
    (d) all of these

24. Where there are two or more air-conditioning units served by the same feeder, it shall be permissible to apply a dwelling unit appliance load demand factor of 75%.

    (a) True
    (b) False

25. The load for electric clothes dryers in a dwelling unit shall be _____ watts or the nameplate rating, whichever is larger, per dryer.

    (a) 1,500
    (b) 4,500
    (c) 5,000
    (d) 8,000

26. Using the standard load calculation method, the feeder demand factor for five household clothes dryers is _____ percent.

    (a) 50
    (b) 70
    (c) 85
    (d) 100

27. To determine the feeder calculated load for ten 3 kW household cooking appliances, use _____ of Table 220.55.

    (a) Column A
    (b) Column B
    (c) Column C
    (d) 125 percent

28. The feeder/service calculated load for a multifamily dwelling containing nine 12 kW ranges is _____.

    (a) 13,000W
    (b) 14,700W
    (c) 16,000W
    (d) 24,000W

29. Table 220.56 may be applied to determine the load for thermostatically controlled or intermittently used _____ and other kitchen equipment in a commercial kitchen.

    (a) commercial electric cooking equipment
    (b) dishwasher booster heaters
    (c) water heaters
    (d) all of these

30. The demand factors of Table 220.56 apply to space-heating, ventilating, or air-conditioning equipment.

    (a) True
    (b) False

31. When applying the demand factors of Table 220.56, the feeder or service demand load shall not be less than the sum of the _____.

    (a) total number of receptacles at 180 VA per receptacle outlet
    (b) VA ratings of all of the small-appliance branch circuits combined
    (c) largest two kitchen equipment loads
    (d) kitchen heating and air-conditioning loads

32. Where it is unlikely that two or more noncoincident loads will be in use simultaneously, only the _____ the loads used at one time is required to be used in computing the total load to a feeder.

    (a) smaller of
    (b) largest of
    (c) difference between
    (d) first 40 percent of

33. Where a motor is part of the noncoincident load and it is not the largest of the noncoincident loads, 125 percent of the motor load shall be used in the calculation if it is the largest motor.

    (a) True
    (b) False

34. A feeder or service supplying household electric ranges, wall-mounted ovens, counter-mounted cooking units, and electric dryers, where the maximum unbalanced load has been determined in accordance with Table 220.55 for ranges and Table 220.54 for dryers shall be permitted to have an additional demand factor of _____ percent applied.

    (a) 50
    (b) 70
    (c) 85
    (d) 115

35. There shall be no reduction in the size of the neutral or grounded conductor on _____ loads supplied from a 4-wire, wye-connected, three-phase system.

    (a) dwelling unit
    (b) hospital
    (c) nonlinear
    (d) motel

36. Under the optional method for calculating a single-family dwelling service, general loads beyond the initial 10 kVA are assessed at a _____ percent demand factor.

    (a) 40
    (b) 50
    (c) 60
    (d) 75

37. A demand factor of _____ percent applies to a multifamily dwelling with ten units if the optional calculation method is used.

    (a) 43
    (b) 50
    (c) 60
    (d) 75

38. Where two dwelling units are supplied by a single feeder and the calculated load under Part III of this article exceeds that for _____ identical units calculated under 220.84, the lesser of the two loads is permitted to be used.

    (a) 2
    (b) 2.50
    (c) 3
    (d) 4

39. When calculating a feeder or service load for existing installations, if the maximum demand data for a 1-year period is not available, the calculated load shall be permitted to be based on the maximum demand (the _____ kilowatts reached and maintained for a 15-minute interval continuously recorded over a minimum 30-day period using a recording ammeter or power meter connected to the highest loaded phase of the feeder or service, based on the initial loading at the start of the recording.

(a) lowest recorded
(b) highest recorded
(c) lowest average
(d) highest average

ARTICLE
225

OUTSIDE BRANCH CIRCUITS AND FEEDERS

Introduction to Article 225—Outside Branch Circuits and Feeders

This article covers the installation requirements for equipment, including overhead and underground branch-circuit and feeder conductors located outdoors on or between buildings, poles, and other structures on the premises. Conductors installed outdoors can serve many purposes such as area lighting, power for outdoor equipment, or for providing power to separate buildings or structures. It is important to remember that the power supply for buildings is not always a service conductor but may be feeder or branch-circuit conductors originating in another building. Never just assume that the conductors supplying power to a building are service conductors until you have identified where the service point is [Article 100] and reviewed the Article 100 definitions for feeders, branch circuits, and service conductors. If you have correctly determined the conductors are service conductors, then use Article 230.

Part II of this article limits the number of feeders plus branch circuits to a building and provides rules regarding their disconnects. These requirements include the disconnect rating, construction characteristics, labeling, where to locate the disconnect, and the grouping of multiple disconnects.

 Please use the 2020 *Code* book to answer the following questions.

1. Article _____ covers requirements for outside branch circuits and feeders run on or between buildings, structures, or poles on the premises.

   (a) 200
   (b) 210
   (c) 220
   (d) 225

2. Open individual conductors shall not be smaller than _____ AWG copper for spans up to 50 ft in length and _____ AWG copper for a longer span, unless supported by a messenger wire.

   (a) 10, 8
   (b) 8, 8
   (c) 6, 8
   (d) 6, 6

3. The point of attachment of overhead premises wiring to a building shall in no case be less than _____ ft above finished grade.

   (a) 8
   (b) 10
   (c) 12
   (d) 15

4. Where a mast is used for overhead branch-circuit or feeder conductor support, it shall have adequate strength or be supported by braces or guys to safely withstand the strain imposed by the conductors.

   (a) True
   (b) False

5. Overhead feeder and/or branch-circuit conductors shall not be attached to a mast where the connection is _____ a weatherhead or the end of the conduit and a coupling where the coupling is located above the last point of securement to the building or other structure, or where the coupling is located above the building or other structure.

    (a) above
    (b) below
    (c) between
    (d) even with

6. Overhead feeder and branch circuit spans of open conductors and open multiconductor cables of not over 1000 volts, nominal, shall have a clearance of not less than _____ over residential property and driveways.

    (a) 10 ft
    (b) 12 ft
    (c) 15 ft
    (d) 18 ft

7. Overhead feeder conductors shall have a minimum vertical clearance of _____ ft over residential property and driveways, as well as those commercial areas not subject to truck traffic, where the voltage does not exceed 300 volts-to-ground.

    (a) 10
    (b) 12
    (c) 15
    (d) 18

8. The minimum clearance for overhead feeder conductors not exceeding 1,000V that pass over commercial areas subject to truck traffic is _____ ft.

    (a) 10
    (b) 12
    (c) 15
    (d) 18

9. Overhead feeder conductors installed over roofs shall have a vertical clearance of not less than _____ above the roof surface, unless otherwise permitted by an exception.

    (a) 3 ft
    (b) 8 ft 6 in.
    (c) 12 ft
    (d) 15 ft 6 in.

10. If a set of 120/240V overhead feeder conductors terminates at a through-the-roof raceway or approved support, with not more than 6 ft of these conductors, 4 ft horizontally, passing over the roof overhang, the minimum clearance above the roof for these conductors is not less than _____.

    (a) 12 in.
    (b) 18 in.
    (c) 2 ft
    (d) 5 ft

11. Overhead feeder and branch circuit clearance from chimneys, radio and television antennas, tanks, and other nonbuilding or nonbridge structures, shall not be less than _____.

    (a) 3 ft
    (b) 6 ft
    (c) 8 ft
    (d) 10 ft

12. The requirement for maintaining a 3-foot vertical clearance from the edge of the roof shall not apply to the final feeder conductor span where the conductors are attached to _____.

    (a) a building pole
    (b) the side of a building
    (c) an antenna
    (d) the base of a building

13. The vertical clearance of final spans of overhead conductors above or within _____ ft measured horizontally of platforms, projections, or surfaces that will permit personal contact shall be maintained in accordance with 225.18.

    (a) 3
    (b) 6
    (c) 8
    (d) 10

14. Outside branch circuits and feeders shall not be installed beneath openings through which materials may be moved and shall not be installed where they will obstruct entrance to these buildings' openings.

    (a) True
    (b) False

15. Raceways on exteriors of buildings or other structures shall be arranged to drain and shall be _____ for use in wet locations.

    (a) labeled
    (b) listed
    (c) approved
    (d) b or c

16. Vegetation such as trees shall not be used for support of _____.

    (a) overhead conductor spans
    (b) surface wiring methods
    (c) luminaires
    (d) electric equipment

17. Underground raceways entering a(n) _____ from outside shall be sealed.

    (a) building or structure
    (b) crawlspace
    (c) highway right-of-way
    (d) easement

18. Raceways entering from outside shall be sealed with a product identified for use with the _____ insulation.

    (a) conductor
    (b) cable
    (c) raceway interior
    (d) conductor or cable

19. A building or structure shall be supplied by a maximum of _____ feeder(s) or branch circuit(s), unless specifically permitted otherwise.

    (a) one
    (b) two
    (c) three
    (d) four

20. Where multiple feeders to a building conductors originate in the same panelboard, switchboard, or other distribution equipment, and each feeder terminates in a single disconnecting means, not more than _____ feeders are permitted to be run to the building.

    (a) 2
    (b) 4
    (c) 6
    (d) 8

21. Where more than one feeder is installed to a building in accordance with this 225.30(B), all feeder disconnects in the building shall be grouped in the same location.

    (a) True
    (b) False

22. The disconnecting means for a building supplied by a feeder shall be installed at a(n) _____ location.

    (a) accessible
    (b) readily accessible
    (c) outdoor
    (d) indoor

23. There shall be no more than _____ switches or circuit breakers to serve as the disconnecting means for a building supplied by a feeder.

    (a) two
    (b) four
    (c) six
    (d) eight

24. The two to six disconnects for a disconnecting means for a building supplied by a feeder shall be _____.

    (a) the same size
    (b) grouped
    (c) in the same enclosure
    (d) of the same manufacturer

25. Where a building has multiple feeders, a permanent _____ shall be installed at each feeder disconnect location denoting all other services and feeders and the area served by each.

    (a) plaque or directory
    (b) map
    (c) label
    (d) guide

26. A building disconnecting means that supplies only limited loads of a single branch circuit shall have a rating of not less than _____.

    (a) 15A
    (b) 20A
    (c) 25A
    (d) 30A

27. For a one-family dwelling, the feeder disconnecting means shall have a rating of not less than _____, 3-wire.

    (a) 60A
    (b) 100A
    (c) 150A
    (d) 200A

28. For all other installations, the feeder or branch-circuit disconnecting means shall have a rating of not less than _____.

    (a) 20A
    (b) 30A
    (c) 40A
    (d) 60A

29. For installations consisting of not more than two 2-wire branch circuits, the building disconnecting means shall have a rating of not less than _____.

    (a) 15A
    (b) 20A
    (c) 25A
    (d) 30A

ARTICLE
230 SERVICES

Introduction to Article 230—Services

This article covers the installation requirements for service conductors and their first means of disconnect. The requirements for service conductors differ from those for other conductors. For one thing, service conductors for one building cannot pass through the interior of another [230.3], and different rules are applied depending on whether a service conductor is inside or outside a building. When are they "outside" as opposed to "inside"? The answer may seem obvious, but 230.6 will help you determine when (and if) service conductors are considered to be outside. Article 230 consists of seven parts:

- ▸ Part I. General
- ▸ Part II. Overhead Service Conductors
- ▸ Part III. Underground Service Conductors
- ▸ Part IV. Service-Entrance Conductors
- ▸ Part V. Service Disconnect
- ▸ Part VI. Disconnecting Means
- ▸ Part VIII. Overcurrent Protection

Please use the 2020 *Code* book to answer the following questions.

1. Service conductors and equipment for control and protection of services and their installation requirements are covered in Article _____.

    (a) 210
    (b) 220
    (c) 230
    (d) 240

2. A building or structure shall be supplied by a maximum of _____ service(s), unless specifically permitted otherwise.

    (a) one
    (b) two
    (c) three
    (d) as many as desired

3. Additional services shall be permitted for a single building or other structure sufficiently large to make two or more services necessary if permitted by _____.

    (a) the registered design professional
    (b) special permission
    (c) the engineer of record
    (d) master electricians

4. Additional services shall be permitted for different voltages, frequencies, or phases, or for different uses, such as for _____.

    (a) gymnasiums
    (b) different rate schedules
    (c) flea markets
    (d) special entertainment events

5. Where a building or structure is supplied by more than one service, a permanent plaque or directory shall be installed at each service disconnect location denoting all other services supplying that building or structure and the area served by each.

(a) True
(b) False

6. Service conductors shall be considered outside of a building or other structure where installed under not less than _____ of concrete beneath a building or other structure.

(a) 2 in.
(b) 4 in.
(c) 5 in.
(d) 6 in.

7. Service conductors supplying a building or other structure shall not _____ of another building or other structure.

(a) be installed on the exterior walls
(b) pass through the interior
(c) be installed underneath
(d) span the roof

8. Conductors other than service conductors shall not be installed in the same _____ in which the service conductors are installed.

(a) service raceway or cable
(b) service drop
(c) enclosure
(d) service lateral

9. Grounding electrode conductors or supply-side bonding jumpers or conductors shall not be permitted within raceways containing service conductors.

(a) True
(b) False

10. Where a service raceway enters a building or structure from a(n) _____, it shall be sealed in accordance with 300.5(G).

(a) transformer vault
(b) underground distribution system
(c) cable tray
(d) overhead rack

11. Service conductors installed as unjacketed multiconductor cable shall have a minimum clearance of _____ ft from windows that are designed to be opened, doors, porches, balconies, ladders, stairs, fire escapes, or similar locations.

(a) 3
(b) 4
(c) 6
(d) 10

12. The vertical clearance of final spans of overhead service conductors above, or within _____ ft measured horizontally of platforms, projections, or surfaces that will permit personal contact shall be maintained in accordance with 230.24(B).

(a) 3
(b) 6
(c) 8
(d) 10

13. Service conductors shall not be installed beneath openings through which materials may be moved and shall not be installed where they will obstruct entrance to these buildings' openings.

(a) True
(b) False

14. Overhead service conductors or service equipment can be supported to hardwood trees.

(a) True
(b) False

15. Service-drop conductors shall have _____.

(a) sufficient ampacity to carry the load
(b) adequate mechanical strength
(c) sufficient ampacity to carry the load or adequate mechanical strength
(d) sufficient ampacity to carry the load and adequate mechanical strength

16. The minimum size service-drop conductor permitted is _____ AWG copper or _____ AWG aluminum or copper-clad aluminum.

(a) 8, 8
(b) 8, 6
(c) 6, 8
(d) 6, 6

17. Overhead service conductors installed over roofs shall have a vertical clearance of not less than _____ ft above the roof surface, unless a lesser distance is permitted by an exception.

    (a) 3
    (b) 8
    (c) 12
    (d) 15

18. If a set of 120/240V overhead service conductors terminate at a through-the-roof raceway or approved support, with less than 6 ft of these conductors passing over the roof overhang, the minimum clearance above the roof for these service conductors shall be _____.

    (a) 12 in.
    (b) 18 in.
    (c) 2 ft
    (d) 5 ft

19. The requirement to maintain a 3-foot vertical clearance from the edge of a roof does not apply to the final conductor span where the service drop is attached to _____.

    (a) a service pole
    (b) the side of a building
    (c) an antenna
    (d) the base of a building

20. Overhead service conductors shall have a minimum clearance from final grade of _____ above areas or sidewalks accessible only to pedestrians, measured from final grade or other accessible surface where the voltage does not exceed 150 volts to ground.

    (a) 8 ft
    (b) 10 ft
    (c) 12 ft
    (d) 15 ft

21. If the voltage between overhead service conductors does not exceed 300V and the roof area is guarded or isolated, a reduction in clearance to 3 ft is permitted.

    (a) True
    (b) False

22. Overhead service conductors shall have a minimum vertical clearance of _____ ft from final grade over residential property and driveways, as well as over commercial areas not subject to truck traffic where the voltage does not exceed 300 volts-to-ground.

    (a) 10
    (b) 12
    (c) 15
    (d) 18

23. The minimum clearance for overhead service conductors not exceeding 1,000V that pass over parking areas subject to truck traffic is _____ ft..

    (a) 10
    (b) 12
    (c) 15
    (d) 18

24. Overhead service conductors shall have a horizontal clearance of not less than _____ ft from a pool.

    (a) 8
    (b) 10
    (c) 12
    (d) 14

25. The minimum point of attachment of overhead service conductors to a building shall not be less than _____ ft above finished grade.

    (a) 8
    (b) 10
    (c) 12
    (d) 15

26. Where conduits are used as service masts, hubs shall be _____ for use with service-entrance equipment.

    (a) identified
    (b) approved
    (c) of a heavy-duty type
    (d) listed

27. Underground service conductors shall be installed in accordance with the applicable requirements of this *Code* covering the type of wiring method used and shall be limited to _____.

    (a) Type RMC conduit
    (b) Type PVC conduit
    (c) Type USE conductors or cables
    (d) any of these

28. Underground service conductors shall have _____.

    (a) adequate mechanical strength
    (b) sufficient ampacity for the loads calculated
    (c) 90°C insulation rating
    (d) adequate mechanical strength and sufficient ampacity for the loads calculated

29. Underground copper service conductors shall not be smaller than _____ AWG copper.

    (a) 3
    (b) 4
    (c) 6
    (d) 8

30. Underground service conductors that supply power to limited loads of a single branch circuit shall not be smaller than _____.

    (a) 14 AWG copper
    (b) 14 AWG aluminum
    (c) 12 AWG copper
    (d) 12 AWG aluminum

31. Underground service conductors shall be protected from damage in accordance with _____ including minimum cover requirements.

    (a) 240.6(A)
    (b) 300.5
    (c) 310.16
    (d) 430.52

32. The general requirement for each service drop, set of overhead service conductors, set of underground service conductors, or service lateral is that it shall supply _____ set(s) of service-entrance conductors.

    (a) only one
    (b) only two
    (c) up to six
    (d) an unlimited number of

33. One set of service-entrance conductors connected to the supply side of the normal service disconnecting means shall be permitted to supply standby power systems, fire pump equipment, and fire and sprinkler alarms covered by 230.82(5).

    (a) True
    (b) False

34. The minimum service-entrance conductor size shall have an ampacity not less than the maximum load to be served after the application of any _____ factors.

    (a) adjustment
    (b) correction
    (c) demand factors
    (d) adjustment and correction

35. Wiring methods permitted for service-entrance conductors include _____.

    (a) rigid metal conduit
    (b) electrical metallic tubing
    (c) PVC conduit
    (d) all of these

36. Service entrance conductors shall be continuous and are not permitted to be spliced or tapped.

    (a) True
    (b) False

37. Underground service-entrance conductors shall be protected against physical damage.

    (a) True
    (b) False

38. Service-entrance cables which are not installed underground, where subject to physical damage, shall be protected by _____.

    (a) rigid metal conduit
    (b) IMC
    (c) Schedule 80 PVC conduit
    (d) any of these

39. Service-entrance cables mounted in contact with a building shall be supported at intervals not exceeding _____.

    (a) 24 in.
    (b) 30 in.
    (c) 3 ft
    (d) 4 ft

40. Where exposed to the weather, raceways enclosing service-entrance conductors shall be _____ for use in wet locations and arranged to drain.

    (a) approved or listed
    (b) listed and identified
    (c) suitable
    (d) listed and labeled

41. Overhead service-entrance cables shall be equipped with a _____.

    (a) raceway
    (b) service head
    (c) cover
    (d) all of these

42. Service-entrance cables shall be equipped with a service head. _____ cable shall be permitted to be formed in a gooseneck and taped with a self-sealing weather-resistant thermoplastic.

    (a) Type NMC
    (b) Type TC
    (c) Type SE
    (d) Type AC

43. Service heads on raceways or service-entrance cables and goosenecks in service-entrance cables shall be located _____ the point of attachment, unless impracticable.

    (a) above
    (b) below
    (c) even with
    (d) any of these

44. To prevent moisture from entering service equipment, service-entrance conductors shall _____.

    (a) be connected to service-drop conductors below the level of the service head
    (b) have drip loops formed on the individual service-entrance conductors
    (c) be connected to service-drop conductors below the level of the service head or have drip loops formed on the individual service-entrance conductors
    (d) be connected to service-drop conductors below the level of the service head and have drip loops formed on the individual service-entrance conductors

45. Service-entrance and overhead service conductors shall be arranged so that _____ will not enter the service raceway or equipment.

    (a) dust
    (b) vapor
    (c) water
    (d) lightning

46. Barriers shall be placed in service equipment such that no uninsulated, ungrounded service busbar or service _____ is exposed to inadvertent contact by persons or maintenance equipment while servicing load terminations.

    (a) phase conductor
    (b) neutral conductor
    (c) terminal
    (d) disconnect

47. On a three-phase, 4-wire, delta-connected service where the midpoint of one phase winding is grounded, the service conductor having the higher phase voltage-to-ground shall be durably and permanently marked by an outer finish that is _____ in color, or by other effective means, at each termination or junction point.

    (a) orange
    (b) red
    (c) blue
    (d) any of these

48. The service disconnecting means rated 1,000V or less shall be marked to identify it as being suitable for use as service equipment and shall be _____.

    (a) weatherproof
    (b) listed or field evaluated
    (c) approved
    (d) acceptable

49. Individual meter socket enclosures shall not be considered service equipment but shall be _____ for the voltage and ampacity of the service.

    (a) listed and rated
    (b) labeled and approved
    (c) inspected and rated
    (d) suitable

50. Meter sockets supplied by and under the exclusive control of an electric utility shall not be required to be _____.

    (a) approved
    (b) rated
    (c) listed
    (d) all of these

51. All services in dwelling units shall be provided with a surge protective device (SPD).

    (a) True
    (b) False

52. The surge protective device, (SPD) required for a dwelling unit shall be an integral part of the service equipment or be located immediately adjacent thereto and is not permitted to be located in the downstream panelboard.

    (a) True
    (b) False

53. The surge protective device (SPD) required for a dwelling unit service shall be _____.

    (a) Type 1 or 2
    (b) Type 2 or 3
    (c) Type 3
    (d) Type 4

54. Where dwelling unit service equipment is replaced, a surge protective device, (SPD), shall be installed.

    (a) True
    (b) False

55. A service disconnecting means shall be installed at a(n) _____ location.

    (a) dry
    (b) readily accessible
    (c) outdoor
    (d) indoor

56. A service disconnecting means shall not be installed in bathrooms.

    (a) True
    (b) False

57. Where a remote-control device actuates the service disconnecting means, the service disconnecting means shall still be at a readily accessible location either outside the building or structure, or nearest the point of entry of the service conductors.

    (a) True
    (b) False

58. Each service disconnecting means shall be permanently _____ to identify it as a service disconnect.

    (a) identified
    (b) positioned
    (c) marked
    (d) arranged

59. There shall be no more than _____ disconnects installed for each service or for each set of service-entrance conductors as permitted in 230.2 and 230.40.

    (a) two
    (b) four
    (c) six
    (d) eight

60. When the service contains two to six service disconnecting means, they shall be _____.

    (a) the same size
    (b) grouped
    (c) in the same enclosure
    (d) the same manufacturer

61. The additional service disconnecting means for fire pumps, emergency systems, legally required standby, or optional standby services, shall be installed remote from the one to six service disconnecting means for normal service to minimize the possibility of _____ interruption of supply.

    (a) intentional
    (b) accidental
    (c) simultaneous
    (d) prolonged

62. When the service disconnecting means is a power-operated switch or circuit breaker, it shall be able to be opened by hand in the event of a _____.

    (a) ground fault
    (b) short circuit
    (c) power surge
    (d) power supply failure

63. For installations that supply only limited loads of a single branch circuit, the service disconnecting means shall have a rating not less than _____.

    (a) 15A
    (b) 20A
    (c) 25A
    (d) 30A

64. For a one-family dwelling, the service disconnecting means shall have a rating of not less than _____ amperes, 3-wire.

    (a) 90A
    (b) 100A
    (c) 125A
    (d) 200A

65. For installations consisting of not more than two 2-wire branch circuits, the service disconnecting means shall have a rating of not less than _____.

    (a) 15A
    (b) 20A
    (c) 25A
    (d) 30A

66. Electrical equipment shall not be connected to the supply side of the service disconnecting means, except for a few specific exceptions such as _____.

    (a) Type 1 surge-protective devices
    (b) taps used to supply standby power systems, fire pump equipment, fire and sprinkler alarms, and load (energy) management devices
    (c) solar photovoltaic systems
    (d) all of these

67. Solar photovoltaic systems, fuel cell systems, wind electric systems, energy storage systems, or interconnected electric power production sources are permitted to be connected to the supply side of the service disconnecting means.

    (a) True
    (b) False

68. For one- and two-family dwelling units, all service conductors shall terminate in an emergency disconnecting means having a short-circuit current rating equal to or greater than the _____, installed in a readily accessible outdoor location.

    (a) demand load
    (b) peak demand load
    (c) available fault current
    (d) service conductor rating

69. A meter-mounted transfer switch shall be listed and be capable of transferring _____.

    (a) the load served
    (b) 125 percent of the continuous load served
    (c) the maximum short-circuit current
    (d) all of these

70. Each _____ service conductor shall have overload protection.

    (a) overhead
    (b) underground
    (c) ungrounded
    (d) individual

71. Where fuses are used as the service overcurrent device, the disconnecting means shall be located ahead of the supply side of the fuses in accordance with 230.91.

    (a) True
    (b) False

72. Ground-fault protection of equipment shall be provided for solidly grounded wye electrical services of more than 150 volts-to-ground, but not exceeding 1,000V phase-to-phase for each service disconnecting means rated _____ or more.

    (a) 1,000A
    (b) 1,500A
    (c) 2,000A
    (d) 2,500A

73. As defined by 230.95, the rating of the service disconnect shall be considered to be the rating of the largest _____ that can be installed or the highest continuous current trip setting for which the actual overcurrent device installed in a circuit breaker is rated or can be adjusted.

    (a) fuse
    (b) circuit
    (c) conductor
    (d) all of these

ARTICLE 240

OVERCURRENT PROTECTION

Introduction to Article 240—Overcurrent Protection

This article provides the requirements for overcurrent protection and selecting and installing overcurrent protective devices—typically circuit breakers or fuses. Overcurrent exists when current exceeds the rating of equipment or the ampacity of a conductor due to an overload, short circuit, or ground fault [Article 100]. ▸Figure 240–1

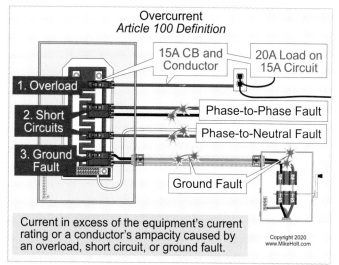

Current in excess of the equipment's current rating or a conductor's ampacity caused by an overload, short circuit, or ground fault.

▸Figure 240–1

▸ *Overload.* An overload is a condition where equipment or conductors carry current exceeding their current rating [Article 100]. A fault, such as a short circuit or ground fault, is not an overload. An example of an overload is plugging two 12.50A (1,500W) hair dryers into a 20A branch circuit.

▸ *Short Circuit.* A short circuit is the unintentional electrical connection between any two normally current-carrying conductors of an electric circuit, either line-to-line or line-to-neutral.

▸ *Ground fault.* A ground fault is an unintentional, electrically conducting connection between a phase conductor of an electric circuit and the normally noncurrent-carrying conductors, metal enclosures, metal raceways, metal equipment, or the Earth [Article 100]. When a ground fault occurs, dangerous voltages is present on metal parts until the circuit overcurrent protective device opens and clears the fault.

Overcurrent protective devices protect conductors and equipment. Selecting the proper overcurrent protection for a specific circuit can be more complicated than it sounds. The general rule for overcurrent protection is that conductors must be protected in accordance with their ampacities at the point where they receive their supply [240.4 and 240.21]. The asterisks next to the small conductor sizes in Table 310.16 refer to a footnote directing you to 240.4(D). That section contains the general rules for small conductors which limit the rating of the overcurrent devices protecting small conductors. There are quite a few circumstances that deviate from this and seem to "break" those rules. Table 240.4(G) lists articles in the *Code* that modify the basic rules of 240.4(D). There are also several rules allowing tap conductors (with much lower ampacities than the overcurrent device protecting them seems to allow) in specific situations [240.21(B)].

Author's Comment:

▸ The tripping action of an overcurrent protective device during an overload is based on a "time-curve," which essentially means that the higher the current, the faster the device will trip. Because of this "time-curve," conductors with lower ampacities than the overcurrent protective device protecting them, may seem to break the rules, but the overcurrent condition will be present only for a very short and safe amount of time.

• • •

An overcurrent protective device must be capable of opening a circuit when an overcurrent situation occurs and must also have an interrupting rating sufficient to avoid damage in fault conditions [110.9]. Carefully study this article to be sure you provide enough overcurrent protection in the correct location(s).

Please use the 2020 *Code* book to answer the following questions.

1. The general requirements for overcurrent protection and over-current protective devices not more than 1000 volts, nominal are provided in Article _____.

   (a) 230
   (b) 240
   (c) 242
   (d) 250

2. Overcurrent protection for conductors and equipment is provided to _____ the circuit if the current reaches a value that will cause an excessive or dangerous temperature in conductors or conductor insulation.

   (a) open
   (b) close
   (c) monitor
   (d) record

3. A device that, when interrupting currents in its current-limiting range, reduces the current flowing in the faulted circuit to a magnitude substantially less than that obtainable in the same circuit if the device were replaced with a solid conductor having comparable impedance, is a(n) "_____ protective device."

   (a) short-circuit
   (b) overload
   (c) ground-fault
   (d) current-limiting overcurrent

4. A conductor, other than a service conductor, that has overcurrent protection ahead of its point of supply that exceeds the ampacity permitted for similar conductors is known as a _____.

   (a) feeder conductor
   (b) service conductor
   (c) tap conductor
   (d) conductor extension

5. Conductor overload protection shall not be required where the interruption of the _____ would create a hazard, such as in a material-handling magnet circuit or fire pump circuit. However, short-circuit protection is required.

   (a) circuit
   (b) line
   (c) phase
   (d) system

6. The next higher standard rating overcurrent device above the ampacity of the ungrounded conductors being protected shall be permitted to be used, provided the _____.

   (a) conductors being protected are not part of a branch circuit supplying more than one receptacle for cord-and-plug-connected portable loads
   (b) ampacity of the conductors does not correspond with the standard ampere rating of a fuse or circuit breaker
   (c) next higher standard rating selected does not exceed 800A
   (d) all of these

7. If the circuit's overcurrent device exceeds _____, the conductor ampacity shall have a rating not less than the rating of the overcurrent device.

   (a) 800A
   (b) 1,000A
   (c) 1,200A
   (d) 2,000A

8. Overcurrent protection shall not exceed _____.

   (a) 15A for 14 AWG copper
   (b) 20A for 12 AWG copper
   (c) 30A for 10 AWG copper
   (d) all of these

9. The standard ampere ratings for fuses include(s) _____.

(a) 1A
(b) 6A
(c) 601A
(d) all of these

10. For adjustable-trip circuit breakers, restricted access is defined as _____.

(a) located behind bolted equipment enclosure doors
(b) located behind locked doors accessible only to qualified personnel
(c) password protected, with password accessible only to qualified personnel
(d) any of these

11. Supplementary overcurrent protection _____.

(a) shall not be used in luminaires
(b) may be used as a substitute for a branch-circuit overcurrent device
(c) may be used to protect internal circuits of equipment
(d) shall be readily accessible

12. Supplementary overcurrent devices used in luminaires or appliances are not required to be readily accessible.

(a) True
(b) False

13. Ground-fault protection of equipment shall be provided for solidly grounded wye electrical systems of more than 150 volts-to-ground, but not exceeding 1,000V phase-to-phase for each individual device used as a building or structure main disconnecting means rated _____ or more, unless specifically exempted.

(a) 1,000A
(b) 1,500A
(c) 2,000A
(d) 2,500A

14. Circuit breakers shall _____ all ungrounded conductors of the circuit both manually and automatically unless specifically permitted otherwise.

(a) open
(b) close
(c) isolate
(d) inhibit

15. Single-pole breakers with identified handle ties can be used to protect each ungrounded conductor for line-to-line connected loads.

(a) True
(b) False

16. Conductors supplied under the tap rules are allowed to supply another conductor using the tap rules.

(a) True
(b) False

17. Feeder taps are permitted to be located at any point on the load side of the feeder overcurrent protective device.

(a) True
(b) False

18. When taps are not over 10 ft in length for field installations, and they leave the enclosure or vault in which the tap is made, the ampacity of the tap conductors cannot be less than _____ the rating of the device protecting the feeder.

(a) $\frac{1}{10}$
(b) $\frac{1}{5}$
(c) $\frac{1}{2}$
(d) $\frac{2}{3}$

19. Tap conductors not over 25 ft in length shall be permitted, providing the _____.

(a) ampacity of the tap conductors is not less than one-third the rating of the overcurrent device protecting the feeder conductors being tapped
(b) tap conductors terminate in a single circuit breaker or set of fuses that limits the load to the ampacity of the tap conductors
(c) tap conductors are suitably protected from physical damage
(d) all of these

20. Outside feeder tap conductors can be of unlimited length without overcurrent protection at the point they receive their supply if the tap conductors _____.

(a) are protected from physical damage
(b) terminate at a single circuit breaker or a single set of fuses that limits the load to the ampacity of the tap conductors
(c) the overcurrent device is part of the building feeder disconnect
(d) all of these

21. Outside secondary conductors can be of unlimited length without overcurrent protection at the point they receive their supply if the conductors _____.

    (a) are protected from physical damage
    (b) terminate at a single overcurrent device equal to or less than their ampacity
    (c) the overcurrent device is part of the building disconnect
    (d) all of these

22. Circuit breakers and switches containing fuses shall be readily accessible and installed so the center of the grip of the operating handle of the switch or circuit breaker, when in its highest position, is not more than _____ above the floor or working platform.

    (a) 2 ft
    (b) 4 ft 6 in.
    (c) 5 ft
    (d) 6 ft 7 in.

23. Overcurrent devices shall not be located _____.

    (a) where exposed to physical damage
    (b) near easily ignitible materials, such as in clothes closets
    (c) in bathrooms of dwelling units
    (d) all of these

24. Overcurrent devices are not permitted to be located in the bathrooms of _____.

    (a) dwelling units
    (b) dormitories
    (c) guest rooms or guest suites of hotels or motels
    (d) all of these

25. _____ shall not be located over the steps of a stairway.

    (a) Disconnect switches
    (b) Overcurrent devices
    (c) Knife switches
    (d) Transformers

26. Cartridge fuses in circuits of _____, and all fuses in circuits over 150 volts to ground, shall be provided with a disconnecting means on their supply side so that each circuit containing fuses can be independently disconnected from the source of power.

    (a) any voltage
    (b) over 250V to ground
    (c) over 600V to ground
    (d) over 1,000V to ground

27. Circuit breaker enclosures shall be permitted to be installed _____ where the circuit breaker is installed in accordance with 240.81

    (a) vertically
    (b) horizontally
    (c) face-up
    (d) face-down

28. Plug fuses of the Edison-base type shall have a maximum rating of _____.

    (a) 20A
    (b) 30A
    (c) 40A
    (d) 50A

29. Plug fuses of the Edison-base type shall be used only _____.

    (a) where over fusing is necessary
    (b) as a replacement in existing installations
    (c) as a replacement for Type S fuses
    (d) if rated 50A and above

30. Fuseholders for cartridge fuses shall be so designed that it is difficult to put a fuse of any given class into a fuseholder that is designed for a _____ lower or a _____ higher than that of the class to which the fuse belongs.

    (a) voltage, wattage
    (b) wattage, voltage
    (c) voltage, current
    (d) current, voltage

31. Fuses shall be marked with their _____.

    (a) ampere and voltage rating
    (b) interrupting rating where other than 10,000A
    (c) name or trademark of the manufacturer
    (d) all of these

32. Where a method to reduce clearing time for fuses rated 1200A or greater is required in accordance with 240.67(B), the _____ reduction system shall be performance tested when first installed on site.

    (a) ground-fault
    (b) short-circuit
    (c) arc-fault
    (d) arc-energy

33. Where the circuit breaker handles are operated vertically, the "up" position of the handle shall be the "_____" position.

(a) on
(b) off
(c) tripped
(d) any of these

34. A circuit breaker having an interrupting current rating of other than _____ shall have its interrupting rating marked on the circuit breaker.

(a) 5,000A
(b) 10,000A
(c) 22,000A
(d) 50,000A

35. Circuit breakers used to switch 120V and 277V fluorescent lighting circuits shall be listed and marked _____.

(a) UL
(b) SWD or HID
(c) Amps
(d) VA

36. Circuit breakers used to switch high-intensity discharge lighting circuits shall be listed and marked as _____.

(a) SWD
(b) HID
(c) SWD or HID
(d) SWD and HID

37. A circuit breaker with a _____ voltage rating, such as 240V or 480V, can be used where the nominal voltage between any two conductors does not exceed the circuit breaker voltage rating.

(a) straight
(b) slash
(c) high
(d) low

38. A circuit breaker with a _____ rating, such as 120/240V or 277/480V can be used on a solidly grounded circuit where the nominal voltage of any conductor to ground does not exceed the lower of the two values, and the nominal voltage between any two conductors does not exceed the higher value.

(a) straight
(b) slash
(c) high
(d) low

39. A circuit breaker with a slash rating, such as 120/240V or 480Y/277V, shall be permitted to be applied in a solidly grounded circuit where the nominal voltage of any conductor to ground _____ the lower of the two values of the circuit breaker's voltage rating and the nominal voltage between any two conductors _____ the higher value of the circuit breaker's voltage rating.

(a) is equal to
(b) is equal to or greater than
(c) does not exceed
(d) is equal to 125 percent of

40. The arc energy reduction protection system shall be performance tested when first installed by _____ in accordance with the manufacturer's instructions.

(a) the manufacturer
(b) electrical contractor
(c) engineer
(d) qualified person

41. Reconditioned circuit breakers shall be listed as "reconditioned" and the original listing mark shall be _____.

(a) removed
(b) struck out
(c) replaced
(d) any of these

42. Molded-case circuit breakers are permitted to be reconditioned.

(a) True
(b) False

43. Only _____ circuit breakers shall be permitted to be reconditioned.

(a) low-voltage power
(b) medium-voltage power
(c) high-voltage
(d) all of these

ARTICLE 242

OVERVOLTAGE PROTECTION

Introduction to Article 242—Overvoltage Protection

Part I of this article provides the general, installation, and connection requirements for overvoltage protection and overvoltage protective devices (surge protective devices or SPDs). Part II covers SPDs rated 1kV or less that are permanently installed on premises wiring systems.

Surge protective devices are designed to reduce transient voltages present on premises power distribution wiring and load-side equipment, particularly electronic equipment such as computers, telecommunications equipment, security systems, and electronic appliances.

These transient voltages can originate from several sources, including anything from lightning to laser printers. Voltage spikes and transients caused by the switching of utility power lines, power factor correction capacitors, or lightning can reach thousands of volts and amperes. ▶Figure 242–1

Voltage spikes and transients produced by premises equipment such as photocopiers, laser printers, and other high reactive loads cycling off can be in the hundreds of volts. ▶Figure 242–2

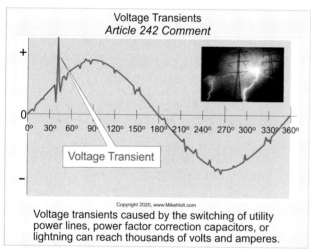

Voltage transients caused by the switching of utility power lines, power factor correction capacitors, or lightning can reach thousands of volts and amperes.

▶Figure 242–1

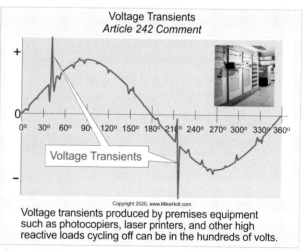

Voltage transients produced by premises equipment such as photocopiers, laser printers, and other high reactive loads cycling off can be in the hundreds of volts.

▶Figure 242–2

The best line of defense for all types of electronic equipment may be the installation of surge protective devices at the electrical service and source of power, as well as at the location of the utilization equipment.

The intent of a surge protective device is to limit transient voltages by diverting or limiting surge current and preventing continued flow of current while remaining capable of repeating these functions [Article 100]. ▶Figure 242–3 and ▶Figure 242–4

• • •

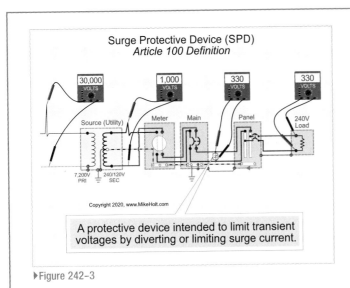

A protective device intended to limit transient voltages by diverting or limiting surge current.

▶Figure 242–3

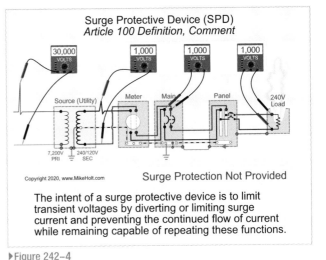

Surge Protection Not Provided

The intent of a surge protective device is to limit transient voltages by diverting or limiting surge current and preventing the continued flow of current while remaining capable of repeating these functions.

▶Figure 242–4

Please use the 2020 *Code* book to answer the following questions.

1. Article(s) _____ provide(s) the general requirements, installation requirements, and connection requirements for overvoltage protection and overvoltage protective devices.

   (a) Article 242
   (b) Article 285
   (c) Article 286
   (d) Article 287

2. A surge protective device shall not be installed in circuits over _____ volts.

   (a) 480V
   (b) 600V
   (c) 1,000V
   (d) 4,160V

3. Surge protective devices shall be listed.

   (a) True
   (b) False

4. Surge protective devices shall be marked with a short-circuit current rating and shall not be installed where the available fault current is in excess of that rating.

   (a) True
   (b) False

5. Type 1 surge protective devices, (SPDs), are permitted to be connected on the load side of the service disconnect overcurrent device.

   (a) True
   (b) False

6. A Type 2 surge protective device is permitted to be connected on either the line or load side of the service equipment.

   (a) True
   (b) False

7. Type 2 surge protective device(s) shall be connected on the load side of the _____ in a separately derived system.

   (a) first overcurrent device
   (b) metering device
   (c) service disconnect
   (d) service entrance

8. For a feeder-supplied building or structure, Type 2 SPDs shall be connected at the building or structure anywhere on the load side of the _____ .

   (a) first overcurrent device
   (b) service attachment point
   (c) meter socket
   (d) transformer

9. The conductors used to connect the surge protective device to the line or bus and to ground shall not be any longer than _____ and shall avoid unnecessary bends.

   (a) 6 in.
   (b) 12 in.
   (c) 18 in.
   (d) necessary

ARTICLE 250

GROUNDING AND BONDING

Introduction to Article 250—Grounding and Bonding

No other article can match this one for misapplication, violation, and misinterpretation. The terminology used in Article 250 has been a source of much confusion but has been improved during the last few *NEC* revisions. It is very important for you to understand the difference between grounding and bonding in order to correctly apply the provisions of this article. Pay careful attention to the definitions of important terms located in Article 100 that apply to grounding and bonding. Article 250 covers the grounding requirements for providing a path to the Earth to reduce overvoltage from lightning strikes, and the bonding requirements that establish a low-impedance fault current path back to the source of the electrical supply to facilitate the operation of overcurrent protective devices in the event of a ground fault.

This article is arranged in a logical manner as illustrated in Figure 250.1 in the *NEC*. It may be a good idea for you to just read through the entire article in *Mike Holt's Understanding the National Electrical Code, Volume 1* textbook first, to get a big picture overview. The illustrations that accompany the text in that textbook will help you better understand the key points. Then, study Article 250 in the *NEC* closely so you understand the details and remember to check Article 100 for the definitions of terms that may be new to you.

Please use the 2020 *Code* book to answer the following questions.

1. General requirements for grounding and bonding of electrical installations and the location of grounding connections are within the scope of _____.

   (a) Article 110
   (b) Article 200
   (c) Article 250
   (d) Article 680

Part I. General

2. Grounded electrical systems shall be connected to earth in a manner that will _____.

   (a) limit voltages due to lightning, line surges, or unintentional contact with higher-voltage lines
   (b) stabilize the voltage-to-ground during normal operation
   (c) facilitate overcurrent device operation in case of ground faults
   (d) limit voltages due to lightning, line surges, or unintentional contact with higher-voltage lines and stabilize the voltage-to-ground during normal operation

3. An important consideration for limiting imposed voltage on electrical systems is to remember that bonding and grounding electrode conductors should not be any longer than necessary and unnecessary bends and loops should be avoided.

   (a) True
   (b) False

4. For grounded systems, normally noncurrent-carrying conductive materials enclosing electrical conductors or equipment shall be connected to earth so as to limit the voltage-to-ground on these materials.

   (a) True
   (b) False

5. For grounded systems, normally noncurrent-carrying conductive materials enclosing electrical conductors or equipment, or forming part of such equipment, shall be connected together and to the _____ to establish an effective ground-fault current path.

   (a) ground
   (b) earth
   (c) electrical supply source
   (d) enclosure

6. In grounded systems, normally noncurrent-carrying electrically conductive materials that are likely to become energized shall be connected _____ in a manner that establishes an effective ground-fault current path.

   (a) together
   (b) to the electrical supply source
   (c) to the closest grounded conductor
   (d) together and to the electrical supply source

7. For grounded systems, electrical equipment and other electrically conductive material likely to become energized shall be installed in a manner that creates a _____ from any point on the wiring system where a ground fault may occur to the electrical supply source.

   (a) circuit facilitating the operation of the overcurrent device
   (b) low-impedance circuit
   (c) circuit capable of safely carrying the ground-fault current likely to be imposed on it
   (d) all of these

8. For grounded systems, the earth is considered an effective ground-fault current path.

   (a) True
   (b) False

9. For ungrounded systems, noncurrent-carrying conductive materials enclosing electrical conductors or equipment shall be connected to the _____ in a manner that will limit the voltage imposed by lightning or unintentional contact with higher-voltage lines.

   (a) ground
   (b) earth
   (c) electrical supply source
   (d) enclosure

10. For ungrounded systems, noncurrent-carrying conductive materials enclosing electrical conductors or equipment, or forming part of such equipment, shall be connected together and to the supply system grounded equipment in a manner that creates a low-impedance path for ground-fault current that is capable of carrying _____.

    (a) the maximum branch-circuit current
    (b) at least twice the maximum ground-fault current
    (c) the maximum fault current likely to be imposed on it
    (d) the equivalent of the main service rating

11. Electrically conductive materials that are likely to _____ in ungrounded systems shall be connected together and to the supply system grounded equipment in a manner that creates a low-impedance path for ground-fault current that is capable of carrying the maximum fault current likely to be imposed on it.

    (a) become energized
    (b) require service
    (c) be removed
    (d) be coated with paint or nonconductive materials

12. In ungrounded systems, electrical equipment, wiring, and other electrically conductive material likely to become energized shall be installed in a manner that creates a low-impedance circuit from any point on the wiring system to the electrical supply source to facilitate the operation of overcurrent devices should a(n) _____ fault from a different phase occur on the wiring system.

    (a) isolated ground
    (b) second ground
    (c) arc
    (d) high impedance

13. The grounding of electrical systems, circuit conductors, surge arresters, surge-protective devices, and conductive normally noncurrent-carrying metal parts of equipment shall be installed and arranged in a manner that will prevent objectionable current.

    (a) True
    (b) False

14. Equipment grounding conductors, grounding electrode conductors, and bonding jumpers shall be connected by _____.

    (a) listed pressure connectors
    (b) terminal bars
    (c) exothermic welding
    (d) any of these

15. Ground clamps and fittings that are exposed to physical damage shall be enclosed in _____ or equivalent protective covering.

    (a) metal or wood
    (b) wood or rubber
    (c) concrete
    (d) metal or plastic

16. _____ on equipment to be grounded shall be removed from contact surfaces to ensure good electrical continuity.

    (a) Paint
    (b) Lacquer
    (c) Enamel
    (d) any of these

Part II. System Grounding

17. Alternating-current circuits of less than 50V shall be grounded if supplied by a transformer whose supply system exceeds 150 volts-to-ground.

    (a) True
    (b) False

18. Alternating-current systems of 50V to 1,000V that supply premises wiring systems shall be grounded where the system is three-phase, 4-wire, wye-connected, with the neutral conductor used as a circuit conductor.

    (a) True
    (b) False

19. Alternating-current systems of 50V to 1,000V that supply premises wiring systems shall be grounded where supplied by a three-phase, 4-wire, delta-connected system in which the midpoint of one phase winding is used as a circuit conductor.

    (a) True
    (b) False

20. _____ alternating-current systems operating at 480V shall have ground detectors installed on the system.

    (a) Grounded
    (b) Solidly grounded
    (c) Effectively grounded
    (d) Ungrounded

21. Ungrounded alternating-current systems from 50V to 1,000V or less that are not required to be grounded in accordance with 250.21(B) shall have _____.

    (a) ground detectors installed for ac systems operating at not less than 100V at 1,000V or les
    (b) the ground detection sensing equipment connected as far as practicable from where the system receives its supply
    (c) ground detectors installed for ac systems operating at not less than 120V and at 1,000V or less, and have the ground detection sensing equipment connected as close as practicable to where the system receives its supply
    (d) ground-fault protection for equipment

22. Ungrounded alternating-current systems from 50V to less than 1,000V shall be legibly marked "Caution: Ungrounded System—Operating _____ Volts Between Conductors" at _____ of the system, with sufficient durability to withstand the environment involved.

    (a) the source
    (b) the first disconnecting means
    (c) every junction box
    (d) the source or the first disconnecting means

23. The grounding electrode conductor connection shall be made at any accessible point from the load end of the overhead service conductors, _____ to, including the terminal or bus to which the grounded service conductor is connected at the service disconnecting means.

    (a) service drop
    (b) underground service conductors
    (c) service lateral
    (d) any of these

24. A grounded conductor shall not be connected to normally non–current-carrying metal parts of equipment, to equipment grounding conductor(s), or be reconnected to ground on the load side of the _____ except as otherwise permitted.

    (a) service disconnecting means
    (b) distribution panel
    (c) switchgear
    (d) switchboard

25. Where the main bonding jumper is a wire or busbar and is installed from the grounded conductor terminal bar or bus to the equipment grounding terminal bar or bus in the service equipment, the _____ shall be permitted to be connected to the equipment grounding terminal, bar, or bus to which the main bonding jumper is connected.

    (a) equipment grounding conductor
    (b) grounded service conductor
    (c) grounding electrode conductor
    (d) system bonding jumper

26. For a grounded system, an unspliced _____ shall be used to connect the equipment grounding conductor(s) and the service disconnect enclosure to the grounded conductor of the system within the enclosure for each service disconnect.

    (a) grounding electrode
    (b) main bonding jumper
    (c) busbar
    (d) insulated copper conductor

27. Where an ac system operating at 1000 volts or less is grounded at any point, a(an) _____ shall connect the grounded conductor(s) to each service disconnecting means enclosure.

    (a) system bonding jumper
    (b) supply-side bonding jumper
    (c) main bonding jumper
    (d) equipment bonding jumper

28. Where an alternating-current system operating at 1,000V or less is grounded at any point, the _____ conductor(s) shall be routed with the ungrounded conductors to each service disconnecting means and shall be connected to each disconnecting means grounded conductor(s) terminal or bus.

    (a) ungrounded
    (b) grounded
    (c) grounding
    (d) paralleled

29. The grounded conductor brought to service equipment shall be routed with the phase conductors and shall not be smaller than specified in Table _____ when the service-entrance conductors are 1,100 kcmil copper and smaller.

    (a) 250.102(C)(1)
    (b) 250.122
    (c) 310.16
    (d) 430.52

30. Where service-entrance conductors are installed in parallel in two or more raceways or cables, the size of the grounded conductor in each raceway or cable shall be based on the total circular mil area of the parallel ungrounded service-entrance conductors in the raceway or cable, sized in accordance with 250.24(C)(1), but not smaller than _____ AWG.

    (a) 1/0
    (b) 2/0
    (c) 3/0
    (d) 4/0

31. A grounding electrode conductor, sized in accordance with 250.66, shall be used to connect the equipment grounding conductors, the service-equipment enclosures, and, where the system is grounded, the grounded service conductor to the grounding electrode(s).

    (a) True
    (b) False

32. A main bonding jumper shall be a _____ or similar suitable conductor.

    (a) wire
    (b) bus
    (c) screw
    (d) any of these

33. Where a main bonding jumper is a screw only, the screw shall be identified with a(n) _____ that shall be visible with the screw installed.

    (a) silver or white finish
    (b) etched ground symbol
    (c) hexagonal head
    (d) green finish

34. Main bonding jumpers and system bonding jumpers shall not be smaller than specified in _____.

    (a) Table 250.102(C)(1)
    (b) Table 250.122
    (c) Table 310.16
    (d) Chapter 9, Table 8

35. Where the supply conductors are larger than 1,100 kcmil copper or 1,750 kcmil aluminum, the main bonding jumper shall have an area that is _____ the area of the largest phase conductor when of the same material.

    (a) at least equal to
    (b) at least 50 percent of
    (c) not less than 12½ percent of
    (d) not more than 12½ percent of

36. A grounded conductor shall not be connected to normally noncurrent-carrying metal parts of equipment on the _____ side of the system bonding jumper of a separately derived system except as otherwise permitted in Article 250.

    (a) supply
    (b) grounded
    (c) high-voltage
    (d) load

37. The connection of an unspliced _____ complying with 250.28(A) through (D) shall be made at any single point on the separately derived system from the source to the first system disconnecting means or overcurrent device, or it shall be made at the source of a separately derived system that has no disconnecting means or overcurrent devices, in accordance with 250.20(A)(1)(a) or (A)(1)(b).

    (a) system bonding jumper
    (b) equipment grounding conductor
    (c) grounded conductor
    (d) grounding electrode conductor

38. The connection of the system bonding jumper for a separately derived system shall be made _____ on the separately derived system from the source to the first system disconnecting means or overcurrent device.

    (a) in at least two locations
    (b) in every location that the grounded conductor is present
    (c) at any single point
    (d) effectively

39. A separately derived ac system supply-side bonding jumper shall be installed to the first disconnecting means enclosure and it is not be required to be larger than the _____.

    (a) neutral conductor
    (b) derived phase conductors
    (c) equipment grounding conductor
    (d) the main service grounding electrode conductor

40. If a building or structure is supplied by a feeder from an outdoor separately derived system, a system bonding jumper at both the source and the first disconnecting means shall be permitted if doing so does not establish a(an) _____ path for the grounded conductor.

    (a) series
    (b) parallel
    (c) conductive
    (d) effective

41. When sizing grounded conductors for parallel raceways installed for a separately derived ac system and the system bonding jumper is not located at the source, they shall also be installed in parallel and not smaller than _____.

    (a) 1 AWG
    (b) 1/0 AWG
    (c) 3/0 AWG
    (d) 250 kcmil

42. If the source of a separately derived system and the first disconnecting means are located in separate enclosures, a supply-side bonding jumper of the wire type shall comply with 250.102(C), based on _____.

(a) the size of the primary conductors
(b) the size of the secondary overcurrent protection
(c) the size of the derived ungrounded conductors
(d) one third the size of the primary grounded conductor

43. The building or structure grounding electrode system shall be used as the _____ electrode for the separately derived system.

(a) grounding
(b) bonding
(c) grounded
(d) bonded

44. For a single separately derived system, the grounding electrode conductor connects the grounded conductor of the derived system to the grounding electrode at the same point on the separately derived system where the _____ is connected.

(a) metering equipment
(b) transfer switch
(c) system bonding jumper
(d) largest circuit breaker

45. Grounding electrode conductor taps from a separately derived system to a common grounding electrode conductor are permitted when a building or structure has multiple separately derived systems, provided that the taps terminate at the same point as the system bonding jumper.

(a) True
(b) False

46. The common grounding electrode conductor installed for multiple separately derived systems shall not be smaller than _____ AWG copper when using a wire-type conductor.

(a) 1/0
(b) 2/0
(c) 3/0
(d) 4/0

47. The common grounding electrode conductor installed for multiple separately derived systems shall be permitted to be a _____ pipe that complies with 250.68(C)(1).

(a) metal gas
(b) metal water
(c) PVC water
(d) any of these

48. The common grounding electrode conductor installed for multiple separately derived systems shall be permitted to be the metal structural frame of the building or structure that complies with 250.68(C)(2) or is connected to the grounding electrode system by a conductor not smaller than _____ or 250 kcmil aluminum.

(a) 6 AWG copper
(b) 1/0 AWG copper
(c) 3/0 AWG copper
(d) 4/0 AWG aluminum

49. Each tap conductor to a common grounding electrode conductor for multiple separately derived systems shall be sized in accordance with _____, based on the derived ungrounded conductors of the separately derived system it serves.

(a) 250.66
(b) 250.118
(c) 250.122
(d) 310.15

50. Tap connections to a common grounding electrode conductor for multiple separately derived systems shall be made at an accessible location by _____.

(a) a connector listed as grounding and bonding equipment
(b) listed connections to aluminum or copper busbars
(c) the exothermic welding process
(d) any of these

51. Tap connections to a common grounding electrode conductor for multiple separately derived systems may be made to a copper or aluminum busbar that is _____ and of sufficient length to accommodate the number of terminations necessary for the installation.

(a) smaller than ¼ in. thick x 4 in. wide
(b) not smaller than ¼ in. thick x 2 in. wide
(c) not smaller than ½ in. thick x 2 in. wide
(d) not smaller than ¼ in. thick x 2½ in. wide

52. In an area served by a separately derived system, the _____ shall be connected to the grounded conductor of the separately derived system.

    (a) structural steel
    (b) metal piping
    (c) metal building skin
    (d) structural steel and metal piping

53. A grounding electrode shall be required if a building or structure is supplied by a feeder.

    (a) True
    (b) False

54. A grounding electrode at a separate building or structure shall be required where one multiwire branch circuit serves the building or structure.

    (a) True
    (b) False

55. When supplying a grounded system at a separate building or structure, an equipment grounding conductor shall be run with the supply conductors and connected to the building or structure disconnecting means and to the grounding electrode(s).

    (a) True
    (b) False

56. For a separate building or structure supplied by a feeder or branch circuit, the grounded conductor can serve as the ground-fault return path for the building/structure disconnecting means for existing installations made in compliance with previous editions of the *Code* as long as the installation continues to meet the condition(s) that _____.

    (a) there are no continuous metallic paths between buildings and structures
    (b) ground-fault protection of equipment is not installed on the supply side of the feeder
    (c) the neutral conductor is sized no smaller than the larger required by 220.61 or 250.122
    (d) all of these

57. For a separate building or structure supplied by a separately derived system when overcurrent protection is provided where the conductors originate, the supply conductors shall contain _____.

    (a) an equipment grounding conductor
    (b) copper conductors only
    (c) GFI protection for the feeder
    (d) all of these

58. For a separate building or structure supplied by a separately derived system when overcurrent protection is not provided for the supply conductors to the building/structure as permitted by 240.21(C)(4), the installation shall be _____ in accordance with 250.30(A).

    (a) AFCI protected
    (b) grounded and bonded
    (c) isolated
    (d) all of these

59. The size of the grounding electrode conductor for a building or structure supplied by a feeder shall not be smaller than that identified in _____, based on the largest ungrounded supply conductor.

    (a) 250.66
    (b) 250.102
    (c) 250.122
    (d) Table 310.16

60. The frame of a portable generator shall not be required to be connected to a(n) _____ if the generator only supplies equipment mounted on the generator, cord-and-plug-connected equipment using receptacles mounted on the generator, or both.

    (a) grounding electrode
    (b) grounded conductor
    (c) ungrounded conductor
    (d) equipment grounding conductor

61. The frame of a vehicle-mounted generator shall not be required to be connected to a(n) _____ if the generator only supplies equipment mounted on the vehicle or cord-and-plug-connected equipment, using receptacles mounted on the vehicle.

    (a) grounding electrode
    (b) grounded conductor
    (c) ungrounded conductor
    (d) equipment grounding conductor

62. High-impedance grounded neutral systems shall be permitted for three-phase ac systems of 480V to 1,000V where _____.

    (a) the conditions of maintenance and supervision ensure that only qualified persons service the installation
    (b) ground detectors are installed on the system
    (c) line-to-neutral loads are not served
    (d) all of these

Part III. Grounding Electrode System and Grounding Electrode Conductor

63. Concrete-encased electrodes of _____ shall not be required to be part of the grounding electrode system where the steel reinforcing bars or rods aren't accessible for use without disturbing the concrete.

    (a) hazardous (classified) locations
    (b) health care facilities
    (c) existing buildings or structures
    (d) agricultural buildings with equipotential planes

64. In order for a metal underground water pipe to be used as a grounding electrode, it shall be in direct contact with the earth for _____.

    (a) 5 ft
    (b) 10 ft or more
    (c) less than 10 ft
    (d) 20 ft or more

65. One or more metal in-ground support structure(s) in direct contact with the earth vertically for _____ ft or more, with or without concrete encasement is permitted to be a grounding electrode in accordance with 250.52.

    (a) 4
    (b) 6
    (c) 8
    (d) 10

66. A bare 4 AWG copper conductor installed horizontally near the bottom or vertically, and within that portion of a concrete foundation or footing that is in direct contact with the earth, can be used as a grounding electrode when the conductor is at least _____ ft in length.

    (a) 10
    (b) 15
    (c) 20
    (d) 25

67. An electrode encased by at least 2 in. of concrete, located horizontally near the bottom or vertically and within that portion of a concrete foundation or footing that is in direct contact with the earth, shall be permitted as a grounding electrode when it consists of _____.

    (a) bare copper conductor not smaller than 8 AWG
    (b) bare copper conductor not smaller than 6 AWG
    (c) bare copper conductor not smaller than 4 AWG
    (d) bare copper conductor not smaller than 1/0 AWG

68. Reinforcing bars for use as a concrete-encased electrode can be bonded together by the usual steel tie wires or other effective means.

    (a) True
    (b) False

69. Concrete-encased grounding electrodes that are installed where the concrete is installed with _____ is not considered to be in direct contact with the earth.

    (a) insulation
    (b) vapor barriers
    (c) films
    (d) any of these

70. Where more than one concrete-encased electrode is present at a building or structure, it shall be permitted to bond only one into the grounding electrode system.

    (a) True
    (b) False

71. Rod and pipe grounding electrodes shall not be less than _____ in length.

    (a) 6 ft
    (b) 8 ft
    (c) 10 ft
    (d) 20 ft

72. A ground ring encircling the building or structure can be used as a grounding electrode when the _____.

    (a) ring is in direct contact with the earth
    (b) ring consists of at least 20 ft of bare copper conductor
    (c) bare copper conductor is not smaller than 2 AWG
    (d) all of these

73. Grounding electrodes of the rod type less than _____ in. in diameter shall be listed.

   (a) ½
   (b) ⅝
   (c) ¾
   (d) 1

74. A buried iron or steel plate used as a grounding electrode shall expose not less than _____ sq ft of surface area to exterior soil.

   (a) 2
   (b) 4
   (c) 9
   (d) 10

75. Grounding electrodes of bare or electrically conductive coated iron or steel plates shall be at least _____ in. thick.

   (a) ⅛
   (b) ¼
   (c) ½
   (d) ¾

76. Local metal underground systems or structures such as underground tanks are permitted to serve as grounding electrodes.

   (a) True
   (b) False

77. _____ shall not be used as grounding electrodes.

   (a) Metal underground gas piping systems
   (b) Aluminum
   (c) Metal well casings
   (d) Metal underground gas piping systems and Aluminum

78. Swimming pool structures and structural _____ [680.26(B)(1) and (B)(2)] shall not be used as a grounding electrode.

   (a) reinforcing steel
   (b) equipotential planes
   (c) pool shells
   (d) pool pump houses

79. Where practicable, rod, pipe, and plate electrodes shall be installed _____.

   (a) directly below the electrical meter
   (b) on the north side of the building
   (c) below permanent moisture level
   (d) all of these

80. If a single rod, pipe, or _____ grounding electrode has a resistance to earth of 25 ohms or less, the supplemental electrode shall not be required.

   (a) plate
   (b) ring type
   (c) grid type
   (d) structural

81. A rod or pipe electrode shall be installed such that at least _____ of length is in contact with the soil.

   (a) 30 in.
   (b) 6 ft
   (c) 8 ft
   (d) 10 ft

82. Where rock bottom is encountered, a rod or pipe electrode shall be driven at an angle not to exceed _____ degrees from the vertical.

   (a) 15
   (b) 30
   (c) 45
   (d) 60

83. Where rock bottom is encountered at an angle up to 45 degrees when driving a rod or pipe electrode, the electrode shall be permitted to be buried in a trench _____ deep.

   (a) 30 in.
   (b) 6 ft
   (c) 8 ft
   (d) 10 ft

84. The upper end of the electrode shall _____ unless the aboveground end and the grounding electrode conductor attachment are protected against physical damage as specified in 250.10.

   (a) no more than 1 in above ground level
   (b) no more than 2 in above ground level
   (c) no more than 3 in above ground level
   (d) flush with or below ground level

85. Where the resistance-to-ground of 25 ohms or less is not achieved for a single rod electrode, _____.

    (a) other means besides electrodes shall be used in order to provide grounding
    (b) the single rod electrode shall be supplemented by one additional electrode
    (c) additional electrodes must be added until 25 ohms is achieved
    (d) any of these

86. Two or more grounding electrodes bonded together are considered a single grounding electrode system.

    (a) True
    (b) False

87. Where bonding jumper(s) are used to connect the grounding electrodes together to form the grounding electrode system, rebar is permitted to be used as a conductor to interconnect the electrodes.

    (a) True
    (b) False

88. Where a metal underground water pipe is used as a grounding electrode, the continuity of the grounding path or the bonding connection to interior piping shall not rely on _____ and similar equipment.

    (a) bonding jumpers
    (b) water meters or filtering devices
    (c) grounding clamps
    (d) all of these

89. Where the supplemental electrode is a rod, that portion of the bonding jumper that is the sole connection to the supplemental grounding electrode shall not be required to be larger than _____ AWG copper wire.

    (a) 8
    (b) 6
    (c) 4
    (d) 1

90. When a ground ring is used as a grounding electrode, it shall be installed at a depth below the earth's surface of not less than _____.

    (a) 18 in.
    (b) 24 in.
    (c) 30 in.
    (d) 8 ft

91. Auxiliary grounding electrodes can be connected to the _____.

    (a) equipment grounding conductor
    (b) grounded conductor
    (c) earth as an effective ground-fault current path
    (d) any of these

92. When installing auxiliary electrodes, the earth shall not be used as an effective ground-fault current path.

    (a) True
    (b) False

93. Two or more common grounding electrodes that are bonded together shall be considered as a single grounding electrode system in this sense.

    (a) True
    (b) False

94. Buildings or structures supplied by multiple services or feeders shall use the same _____ to ground enclosures and equipment in or on that building.

    (a) service
    (b) disconnect
    (c) grounding electrode system
    (d) any of these

95. Grounding electrode conductors of the wire type shall be _____.

    (a) solid
    (b) stranded
    (c) insulated or bare
    (d) any of these

96. Where used outside, aluminum or copper-clad aluminum grounding electrode conductors shall not be terminated within _____ in. of the earth.

    (a) 6
    (b) 12
    (c) 15
    (d) 18

97. Bare or covered aluminum or copper-clad aluminum grounding electrode conductors without an extruded polymeric covering shall not be installed where subject to corrosive conditions or be installed in direct contact with _____.

    (a) concrete
    (b) bare copper conductors
    (c) wooden framing members
    (d) all of these

98. Aluminum or copper-clad aluminum conductors external to buildings or equipment enclosures shall not be terminated within _____ of the earth.

    (a) 12 in.
    (b) 16 in.
    (c) 18 in.
    (d) 24 in.

99. Grounding electrode conductors that are not subject to physical damage can be run exposed along the surface of the building construction if securely fastened to the surface on which they are carried.

    (a) True
    (b) False

100. Grounding electrode conductors _____ AWG and larger that are not exposed to physical damage can be run along the surface of the building construction without metal covering or protection.

    (a) 10
    (b) 8
    (c) 6
    (d) 4

101. A(n) _____ AWG or larger copper or aluminum grounding electrode conductor exposed to physical damage shall be protected in rigid metal conduit, IMC, Schedule 80 PVC conduit, reinforced thermosetting resin conduit Type XW (RTRC-XW), EMT, or cable armor.

    (a) 10
    (b) 8
    (c) 6
    (d) 4

102. Grounding electrode conductors smaller than _____ AWG shall be protected in rigid metal conduit, IMC, PVC conduit, electrical metallic tubing, or cable armor.

    (a) 10
    (b) 8
    (c) 6
    (d) 4

103. Grounding electrode conductors and grounding electrode bonding jumpers in contact with _____ shall not be required to comply with 300.5 but shall be buried or otherwise protected if subject to physical damage.

    (a) water
    (b) the earth
    (c) metal
    (d) all of these

104. Grounding electrode conductors shall be installed in one continuous length without a splice or joint, unless spliced by _____.

    (a) connecting together sections of a busbar
    (b) irreversible compression-type connectors listed as grounding and bonding equipment
    (c) the exothermic welding process
    (d) any of these

105. If a building or structure is supplied by a service or feeder with _____ or more disconnecting means in separate enclosures, the grounding electrode connections shall be made in accordance with 250.64(D)(1), 250.64(D)(2), or 250.64(D)(3).

    (a) one
    (b) two
    (c) three
    (d) four

106. Where a building or structure contains more than one service disconnect in separate enclosures, grounding electrode conductor connections shall be permitted to be _____.

    (a) multiple individual grounding electrode conductors
    (b) one grounding electrode conductor at a common location
    (c) a common grounding electrode conductor and taps
    (d) any of these

107. Ferrous metal raceways and enclosures for grounding electrode conductors shall be electrically continuous from the point of attachment to cabinets or equipment to the grounding electrode.

    (a) True
    (b) False

108. Ferrous metal raceways and enclosures for grounding electrode conductors shall be bonded at each end of the raceway or enclosure to the grounding electrode or grounding electrode conductor to create a(n) _____ parallel path.

    (a) mechanically
    (b) electrically
    (c) physically
    (d) effective

109. The grounding electrode conductor shall be permitted to be run to any _____ available in the grounding electrode system.

    (a) panelboards
    (b) bonding jumper
    (c) switchgear
    (d) convenient grounding electrode

110. A grounding electrode conductor shall be permitted to be run to any convenient grounding electrode available in the grounding electrode system where the other electrode(s), if any, is connected by bonding jumpers that are installed in accordance with 250.53(C).

    (a) True
    (b) False

111. Bonding jumper(s) from grounding electrode(s) shall be permitted to be connected to an aluminum or copper busbar not less than _____ and of sufficient length to accommodate the number of terminations necessary for the installation in accordance with 250.64(F).

    (a) ⅛ in. thick x 1 in. wide
    (b) ⅛ in. thick x 2 in. wide
    (c) ¼ in. thick x 1 in. wide
    (d) ¼ in. thick x 2 in. wide

112. A service consisting of 12 AWG service-entrance conductors requires a grounding electrode conductor sized no less than _____ AWG.

    (a) 10
    (b) 8
    (c) 6
    (d) 4

113. The largest size grounding electrode conductor required is _____ copper.

    (a) 6 AWG
    (b) 1/0 AWG
    (c) 3/0 AWG
    (d) 250 kcmil

114. What size copper grounding electrode conductor is required for a service that has three sets of 600 kcmil copper conductors per phase?

    (a) 1 AWG
    (b) 1/0 AWG
    (c) 2/0 AWG
    (d) 3/0 AWG

115. If the grounding electrode conductor or bonding jumper connected to a single or multiple rod, pipe, or plate electrode(s), or any combination thereof, as described in 250.52(A)(5) or (A)(7), does not extend on to other types of electrodes that require a larger size conductor, the grounding electrode conductor shall not be required to be larger than _____ AWG copper wire.

    (a) 10
    (b) 8
    (c) 6
    (d) 4

116. In an ac system, if the size of the grounding electrode conductor or bonding jumper connected to a concrete-encased electrode does not extend on to other types of electrodes that require a larger size of conductor, the grounding electrode conductor shall not be required to be larger than _____ AWG copper.

    (a) 10
    (b) 8
    (c) 6
    (d) 4

117. Mechanical elements used to terminate a grounding electrode conductor to a grounding electrode shall be accessible.

    (a) True
    (b) False

118. An encased or buried connection to a concrete-encased, driven, or buried grounding electrode shall be accessible.

    (a) True
    (b) False

119. Exothermic or irreversible compression connections, together with the mechanical means used to attach to fireproofed structural metal, shall not be required to be accessible.

    (a) True
    (b) False

120. When an underground metal water piping system is used as a grounding electrode, bonding shall be provided around insulated joints and around any equipment that is likely to be disconnected for repairs or replacement.

    (a) True
    (b) False

121. Interior metal water piping that is electrically continuous with a metal underground water pipe electrode and is located not more than _____ ft from the point of entrance to the building shall be permitted to extend the connection to an electrode(s).

    (a) 2
    (b) 4
    (c) 5
    (d) 6

122. The metal structural frame of a building shall be permitted to be used as a conductor to interconnect electrodes that are part of the grounding electrode system, or as a grounding electrode conductor. Hold-down bolts securing the structural steel column that are connected to a concrete-encased electrode that complies with 250.52(A)(3) and is located in the support footing or foundation shall be permitted to connect the metal structural frame of a building or structure to the concrete-encased grounding electrode.

    (a) True
    (b) False

123. A rebar-type concrete-encased electrode installed in accordance with 250.52(A)(3) with an additional rebar section extended from its location within the concrete foundation or footing to an accessible location that is not subject to _____ shall be permitted for connection of grounding electrode conductors and bonding jumpers.

    (a) physical damage
    (b) moisture
    (c) corrosion
    (d) any of these

124. A rebar-type concrete-encased electrode installed in accordance with 250.52(A)(3) with an additional rebar section extended from its location within the concrete foundation or footing to an accessible location that is not subject to corrosion is permitted for connection of grounding electrode conductors and bonding jumpers providing _____.

    (a) the rebar is continuous or effectively connected to the grounding electrode rebar
    (b) the rebar extension is not in direct contact with the earth without corrosion protection
    (c) the rebar is not used as a conductor to interconnect the grounding electrode system
    (d) all of these

125. The grounding conductor connection to the grounding electrode shall be made by _____.

    (a) listed lugs
    (b) exothermic welding
    (c) listed pressure connectors
    (d) any of these

Part IV. Enclosure, Raceway, and Service Cable Connections

126. Metal enclosures and raceways containing service conductors shall be connected to the grounded system conductor if the electrical system is grounded.

    (a) True
    (b) False

127. Metal enclosures and raceways for other than service conductors shall be connected to the neutral conductor.

    (a) True
    (b) False

128. Short sections of metal enclosures or raceways used to provide support or protection of _____ from physical damage shall not be required to be connected to the equipment grounding conductor.

    (a) conduit
    (b) feeders under 600V
    (c) cable assemblies
    (d) grounding electrode conductors

Part V. Bonding

129. Bonding shall be provided where necessary to ensure _____ and the capacity to conduct safely any fault current likely to be imposed.

    (a) electrical continuity
    (b) fiduciary responsibility
    (c) listing requirements are met
    (d) sufficient electrical demand

130. The normally noncurrent-carrying metal parts of service equipment, such as service _____, shall be bonded together.

    (a) raceways or service cable armor
    (b) equipment enclosures containing service conductors, including meter fittings, boxes, or the like, interposed in the service raceway or armor
    (c) cable trays
    (d) all of these

131. Bonding jumpers for service raceways shall be used around impaired connections such as _____.

    (a) oversized concentric knockouts
    (b) oversized eccentric knockouts
    (c) reducing washers
    (d) any of these

132. Electrical continuity at service equipment, service raceways, and service conductor enclosures shall be ensured by _____.

    (a) bonding equipment to the grounded service conductor
    (b) connections utilizing threaded couplings on enclosures, if made up wrenchtight
    (c) other listed bonding devices, such as bonding-type locknuts, bushings, or bushings with bonding jumpers
    (d) any of these

133. Service raceways threaded into metal service equipment such as bosses (hubs) are considered to be effectively _____ to the service metal enclosure.

    (a) attached
    (b) bonded
    (c) grounded
    (d) secured

134. Service metal raceways and metal-clad cables are considered effectively bonded when using threadless couplings and connectors that are _____.

    (a) nonmetallic
    (b) made up tight
    (c) sealed
    (d) classified

135. A means external to enclosures for connecting intersystem _____ conductors shall be provided at the service equipment or metering equipment enclosure and disconnecting means of buildings or structures supplied by a feeder.

    (a) bonding
    (b) ungrounded
    (c) secondary
    (d) bonding and ungrounded

136. The intersystem bonding termination shall _____.

    (a) be accessible for connection and inspection
    (b) consist of a set of terminals with the capacity for connection of not less than three intersystem bonding conductors
    (c) not interfere with opening the enclosure for a service, building/structure disconnecting means, or metering equipment
    (d) all of these

137. The intersystem bonding termination shall _____.

    (a) be securely mounted and electrically connected to service equipment, the meter enclosure, or exposed nonflexible metallic service raceway, or be mounted at one of these enclosures and be connected to the enclosure or grounding electrode conductor with a minimum 6 AWG copper conductor
    (b) be securely mounted to the building/structure disconnecting means, or be mounted at the disconnecting means and be connected to the metallic enclosure or grounding electrode conductor with a minimum 6 AWG copper conductor
    (c) have terminals that are listed as grounding and bonding equipment
    (d) all of these

138. At existing buildings or structures, an intersystem bonding termination is not required if other acceptable means of bonding exists. An external accessible means for bonding communications systems together can be by the use of a(n) _____.

    (a) nonflexible metallic raceway
    (b) exposed grounding electrode conductor
    (c) connection to a grounded raceway or equipment approved by the authority having jurisdiction
    (d) any of these

139. When bonding enclosures, metal raceways, frames, and fittings, any nonconductive paint, enamel, or similar coating shall be removed at _____.

    (a) contact surfaces
    (b) threads
    (c) contact points
    (d) all of these

140. For circuits over 250 volts-to-ground, electrical continuity can be maintained between a box or enclosure where no oversized, concentric or eccentric knockouts are encountered, and a metal conduit by _____.

    (a) threadless fittings for cables with metal sheaths
    (b) double locknuts on threaded conduit (one inside and one outside the box or enclosure)
    (c) fittings that have shoulders that seat firmly against the box with a locknut on the inside or listed fittings
    (d) all of these

141. Expansion, expansion-deflection, or deflection fittings and telescoping sections of metal raceways shall be made _____ continuous by equipment bonding jumpers or other means.

    (a) physically
    (b) mechanically
    (c) electrically
    (d) directly

142. Supply-side bonding jumpers shall be no smaller than the sizes specified in _____.

    (a) Table 250.102(C)(1)
    (b) Table 250.122
    (c) Table 310.16
    (d) Table 250.66

143. The supply-side bonding jumper on the supply side of services shall be sized according to the _____.

    (a) overcurrent device rating
    (b) ungrounded supply conductor size
    (c) service-drop size
    (d) load to be served

144. What is the minimum size copper supply-side bonding jumper for a service raceway containing 4/0 THHN aluminum conductors?

    (a) 6 AWG aluminum
    (b) 4 AWG aluminum
    (c) 4 AWG copper
    (d) 3 AWG copper

145. Where ungrounded supply conductors are paralleled in two or more raceways or cables, the bonding jumper for each raceway or cable shall be based on the size of the _____ in each raceway or cable.

    (a) overcurrent protection for conductors
    (b) grounded conductors
    (c) ungrounded supply conductors
    (d) sum of all conductors

146. Service conductors are parallel in three separate metal raceways, the ungrounded conductors in each raceway are 600 kcmil per phase. Determine the copper supply-side bonding jumper size for each service raceway.

    (a) 1/0 AWG
    (b) 3/0 AWG
    (c) 250 kcmil
    (d) 500 kcmil

147. What is the minimum size copper equipment bonding jumper for a 40A rated circuit?

    (a) 14 AWG
    (b) 12 AWG
    (c) 10 AWG
    (d) 8 AWG

148. An equipment bonding jumper can be installed on the outside of a raceway, providing the length of the equipment bonding jumper is not more than _____ in. and the equipment bonding jumper is routed with the raceway.

   (a) 12
   (b) 24
   (c) 36
   (d) 72

149. The bonding jumper used to bond the metal water piping system shall be installed in accordance with 250.64(A), 250.64(B), and 250.64(E) and the points of attachment of the bonding jumper(s) shall be _____.

   (a) readily accessible
   (b) accessible
   (c) enclosed
   (d) secured

150. The bonding jumper used to bond the metal water piping system shall be sized in accordance with _____ except as permitted in 250.104(A)(2) and 250.104(A)(3).

   (a) Table 250.102(C)(1)
   (b) Table 250.122
   (c) Table 310.16
   (d) Table 310.15(6)

151. Metal water piping system(s) shall be bonded to the _____, or to one or more grounding electrodes used, if the grounding electrode conductor or bonding jumper to the grounding electrode is of sufficient size.

   (a) grounded conductor at the service
   (b) service equipment enclosure
   (c) grounding electrode conductor if of sufficient size
   (d) any of these

152. Bonding jumper(s) for the bonding of metal water piping systems shall be sized in accordance with Table 250.102(C)(1) and are not required to be larger than _____ AWG copper or 250 kcmil aluminum or copper-clad aluminum

   (a) 1/0
   (b) 2/0
   (c) 3/0
   (d) 4/0

153. Where isolated metal water piping systems are installed in a multiple-occupancy building, the water pipes can be bonded with bonding jumpers sized in accordance with 250.104(D).

   (a) True
   (b) False

154. The metal water piping system(s) installed in or attached to a building or structure [250.104(A)(3)] shall be bonded to _____.

   (a) the building or structure disconnecting means enclosure where located at the building or structure
   (b) the equipment grounding conductor run with the supply conductors
   (c) one or more grounding electrodes used
   (d) any of these

155. The bonding jumper(s) required for the metal water piping system(s) installed in or attached to a building or structure supplied by a feeder(s) or branch circuit(s) shall be sized in accordance with _____.

   (a) 250.66
   (b) 250.102(D)
   (c) 250.122
   (d) 310.16

156. Metal piping, including gas piping shall be considered bonded by the equipment grounding conductor for the circuit that is likely to energize the piping system.

   (a) True
   (b) False

157. Exposed structural metal interconnected to form a metal building frame that is not intentionally grounded or bonded and is likely to become energized, shall be bonded to the _____.

   (a) service equipment enclosure or building disconnecting means
   (b) grounded conductor at the service
   (c) grounding electrode conductor where of sufficient size
   (d) any of these

158. Metal water piping systems and structural metal that is interconnected to form a building frame shall be bonded to separately derived systems in accordance with 250.104(D)(1) through 250.104(D)(3).

   (a) True
   (b) False

159. The grounded conductor of each separately derived system shall be bonded to the nearest available point of the metal water piping system(s) in the area served by each separately derived system and each bonding jumper shall be sized in accordance with Table 250.102(C)(1) based on the largest ungrounded conductor of the separately derived system.

    (a) True
    (b) False

160. A separate water piping bonding jumper shall be required if the metal frame of a building or structure is used as the grounding electrode for a separately derived system and is bonded to the metal water piping in the area served by the separately derived system.

    (a) True
    (b) False

161. If exposed structural metal that is interconnected to form the building frame exists in the area served by the separately derived system, it shall be bonded to the grounded conductor of each separately derived system and each bonding jumper shall be sized in accordance with Table 250.102(C)(1) based on the largest ungrounded conductor of the service.

    (a) True
    (b) False

162. A separate bonding jumper to the building structural metal shall not be required if the metal frame of a building or structure is used as the _____ for the separately derived system.

    (a) bonding jumper
    (b) ground-fault current path
    (c) grounding electrode
    (d) lightning protection

163. Lightning protection system ground terminals _____ bonded to the building or structure grounding electrode system.

    (a) shall be
    (b) shall not be
    (c) shall be permitted to be
    (d) must be effectively

Part VI. Equipment Grounding and Equipment Grounding Conductors

164. Exposed, normally non–current-carrying metal parts of cord-and-plug-connected equipment shall be connected to the equipment grounding conductor where operated at over _____ to ground.

    (a) 24V
    (b) 50V
    (c) 120V
    (d) 150V

165. Metal enclosures shall be permitted to be used to connect bonding jumpers or _____, or both, together to become a part of an effective ground-fault current path.

    (a) grounded conductors
    (b) neutral conductors
    (c) equipment grounding conductors
    (d) grounded phase conductors

166. Listed FMC can be used as the equipment grounding conductor if the length in any ground return path does not exceed 6 ft and the circuit conductors contained in the conduit are protected by overcurrent devices rated at _____ or less.

    (a) 15A
    (b) 20A
    (c) 30A
    (d) 60A

167. Listed FMC can be used as the equipment grounding conductor if the conduit does not exceed trade size _____.

    (a) 1¼
    (b) 1½
    (c) 2
    (d) 2¼

168. Listed FMC and LFMC is permitted as an equipment grounding conductor at lengths, _____.

    (a) no greater than 2 ft
    (b) no greater than 3 ft
    (c) up to 6 ft
    (d) up to 10 ft

169. The *Code* requires the installation of an equipment grounding conductor of the wire type in _____.

    (a) electrical nonmetallic tubing (ENT)
    (b) rigid metal conduit (RMC)
    (c) intermediate metal conduit (IMC)
    (d) electrical metallic tubing (EMT)

170. Listed liquidtight flexible metal conduit (LFMC) is acceptable as an equipment grounding conductor when it terminates in listed fittings and is protected by an overcurrent device rated 60A or less for trade sizes ⅜ through ½.

    (a) True
    (b) False

171. The armor of Type AC cable is recognized by the *NEC* as an equipment grounding conductor.

    (a) True
    (b) False

172. Type MC cable provides an effective ground-fault current path and is recognized by the *NEC* as an equipment grounding conductor when _____.

    (a) it contains an insulated or uninsulated equipment grounding conductor in compliance with 250.118(1)
    (b) the cable assembly contains a bare copper conductor
    (c) only when it is hospital grade Type MC cable
    (d) it is terminated with bonding bushings

173. An equipment grounding conductor shall be identified by _____.

    (a) a continuous outer finish that is green
    (b) being bare
    (c) a continuous outer finish that is green with one or more yellow stripes
    (d) any of these

174. An insulated or covered conductor _____ and larger shall be permitted, at the time of installation, to be permanently identified as an equipment grounding conductor at each end and at every point where the conductor is accessible.

    (a) 8 AWG
    (b) 6 AWG
    (c) 4 AWG
    (d) 1/0 AWG

175. One or more insulated conductors in a multiconductor cable, at the time of installation, shall be permitted to be permanently identified as equipment grounding conductors at each end and at every point where the conductors are accessible by coloring the insulation _____.

    (a) green
    (b) grey
    (c) green with a yellow stripe
    (d) white or silver

176. Unless part of a suitable Chapter 3 cable wiring method, equipment grounding conductors of bare or covered copper-clad aluminum, shall not be installed where subject to corrosive conditions or be installed in direct contact with concrete, masonry, or the earth.

    (a) True
    (b) False

177. Where not routed with circuit conductors as permitted in 250.130(C) and 250.134(A) Exception No. 2, equipment grounding conductors smaller than _____ shall be protected from physical damage by an identified raceway or cable armor.

    (a) 10 AWG
    (b) 8 AWG
    (c) 6 AWG
    (d) 4 AWG

178. Conductors with the color _____ insulation shall not be used for ungrounded or grounded conductors.

    (a) green or green with one or more yellow stripes
    (b) grey
    (c) black with a white stripe
    (d) white

179. An equipment grounding conductor is not permitted to be used as a grounding electrode conductor under any circumstance(s).

    (a) True
    (b) False

180. The structural metal frame of a _____ shall not be used as an equipment grounding conductor.

    (a) roof or crawl space
    (b) wall or ceiling
    (c) building or structure
    (d) door or window

181. Equipment grounding conductors of the wire type shall not be required to be larger than the circuit conductors.

(a) True
(b) False

182. When ungrounded circuit conductors are increased in size to account for voltage drop, the wire-type equipment grounding conductor shall be proportionately increased in size according to the increase in size of the ungrounded conductors using their _____.

(a) ampacity
(b) circular mil area
(c) diameter
(d) temperature rating

183. When a single equipment grounding conductor is used for multiple circuits in the same raceway, cable, or cable tray, the single equipment grounding conductor shall be sized according to the _____.

(a) combined rating of all the overcurrent devices
(b) largest overcurrent device protecting the circuit conductors
(c) combined rating of all the loads
(d) any of these

184. Equipment grounding conductors for motor branch circuits shall be sized in accordance with Table 250.122(A), based on the rating of the _____ device.

(a) motor overload
(b) motor over-temperature
(c) branch-circuit short-circuit and ground-fault protective
(d) feeder overcurrent protection

185. If conductors are installed in parallel in the same raceway or cable tray, a single wire-type conductor shall be permitted as the equipment grounding conductor and sized in accordance with 250.122, based on the _____.

(a) feeder
(b) branch circuit
(c) overcurrent protective device
(d) service conductors

186. Where circuit conductors are installed in parallel in multiple raceways or cables and include an EGC of the wire type, the equipment grounding conductor shall be installed in parallel in each raceway or cable, sized in compliance with 250.122 based on the overcurrent protective device for the feeder or branch circuit.

(a) True
(b) False

187. Except as provided in 250.122(F)(2)(c) for raceway or cable tray installations, the equipment grounding conductor in each multiconductor cable shall be sized in accordance with 250.122 based on the _____.

(a) largest circuit conductor
(b) overcurrent protective device for the feeder or branch circuit
(c) smallest branch-circuit conductor
(d) overcurrent protective device for the service

188. If multiconductor cables are installed in parallel in the same raceway, auxiliary gutter, or cable tray, _____ equipment grounding conductor(s) that is(are) sized in accordance with 250.122 shall be permitted in combination with the equipment grounding conductors provided within the multiconductor cables and shall all be connected together.

(a) one
(b) two
(c) three
(d) four

189. Equipment grounding conductors for feeder taps are not required to be larger than the tap conductors.

(a) True
(b) False

Part VII. Methods of Equipment Grounding

190. Electrical equipment secured to and in _____ contact with a metal rack or structure provided for its support shall be permitted to be considered as being connected to an equipment grounding conductor if the metal rack or structure is connected to an equipment grounding conductor by one of the means indicated in 250.134.

(a) electrical
(b) direct
(c) metal to metal
(d) mechanical

191. Metal parts of cord-and-plug-connected equipment, if grounded, shall be connected to an equipment grounding conductor that terminates to a grounding-type attachment plug.

    (a) True
    (b) False

192. Frames of electric ranges, wall-mounted ovens, counter-mounted cooking units, _____, shall be connected to the equipment grounding conductor.

    (a) washing machines
    (b) dishwashers
    (c) microwaves
    (d) clothes dryers

193. Load side equipment such as the frames of ranges or dryers in existing installations, are permitted to be connected to the grounded circuit conductor.

    (a) True
    (b) False

194. A grounded circuit conductor is permitted to ground noncurrent-carrying metal parts of equipment, raceways, and other enclosures on the supply side or within the enclosure of the ac service disconnecting means.

    (a) True
    (b) False

195. It shall be permissible to ground meter enclosures immediately adjacent to the service disconnecting means to the _____ circuit conductor on the load side of the service disconnect, if service ground-fault protection is not provided.

    (a) grounding
    (b) bonding
    (c) grounded
    (d) phase

196. A(n) _____ shall be used to connect the grounding terminal of a grounding-type receptacle to a metal box that is connected to an equipment grounding conductor.

    (a) equipment bonding jumper
    (b) grounded conductor jumper
    (c) equipment bonding jumper or grounded conductor jumper
    (d) equipment bonding jumper and grounded conductor jumper

197. Where the box is mounted on the surface, direct metal-to-metal contact between the device yoke and the box shall be permitted to ground the receptacle to the box if at least _____ of the insulating washers of the receptacle is (are) removed.

    (a) one
    (b) two
    (c) three
    (d) four

198. A listed exposed work cover can be the grounding and bonding means when the device is attached to the cover with at least _____ permanent fastener(s) and the cover mounting holes are located on a non-raised portion of the cover.

    (a) one
    (b) two
    (c) three
    (d) four

199. Where a metal box is surface mounted, the direct metal-to-metal contact between the receptacle yoke or strap to the box is permitted to provide the required effective ground-fault current path provided that _____.

    (a) at least one of the mounting screw retaining washers is removed
    (b) the device is attached to the box with at least two screws
    (c) the raised cover mounting holes are located on a flat portion of the cover
    (d) all of these

200. Receptacle yokes designed and _____ as self-grounding can, in conjunction with the supporting screws, establish the equipment bonding between the device yoke and a flush-type box.

    (a) approved
    (b) advertised
    (c) listed
    (d) installed

201. The receptacle grounding terminal of an isolated ground receptacle shall be connected to a(n) _____ equipment grounding conductor run with the circuit conductors.

    (a) insulated
    (b) covered
    (c) bare
    (d) solid

202. The arrangement of grounding connections shall ensure that the disconnection or the removal of a luminaire, receptacle, or other device fed from the box does not interrupt the electrical continuity of the _____ providing an effective ground-fault current path.

    (a) grounded conductor(s)
    (b) ungrounded conductor(s)
    (c) equipment grounding conductor(s)
    (d) all of these

203. One or more equipment grounding conductors brought into a nonmetallic outlet box shall be arranged such that a connection can be made to _____ in that box requiring connection to an equipment grounding conductor.

    (a) any fitting or device
    (b) a ground-clip
    (c) clamp(s)
    (d) the grounded conductor

204. A connection between equipment grounding conductors and a metal floor box shall be by _____.

    (a) a grounding screw used for no other purpose
    (b) equipment listed for grounding
    (c) a listed grounding device
    (d) any of these

CHAPTER 3

WIRING METHODS AND MATERIALS

Introduction to Chapter 3—Wiring Methods and Materials

Chapter 3 focuses on wiring methods and materials, and provides some very specific installation requirements for conductors, cables, boxes, raceways, and fittings. This chapter includes detailed information about the installations and restrictions involved with wiring methods. Not fully understanding the information in this chapter may be the reason many people incorrectly apply these rules. Pay careful attention to each and every detail to be sure your installations comply with these requirements. Disregarding the rules for the wiring methods found in Chapter 3 can result in problems with power quality and can lead to fire, shock, and overall poor installations. The type of wiring method you will use depends on several factors; job specifications, *Code* requirements, the environment, need, the type of building construction, and cost effectiveness just to name a few.

Chapter 3 begins with rules that are common to most wiring methods [Article 300]. It then covers conductors [Article 310], boxes [Article 312], and enclosures [Article 314]. The articles that follow become more specific and deal more in-depth with individual wiring methods such as specific types of cables [Articles 320 through 340] and various raceways [Articles 342 through 390]. The chapter winds up with Article 392, a support system.

Notice as you read through the various wiring methods that the *Code* attempts to use similar section numbering for similar topics from one article to the next, using the same digits after the decimal point in the section number for the same topic. This makes it easier to locate the specific requirements of a particular article. For example, the rules for securing and supporting can be found in the section that ends with ".30" of each article.

Wiring Method Articles

▶ **Article 300—General Requirements for Wiring Methods and Materials.** Article 300 contains the general requirements for all wiring methods included in the *NEC*, except for signaling and communications systems (communications, antennas, and coaxial cable), which are covered in Chapters 7 and 8.

▶ **Article 310—Conductors for General Wiring.** This article contains the general requirements for conductors, such as insulation markings, ampacity ratings, and conductor use. There is also a section that addresses single family dwelling service and feeder conductors exclusively. Article 310 does not apply to conductors that are part of flexible cords, fixture wires, or conductors that are an integral part of equipment [90.6 and 300.1(B)].

▶ **Article 312—Cabinets and Meter Socket Enclosures.** Article 312 covers the installation and construction specifications for cabinets and meter socket enclosures.

▶ **Article 314—Outlet, Device, Pull, and Junction Boxes; Conduit Bodies; Fittings; and Handhole Enclosures.** Installation requirements for outlet boxes, pull and junction boxes, as well as conduit bodies and handhole enclosures are contained in this article.

• • •

Cable Articles

Articles 320 through 340 address specific types of cables. If you take the time to become familiar with the various types of cables, you will be able to:

▸ Understand what is available for doing the work.

▸ Recognize cable types that have special *NEC* requirements.

▸ Avoid buying cable you cannot install due to *Code* requirements you cannot meet with that particular wiring method.

Here is a brief overview of those included in this book:

▸ **Article 320—Armored Cable (Type AC).** Armored cable is an assembly of insulated conductors, 14 AWG through 1 AWG, individually wrapped with wax paper. The conductors are contained within a flexible metal (steel or aluminum) spiral sheath that interlocks at the edges. Armored cable looks like flexible metal conduit. Many electricians call this metal cable "BX®."

▸ **Article 330—Metal-Clad Cable (Type MC).** Metal-clad cable encloses insulated conductors in a metal sheath of either corrugated or smooth copper or aluminum tubing, or spiral interlocked steel or aluminum. The physical characteristics of Type MC cable make it a versatile wiring method permitted in almost any location and for almost any application. The most commonly used Type MC cable is the interlocking kind, which looks similar to armored cable or flexible metal conduit.

▸ **Article 334—Nonmetallic-Sheathed Cable (Type NM).** Nonmetallic-sheathed cable is commonly referred to by its trade name "Romex®." It encloses two, three, or four insulated conductors, 14 AWG through 2 AWG, within a nonmetallic outer jacket. Because this cable is manufactured in this manner, it contains a separate (usually bare) equipment grounding conductor. Nonmetallic-sheathed cable is most commonly used for residential wiring applications but may sometimes be permitted for use in commercial occupancies.

▸ **Article 336—Power and Control Tray Cable (Type TC).** Power and control tray cable is flexible, inexpensive, and easily installed. It provides very limited physical protection for the conductors, so the installation restrictions are rigorous. Its low cost and relative ease of installation make it a common wiring method for industrial applications.

▸ **Article 338—Service-Entrance Cable (Types SE and USE).** Service-entrance and underground service-entrance cables can be a single conductor or a multiconductor assembly within an overall nonmetallic outer jacket or covering. These cables are most often used for services not over 1,000V, but are also permitted for feeders and branch circuits. When used as a service conductor(s) or a service-entrance conductor(s), pre-manufactured Type "SE" cable assemblies will typically contain two insulated phase conductors and a bare neutral conductor. When permitted for use as a feeder or branch circuit, Type SE cable is usually designated as Type "SER" and will contain the same three conductors as Type SE but a fourth conductor (which is insulated) will be added to serve as the neutral conductor.

▸ **Article 340—Underground Feeder and Branch-Circuit Cable (Type UF).** Underground feeder cable is a moisture-, fungus-, and corrosion-resistant cable suitable for direct burial in the earth, and it comes in sizes 14 AWG through 4/0 AWG [340.104]. Multiconductor UF cable is covered in molded plastic that surrounds the insulated conductors.

Raceway Articles

Articles 342 through 390 address specific types of raceways. Refer to Article 100 for the definition of a raceway. If you take the time to become familiar with the various types of raceways, you will be able to:

▸ Understand what is available for doing the work.

▸ Recognize raceway types that have special *Code* requirements.

▸ Avoid buying a raceway you cannot install due to *NEC* requirements you cannot meet with that particular wiring method.

Here is a brief overview of each those included in this book:

▶ **Article 342—Intermediate Metal Conduit (Type IMC).** Intermediate metal conduit is a circular metal raceway with the same outside diameter as rigid metal conduit. The wall thickness of intermediate metal conduit is less than that of rigid metal conduit, so it has a larger interior cross-sectional area for holding conductors. Intermediate metal conduit is lighter and less expensive than rigid metal conduit and is approved by the *NEC* for use in the same applications as rigid metal conduit. Intermediate metal conduit also uses a different steel alloy, which makes it stronger than rigid metal conduit, even though the walls are thinner.

▶ **Article 344—Rigid Metal Conduit (Type RMC).** Rigid metal conduit is similar to intermediate metal conduit, except the wall thickness is greater, so it has a smaller interior cross-sectional area. Rigid metal conduit is heavier than intermediate metal conduit and is permitted for use in the same applications as intermediate metal conduit (Type IMC).

▶ **Article 348—Flexible Metal Conduit (Type FMC).** Flexible metal conduit is a raceway of circular cross section made of a helically wound, interlocked metal strip of either steel or aluminum. It is commonly called "Greenfield" (after its inventor) or "Flex."

▶ **Article 350—Liquidtight Flexible Metal Conduit (Type LFMC).** Liquidtight flexible metal conduit is a raceway of circular cross section with an outer liquidtight, nonmetallic, sunlight-resistant jacket over an inner flexible metal core, with associated couplings, connectors, and fittings. It is listed for the installation of electrical conductors. Liquidtight flexible metal conduit is commonly called "Sealtite®" or simply "liquidtight." Liquidtight flexible metal conduit is similar in construction to flexible metal conduit, but it has an outer thermoplastic covering.

▶ **Article 352—Rigid Polyvinyl Chloride Conduit (Type PVC).** Rigid polyvinyl chloride conduit is a nonmetallic raceway of circular cross section with integral or associated couplings, connectors, and fittings. It is listed for the installation of electrical conductors.

▶ **Article 356—Liquidtight Flexible Nonmetallic Conduit (Type LFNC).** Liquidtight flexible nonmetallic conduit (most commonly referred to as "Carflex®") is a raceway of circular cross section with an outer liquidtight, nonmetallic, sunlight-resistant jacket over an inner flexible core, with associated couplings, connectors, and fittings.

▶ **Article 358—Electrical Metallic Tubing (EMT).** Electrical metallic tubing is a nonthreaded thinwall raceway of circular cross section designed for the physical protection and routing of conductors and cables. Compared to rigid metal conduit and intermediate metal conduit, electrical metallic tubing is relatively easy to bend, cut, and ream. EMT is not threaded, so all connectors and couplings are of the threadless type. It is available in a range of colors, such as red and blue.

▶ **Article 362—Electrical Nonmetallic Tubing (ENT).** Electrical nonmetallic tubing is a pliable, corrugated, circular raceway made of PVC. ENT resembles flexible tubing and is often referred to as "Smurf Pipe" or "Smurf Tube," because it was only available in blue when it first came out, and the nickname is a reference to the children's cartoon characters "The Smurfs." It is now available in additional colors such as red and yellow.

▶ **Article 376—Metal Wireways.** A metal wireway is a sheet metal trough with hinged or removable covers making the electrical conductors and cables housed and protected inside accessible. Metal wireways must be installed as a complete and contiguous system.

▶ **Article 380—Multioutlet Assemblies.** A multioutlet assembly is a surface, flush, or freestanding raceway designed to hold conductors and receptacles. It is assembled in the field or at the factory.

▶ **Article 386—Surface Metal Raceways.** A surface metal raceway is a metal raceway intended to be mounted to the surface with associated accessories, in which conductors are placed after the raceway has been installed as a complete system.

Cable Tray

▶ **Article 392—Cable Trays.** A cable tray system is a unit or assembly of units or sections with associated fittings that form a structural system used to securely fasten or support cables and raceways. A cable tray is not a raceway; it is a support system for raceways, cables, and enclosures.

ARTICLE 300

GENERAL REQUIREMENTS FOR WIRING METHODS AND MATERIALS

Introduction to Article 300—General Requirements for Wiring Methods and Materials

Article 300 contains the general requirements for all wiring methods included in the *NEC*. However, it does not apply to twisted-pair cable and coaxial cable (which are covered in Chapters 7 and 8) unless Article 300 is specifically referenced.

This article is primarily concerned with how to install, route, splice, protect, and secure conductors and raceways. How well you understand and apply the requirements of Article 300 will usually be evident in the finished work. Many of its requirements will affect the appearance, longevity, and even the safety of the installation. Imagine your surprise if you are shoveling some soil onto a plant in the garden and your shovel hits an electrical service cable! After studying and learning the rules in this article, you will immediately realize that the burial depth requirements of 300.5 were possibly overlooked or ignored. Even worse, they might not even have been known at the time of installation.

A good understanding of this article will start you on the path to correctly and safely installing the wiring methods included in Chapter 3, and refer to the definitions in Article 100 as needed.

Please use the 2020 *Code* book to answer the following questions.

1. The provisions of Article 300 apply to the conductors that form an integral part of equipment or listed utilization equipment.

   (a) True
   (b) False

2. All conductors of the same circuit, including the grounded and equipment grounding conductors and bonding conductors shall be contained within the same _____, unless otherwise permitted elsewhere in the *Code*.

   (a) raceway
   (b) cable
   (c) trench
   (d) all of these

3. The requirement to run all paralleled circuit conductors within the same _____ applies separately to each portion of the paralleled installation.

   (a) raceway or auxiliary gutter
   (b) cable tray or trench
   (c) cable or cord
   (d) all of these

4. Connections, taps, or extensions made from paralleled conductors shall connect to all conductors of the paralleled set.

   (a) True
   (b) False

5. Conductors installed in nonmetallic raceways run underground shall be permitted to be arranged as _____ installations. The raceways shall be installed in close proximity, and the conductors shall comply with 300.20(B).

   (a) neutral
   (b) grounded conductor
   (c) isolated phase
   (d) all of these

6. Conductors of ac and dc circuits, rated 1,000V or less, shall be permitted to occupy the same _____ provided that all conductors have an insulation rating equal to the maximum voltage applied to any conductor.

   (a) enclosure
   (b) cable
   (c) raceway
   (d) any of these

7. Where cables or nonmetallic raceways are installed through bored holes in joists, rafters, or wood members, holes shall be bored so that the edge of the hole is _____ the nearest edge of the wood member.

   (a) not less than 1¼ in. from
   (b) immediately adjacent to
   (c) not less than ¹⁄₁₆ in. from
   (d) 90 degrees away from

8. Cables laid in wood notches require protection against nails or screws by using a steel plate at least _____ thick, installed before the building finish is applied.

   (a) ¹⁄₁₆ in.
   (b) ⅛ in.
   (c) ¼ in.
   (d) ½ in.

9. Where Type NM cable passes through factory or field openings in metal members, it shall be protected by _____ bushings or _____ grommets that cover metal edges.

   (a) approved
   (b) identified
   (c) listed
   (d) marked

10. Where Type NM cables pass through cut or drilled slots or holes in metal members, the cable shall be protected by _____ which are installed in the opening prior to the installation of the cable and which securely cover all metal edges.

    (a) anti-shorts
    (b) sleeves
    (c) plates
    (d) listed bushings or grommets

11. Where nails or screws are likely to penetrate nonmetallic-sheathed cable or ENT installed through metal framing members, a steel sleeve, steel plate, or steel clip not less than _____ in thickness shall be used to protect the cable or tubing.

    (a) ¹⁄₁₆ in.
    (b) ⅛ in.
    (c) ½ in.
    (d) ¾ in.

12. Wiring methods installed behind panels that allow access shall be _____ according to their applicable articles.

    (a) supported
    (b) painted
    (c) in a metal raceway
    (d) all of these

13. Where cables and nonmetallic raceways are installed parallel to framing members, the nearest outside surface of the cable or raceway shall be _____ the nearest edge of the framing member where nails or screws are likely to penetrate.

    (a) not less than 1¼ in. from
    (b) immediately adjacent to
    (c) not less than ¹⁄₁₆ in. from
    (d) 90 degrees away from

14. A cable, raceway, or box installed under metal-corrugated sheet roof decking shall be supported so the top of the cable, raceway, or box is not less than _____ from the lowest surface of the roof decking to the top of the cable, raceway, or box.

    (a) ½ in.
    (b) 1 in.
    (c) 1½ in.
    (d) 2 in.

15. When installed under metal-corrugated sheet roof decking, the rules for spacing from roof decking apply equally to rigid metal conduit and intermediate metal conduit.

    (a) True
    (b) False

16. Where raceways contain insulated circuit conductors _____ and larger, the conductors shall be protected from abrasion during and after installation by an identified fitting providing a smoothly rounded insulating surface.

    (a) 8 AWG
    (b) 6 AWG
    (c) 4 AWG
    (d) 2 AWG

17. Where raceways contain 4 AWG or larger insulated circuit conductors entering a cabinet, box, enclosure, or raceway, the conductors shall be protected by _____.

    (a) an identified fitting that provides a smooth rounded insulating surface
    (b) a listed metal fitting that has smooth rounded edges
    (c) threaded hubs that provide a smooth rounded or flared entry
    (d) any of these

18. A listed expansion/deflection fitting or other approved means shall be used where a raceway crosses a _____ intended for expansion, contraction or deflection used in buildings, bridges, parking garages, or other structures.

    (a) junction box
    (b) structural joint
    (c) cable tray
    (d) unistrut hanger

19. What is the minimum cover requirement for direct burial Type UF cable installed outdoors that supplies a 120V, 30A circuit?

    (a) 6 in.
    (b) 12 in.
    (c) 18 in.
    (d) 24 in.

20. Rigid metal conduit that is directly buried outdoors shall have at least _____ of cover.

    (a) 6 in.
    (b) 12 in.
    (c) 18 in.
    (d) 24 in.

21. When installing PVC conduit underground without concrete cover, there shall be a minimum _____ of cover.

    (a) 6 in.
    (b) 12 in.
    (c) 18 in.
    (d) 22 in.

22. What is the minimum cover requirement for Type UF cable supplying power to a 120V, 15A GFCI-protected circuit outdoors under a driveway of a one-family dwelling?

    (a) 6 in.
    (b) 12 in.
    (c) 16 in.
    (d) 24 in.

23. Type UF cable used with a 24V landscape lighting system can have a minimum cover of _____.

    (a) 6 in.
    (b) 12 in.
    (c) 18 in.
    (d) 24 in.

24. For locations not specifically identified in Table 300.5, a cover depth of _____ shall be permitted for pool, spa, and fountain lighting, installed in a nonmetallic raceway, limited to not more than 30V where part of a listed low-voltage lighting system.

    (a) 6 in.
    (b) 12 in.
    (c) 18 in.
    (d) 24 in.

25. "_____" is defined as the shortest distance measured between a point on the top surface of direct-burial cable and the top surface of the finished grade.

    (a) Notch
    (b) Cover
    (c) Gap
    (d) Spacing

26. The interior of underground raceways shall be considered a _____ location.

    (a) wet
    (b) dry
    (c) damp
    (d) corrosive

27. Underground cable and conductors installed under a building shall be _____.

    (a) the same trench
    (b) in a raceway
    (c) encased in concrete
    (d) under at least 2 in. of concrete

28. Type MC Cable _____ for direct burial or concrete encasement shall be permitted under a building without installation in a raceway in accordance with 330.10(A)(5).

    (a) listed
    (b) identified
    (c) tagged
    (d) labeled

29. Where direct-buried conductors and cables emerge from grade, they shall be protected by enclosures or raceways to a point at least _____ above finished grade.

    (a) 3 ft
    (b) 6 ft
    (c) 8 ft
    (d) 10 ft

30. Direct-buried service conductors that are not encased in concrete and that are buried 18 in. or more below grade shall have their location identified by a warning ribbon placed in the trench at least _____ above the underground installation.

    (a) 6 in.
    (b) 10 in.
    (c) 12in.
    (d) 18 in.

31. Direct-buried conductors or cables can be spliced or tapped without the use of splice boxes when the splice or tap is made in accordance with 110.14(B).

    (a) True
    (b) False

32. Backfill used for underground wiring shall not damage _____ or prevent adequate compaction of fill or contribute to corrosion.

    (a) raceways
    (b) cables
    (c) conductors
    (d) all of these

33. Conduits or raceways through which moisture may contact live parts shall be _____ at either or both ends.

    (a) crimped
    (b) taped
    (c) bushed
    (d) sealed or plugged

34. Spare or unused raceways shall be sealed with sealants _____ for use with the cable insulation, conductor insulation, bare conductor, shield, or other components.

    (a) listed
    (b) identified
    (c) approved
    (d) any of these

35. A(An) _____, with an integral bushed opening shall be used at the end of a conduit or other raceway that terminates underground where the conductors or cables emerge as a direct burial wiring method.

    (a) splice kit
    (b) connector
    (c) adapter
    (d) bushing or terminal fitting

36. All conductors of the same circuit shall be _____, unless otherwise specifically permitted in the *Code*.

    (a) bonded
    (b) grounded
    (c) the same size
    (d) in the same raceway or cable or be in close proximity in the same trench

37. Each direct-buried single conductor cable shall be located _____ in the trench to the other single conductor cables in the same parallel set of conductors, including equipment grounding conductors.

    (a) perpendicular
    (b) bundled together
    (c) in close proximity
    (d) spaced apart

38. Direct-buried conductors, cables, or raceways, which are subject to movement by settlement or frost, shall be arranged to prevent damage to the _____ or to equipment connected to the raceways.

    (a) siding of the building mounted on
    (b) landscaping around the cable or raceway
    (c) enclosed conductors
    (d) expansion fitting

39. Raceways, cable trays, cablebus, auxiliary gutters, cable armor, boxes, cable sheathing, cabinets, elbows, couplings, fittings, supports, and support hardware shall be of materials suitable for _____.

    (a) corrosive locations
    (b) wet locations
    (c) the environment in which they are to be installed
    (d) damp locations

40. Where corrosion protection is necessary for ferrous metal equipment and the conduit is threaded in the field, the threads shall be coated with a(n) _____ electrically conductive, corrosion-resistant compound.

    (a) marked
    (b) listed
    (c) labeled
    (d) approved

41. Which of the following metal parts shall be protected from corrosion?

    (a) Ferrous metal raceways
    (b) Ferrous metal elbows
    (c) Ferrous boxes
    (d) all of these

42. Where portions of cable raceways or sleeves are required to be sealed due to different temperatures, sealants shall be identified for use with _____, a bare conductor, a shield, or other components.

    (a) low temperature conditions
    (b) high temperature conditions
    (c) a stranded conductor
    (d) cable and conductor insulation

43. Where portions of a cable raceway or sleeve are subjected to different temperatures and condensation is known to be a problem, the _____ shall be sealed to prevent the circulation of warm air to a colder section of the raceway or sleeve.

    (a) opening
    (b) cable
    (c) space
    (d) raceway or sleeve

44. Raceways shall be provided with expansion, expansion-deflection, or deflection fittings where necessary to compensate for thermal expansion, deflection, and contraction.

    (a) True
    (b) False

45. Where raceways are installed in wet locations above grade, the interior of these raceways shall be considered a _____ location.

    (a) wet
    (b) dry
    (c) damp
    (d) corrosive

46. Metal raceways, cable armor, and other metal enclosures shall be _____ joined together into a continuous electric conductor so as to provide effective electrical continuity.

    (a) electrically
    (b) permanently
    (c) metallically
    (d) physically

47. Raceways, cable assemblies, boxes, cabinets, and fittings shall be securely fastened in place.

    (a) True
    (b) False

48. Where independent support wires of a suspended ceiling assembly are used to support raceways, cable assemblies, or boxes above a ceiling, they shall be secured at _____ end(s).

    (a) one
    (b) both
    (c) the line and load
    (d) at the attachment to the structural member

49. Electrical wiring within the cavity of a fire-rated floor-ceiling or roof-ceiling assembly shall not be supported by the ceiling assembly or ceiling support wires.

    (a) True
    (b) False

50. The independent support wires for supporting electrical wiring methods in a fire-rated ceiling assembly shall be distinguishable from fire-rated suspended-ceiling framing support wires by _____.

    (a) color
    (b) tagging
    (c) other effective means
    (d) any of these

51. Raceways can be used as a means of support of Class 2 circuit conductors or cables that connect to the same equipment.

    (a) True
    (b) False

52. Cable wiring methods shall not be used as a means of support for _____.

    (a) other cables
    (b) raceways
    (c) nonelectrical equipment
    (d) all of these

53. Raceways, cable armors, and cable sheaths shall maintain _____ continuity between cabinets, boxes, fittings, or other enclosures or outlets.

    (a) mechanical
    (b) physical
    (c) effective
    (d) electrical

54. Mechanical continuity of raceways, cable armors, and cable sheaths as required by 300.12 does not apply to _____.

    (a) Type MI cable
    (b) Type MC cable
    (c) short sections of raceways used for support or protection of cable assemblies
    (d) any of these

55. Conductors in raceways shall be _____ between outlets, boxes, devices, and so forth.

    (a) continuous
    (b) installed
    (c) copper
    (d) in conduit

56. In multiwire branch circuits, the continuity of the _____ shall not be dependent upon the device connections.

    (a) ungrounded conductor
    (b) grounded conductor
    (c) grounding electrode
    (d) raceway

57. When the opening to an outlet, junction, or switch point is less than 8 in. in any dimension, each conductor shall be long enough to extend at least _____ in. outside the opening of the enclosure.

    (a) 1
    (b) 3
    (c) 6
    (d) 12

58. Fittings and connectors shall be used only with the specific wiring methods for which they are designed and listed.

    (a) True
    (b) False

59. A box or conduit body shall not be required where cables enter or exit from conduit or tubing that is used to provide cable support or protection against physical damage.

    (a) True
    (b) False

60. A box or conduit body shall not be required for splices and taps in direct-buried conductors and cables as long as the splice is made with a splicing device that is identified for the purpose.

    (a) True
    (b) False

61. A box or conduit body shall not be required for conductors in handhole enclosures, except where connected to electrical equipment.

    (a) True
    (b) False

62. The number and size of conductors permitted in a raceway is limited to _____.

    (a) permit heat to dissipate
    (b) prevent damage to insulation during installation
    (c) prevent damage to insulation during removal of conductors
    (d) all of these

63. Raceways shall be _____ between outlet, junction, or splicing points prior to the installation of conductors.

    (a) installed complete
    (b) tested for ground faults
    (c) a minimum of 80 percent complete
    (d) torqued

64. Prewired raceway assemblies shall be used only where specifically permitted in the *NEC* for the applicable wiring method.

    (a) True
    (b) False

65. Short sections of raceways used for _____ shall not be required to be installed complete between outlet, junction, or splicing points.

    (a) meter to service enclosure connection
    (b) protection of cables from physical damage
    (c) nipples
    (d) separately derived systems

66. At least _____ support method(s) shall be provided for each conductor at the top of the vertical raceway or as close to the top as practical if the vertical rise exceeds the values in Table 300.19(A).

    (a) one
    (b) two
    (c) three
    (d) four

67. A vertical run of 4/0 AWG copper shall be supported at intervals not exceeding _____.

    (a) 40 ft
    (b) 80 ft
    (c) 100 ft
    (d) 120 ft

68. Conductors in ferrous metal raceways or enclosures shall be arranged so as to avoid heating the surrounding ferrous metal by alternating-current induction. To accomplish this, the _____ conductor(s) shall be grouped together.

    (a) phase
    (b) grounded
    (c) equipment grounding
    (d) all of these

69. _____ is a nonferrous, nonmagnetic metal that has no heating due to hysteresis heating.

    (a) Steel
    (b) Iron
    (c) Aluminum
    (d) all of these

70. Electrical installations in hollow spaces, vertical shafts, and ventilation or air-handling ducts shall be made so that the possible spread of fire or products of combustion will not be _____.

    (a) substantially increased
    (b) allowed
    (c) inherent
    (d) possible

71. Openings around electrical penetrations into or through fire-resistant-rated walls, partitions, floors, or ceilings shall _____ to maintain the fire-resistance rating.

    (a) be documented
    (b) not be permitted
    (c) be firestopped using approved methods
    (d) be enlarged

72. Electrical installations in hollow spaces shall be made so not to increase the spread of fire. Such as boxes installed in a wall cavity on opposite sides of a fire rated wall where a minimum horizontal separation of _____ usually applies between boxes.

    (a) 6 in.
    (b) 12 in.
    (c) 18 in.
    (d) 24 in.

73. No wiring of any type shall be installed in ducts used to transport _____.

    (a) dust
    (b) flammable vapors
    (c) loose stock
    (d) all of these

74. Wiring methods that are permitted to be installed in ducts fabricated for environmental air include _____.

    (a) MC cable without an overall nonmetallic covering
    (b) EMT (electrical metallic tubing)
    (c) RMC (rigid metal conduit)
    (d) all of these

75. Equipment and devices shall only be permitted within ducts or plenum chambers specifically fabricated to transport environmental air if necessary for their direct action upon, or sensing of, the _____.

    (a) contained air
    (b) air quality
    (c) air temperature
    (d) humidity

76. Wiring methods and cabling systems, listed for use in other spaces used for environmental air (plenums), shall be permitted to be installed in ducts specifically fabricated for environmental air-handling purposes _____.

    (a) only if necessary to connect to equipment or devices associated with the direct action upon or sensing of the contained air
    (b) if the total length of such wiring methods or cabling systems does not exceed 4 ft
    (c) where illumination is necessary to facilitate maintenance and repair
    (d) any of these

77. Section 300.22(C) applies to spaces not specifically fabricated for environmental air-handling purposes but used for air-handling purposes such as the space over a hung ceiling.

    (a) True
    (b) False

78. The space above a hung ceiling used for environmental air-handling purposes is an example of _____, and the wiring limitations of _____ apply.

    (a) a specifically fabricated duct used for environmental air, 300.22(B)
    (b) other space used for environmental air (plenum), 300.22(C)
    (c) a supply duct used for environmental air, 300.22(B)
    (d) a supplemental return duct used for environmental air, 300.22(C)

79. In accordance with Article 300, a(n) _____ is considered a plenum space.

    (a) office space
    (b) mechanical room
    (c) space over a hung ceiling used for environmental air-handling purposes
    (d) space with supply and return vents

80. Wiring methods permitted in the ceiling areas used for environmental air include _____.

    (a) electrical metallic tubing
    (b) FMC of any length
    (c) RMC without an overall nonmetallic covering
    (d) all of these

81. _____ shall be permitted to support the wiring methods and equipment permitted to be used in other spaces used for environmental air (plenum).

    (a) Metal cable tray systems
    (b) Nonmetallic wireways
    (c) PVC conduit
    (d) Surface nonmetallic raceways

82. Electrical equipment with a metal or nonmetallic enclosure listed for use within an air-handling space and having low _____ properties, and associated wiring material suitable for the ambient temperature can be installed within an air-handling space (plenum).

    (a) resistance
    (b) impedance
    (c) and high temperature
    (d) smoke and heat release

83. Where an exit enclosure is required to be separated from the building, only electrical wiring methods serving equipment permitted by the _____ in the exit enclosure shall be installed within the exit enclosure.

    (a) fire *code* official
    (b) building *code* official
    (c) authority having jurisdiction
    (d) electrical engineer

84. Wiring methods and equipment installed behind suspended-ceiling panels shall be arranged and secured to allow access to the electrical equipment.

    (a) True
    (b) False

Introduction to Article 310—Conductors for General Wiring

This article contains the general requirements for conductors such as their insulation markings, ampacity ratings, and conditions of use. It does not apply to conductors that are part of flexible cords, fixture wires, or to those that are an integral part of equipment [90.7 and 300.1(B)].

Why does Article 310 contain so many tables? Why does Table 310.17 list the ampacity of 6 THHN as 105A, while Table 310.16 lists the same conductor as having an ampacity of only 75A? To answer that, go back to Article 100, review the definition of "Ampacity" and notice the phrase "conditions of use." These tables set a maximum current value at which premature failure of the conductor insulation should not occur during normal use, under the conditions described in the tables. Tables throughout the *NEC* are accompanied by a section of text with information about that table. For example, section 310.16 says that Table 310.16 applies to conductors carrying voltages rated 0V through 2,000V. It can be easy to overlook that limitation if you are not careful! It is imperative for you to read the *Code* section pertaining to each table and any of the Table's footnotes before you decide what is necessary for your particular application.

THHN, THHW-2, RHH, and so on, are insulation types. Those containing a "W" are suitable for use in wet locations. Every type of insulation has a limit as to how much heat it can withstand. When current flows through a conductor, it creates heat. How well the insulation around a conductor can dissipate that heat depends on factors such as whether the conductor is in free air or not. Think about what happens when you put on a sweater, a jacket, and then a coat—all at the same time. You heat up. Your skin cannot dissipate heat with all that clothing on nearly as well as it can in free air. The same principle applies to conductors.

Conductor insulation degrades with age and is called "aging." Its failure takes decades under normal use and becomes a maintenance issue for the appropriate personnel to manage. However, if a conductor is forced to exceed the ampacity listed in the appropriate table (and as a result its design temperature is exceeded) insulation failure happens much sooner and is often catastrophic. Consequently, exceeding the ampacity of a conductor is a serious safety issue.

Please use the 2020 *Code* book to answer the following questions.

1. The minimum size copper conductor permitted for voltage ratings up to 2000V _____ AWG.

    (a) 14
    (b) 12
    (c) 10
    (d) 8

2. In general, where installed in raceways, conductors _____ and larger shall be stranded.

    (a) 2 AWG
    (b) 4 AWG
    (c) 6 AWG
    (d) 8 AWG

3. Conductors for general wiring not specifically permitted elsewhere in this *Code* to be covered or bare shall _____.

    (a) not be permitted
    (b) be insulated
    (c) be rated
    (d) be listed

4. Insulated conductors rated 600 volts with the letters "HH" in their designation have a _____ insulation rating.

    (a) 60°C
    (b) 75°C
    (c) 90°C
    (d) 105°C

5. Conductors that are intended for use as ungrounded conductors, whether used as a single conductor or in multiconductor cables, shall be finished to be clearly distinguishable from _____ conductors.

    (a) grounded
    (b) ungrounded
    (c) equipment grounding
    (d) grounded and equipment grounding

6. Where installed in raceways, conductors _____ and larger shall be stranded, unless specifically permitted or required elsewhere in the *NEC*.

    (a) 10 AWG
    (b) 8 AWG
    (c) 6 AWG
    (d) 4 AWG

7. The conductors described in _____ shall be permitted for use in any of the wiring methods covered in Chapter 3 and as specified in their respective tables or as permitted elsewhere in this *Code*.

    (a) 310.4
    (b) 310.10
    (c) 310.15
    (d) 310.20

8. In general, the minimum size conductor permitted for use in parallel installations is _____.

    (a) 10 AWG
    (b) 4 AWG
    (c) 1 AWG
    (d) 1/0 AWG

9. Parallel conductors shall have the same _____.

    (a) length
    (b) material
    (c) size in circular mil area
    (d) all of these

10. Where conductors in parallel are run in separate raceways, the raceways shall have the same electrical characteristics.

    (a) True
    (b) False

11. Sectioned equipment grounding conductors smaller than _____ shall be permitted in multiconductor cables, if the combined circular mil area of the sectioned equipment grounding conductors in each cable complies with 250.122.

    (a) 3 AWG
    (b) 2 AWG
    (c) 1 AWG
    (d) 1/0 AWG

12. Where there are no adjustment or correction factors required, the service conductors for a rated service of _____ supplying the entire load associated with an individual dwelling unit, may be sized applying Table 310.12.

    (a) 100A
    (b) 200A
    (c) 400A
    (d) all of these

13. Where there are no adjustment or correction factors required, the feeder conductors for a rated service of between 100A and _____ supplying the entire load associated with an individual dwelling unit, may be sized applying Table 310.12.

    (a) 150A
    (b) 200A
    (c) 300A
    (d) 400A

14. No conductor shall be used where its operating temperature exceeds that designated for the type of insulated conductor involved.

    (a) True
    (b) False

15. The _____ rating of a conductor is the maximum temperature, at any location along its length, which the conductor can withstand over a prolonged period of time without serious degradation.

    (a) ampacity
    (b) temperature
    (c) conductivity
    (d) short-circuit

16. There are four principal determinants of conductor operating temperature, one of which is _____ generated internally in the conductor as the result of load current flow, including fundamental and harmonic currents.

    (a) friction
    (b) magnetism
    (c) heat
    (d) compatibility

17. In accordance with Article 310, temperature correction and adjustment factors are permitted to be applied to the ampacity for the temperature rating of the _____, if the corrected and adjusted ampacity does not exceed the ampacity for the temperature rating of the termination in accordance with the provisions of 110.14(C).

    (a) conductor
    (b) feeder
    (c) service
    (d) termination

18. Each current-carrying conductor of a paralleled set of conductors shall be counted as a current-carrying conductor for the purpose of applying the adjustment factors of 310.15(C)(1).

    (a) True
    (b) False

19. Where six current-carrying conductors are run in the same conduit or cable, the ampacity of each conductor shall be lowered to _____ percent of its ampacity.

    (a) 40
    (b) 60
    (c) 80
    (d) 90

20. Conductor adjustment factors shall not apply to conductors in raceways having a length not exceeding _____.

    (a) 12 in.
    (b) 24 in.
    (c) 36 in.
    (d) 48 in.

21. The ampacity adjustment factors of Table 310.15(C)(1) do not apply to Type AC or Type MC cable without an overall outer jacket, if which of the following condition(s) is(are) met.

    (a) Each cable has not more than three current-carrying conductors.
    (b) The conductors are 12 AWG copper.
    (c) No more than 20 current-carrying conductors are installed without maintaining spacing.
    (d) all of these

22. If cables meeting the requirements in 310.15(C)(1)(d)(1) through (C)(1)(d)(3) with more than 20 current-carrying conductors are installed longer than 24 in. without maintaining spacing, are stacked, or are supported on bridle rings, a _____ percent adjustment factor shall be applied.

    (a) 30
    (b) 40
    (c) 50
    (d) 60

23. Where raceways or cables are exposed to direct sunlight on or above rooftops and where the distance above the roof to the bottom of the raceway is less than _____, a temperature adder of 60°F shall be added to the outdoor temperature to determine the applicable ambient temperature for application of the correction factors in Table 310.15(B)(1) or Table 310.15(B)(2).

    (a) ¼ in.
    (b) ⅓ in.
    (c) ½ in.
    (d) ⅞ in.

24. Where conductors are installed in raceways or cables exposed to direct sunlight on or above rooftops, a temperature adder of _____ shall be added to the outdoor temperature where the conduits are less than ⅞ in. from the rooftop.

    (a) 30°F
    (b) 40°F
    (c) 50°F
    (d) 60°F

25. Type _____ insulated conductors shall not be subject to ampacity adjustment where installed exposed to direct sunlight on a rooftop.

    (a) THW-2
    (b) XHHW-2
    (c) THWN-2
    (d) RHW-2

26. A(n) _____ conductor that carries only the unbalanced current from other conductors of the same circuit shall not be required to be counted when applying the provisions of 310.15(C)(1).

    (a) neutral
    (b) ungrounded
    (c) grounding
    (d) bonded

27. In a 3-wire circuit consisting of two phase conductors and the neutral conductor of a 4-wire, 3-phase, wye-connected system, the common conductor is not a current carrying conductor and not subject to the adjustment provisions of 310.15(C)(1).

    (a) True
    (b) False

28. In a 3-wire circuit consisting of two phase conductors and the neutral conductor of a 4-wire, 3-phase, wye-connected system, the common conductor _____ a current-carrying conductor.

    (a) shall be counted as
    (b) is not
    (c) shall be considered to be
    (d) shall not be considered

29. In a 3-wire circuit consisting of two phase conductors and the neutral conductor of a 4-wire, 3-phase, _____ connected system, the common conductor is not a current carrying conductor and not subject to the adjustment provisions of 310.15(C)(1).

    (a) delta
    (b) delta-wye
    (c) delta-delta
    (d) wye

30. On a 4-wire, 3-phase wye circuit where the major portion of the neutral load consists of _____ loads, the neutral conductor shall be considered a current-carrying conductor.

    (a) 240V
    (b) 277V
    (c) nonlinear
    (d) linear

31. When determining the number of current-carrying conductors, a grounding or bonding conductor shall not be counted when applying the provisions of 310.15(C)(1).

    (a) True
    (b) False

32. For one-family dwellings and the individual dwelling units of two-family and multifamily dwellings, single-phase feeder conductors consisting of _____ ungrounded conductor(s) and the neutral conductor from a 208Y/120 volt system shall be permitted to be sized in accordance with 310.12(A) through (D).

    (a) 1
    (b) 2
    (c) 3
    (d) 4

33. Where correction or adjustment factors are required by 310.15(B) or (C), for single-phase feeder conductors installed for _____ dwellings, they shall be permitted to be applied to the ampacity associated with the temperature rating of the conductor.

    (a) one-family
    (b) the individual dwelling units of two-family
    (c) the individual dwelling units of multifamily
    (d) all of these

34. The ampacities specified in Table 310.16 are based on _____.

    (a) conductors are rated 60°C, 75°C, or 90°C
    (b) an ambient temperature of 86°F
    (c) no more than three current-carrying conductors
    (d) all of these

ARTICLE 312 CABINETS

Introduction to Article 312—Cabinets

Conditions of use effect the selection and application of cabinets. For example, you cannot use just any enclosure in a wet or a hazardous location. The conditions of use impose special requirements for these situations.

For all such enclosures, certain requirements apply—regardless of the use. For example, you must cover any openings, protect conductors from abrasion, and allow sufficient bending room for conductors.

Notice that Article 408 covers switchboards, switchgear, and panelboards, with the primary emphasis on the interior (or "guts") while the cabinet used to enclose a panelboard is covered here in Article 312. Therefore, you will find that some important considerations such as wire-bending space at the terminals of panelboards are included in this article.

Please use the 2020 *Code* book to answer the following questions.

1. Article _____ covers the installation and construction specifications of cabinets, cutout boxes, and meter socket enclosures.

    (a) 300
    (b) 310
    (c) 312
    (d) 314

2. Cabinets, cutout boxes, and meter socket enclosures installed in wet locations shall be _____.

    (a) waterproof
    (b) raintight
    (c) weatherproof
    (d) watertight

3. Where raceways or cables enter above the level of uninsulated live parts of cabinets, cutout boxes, and meter socket enclosures in a wet location, a(n) _____ shall be used.

    (a) fitting listed for wet locations
    (b) explosionproof seal
    (c) fitting listed for damp locations
    (d) insulated fitting

4. In walls constructed of wood or other _____ material, electrical cabinets shall be flush with the finished surface or project therefrom.

    (a) nonconductive
    (b) porous
    (c) fibrous
    (d) combustible

5. Noncombustible surfaces that are broken or incomplete shall be repaired so there will be no gaps or open spaces greater than _____ at the edge of a cabinet or cutout box employing a flush-type cover.

    (a) 1/32 in.
    (b) 1/16 in.
    (c) 1/8 in.
    (d) 1/4 in.

6. Each cable entering a cutout box _____.

    (a) shall be secured to the cutout box
    (b) can be sleeved through a chase
    (c) shall have a maximum of two cables per connector
    (d) all of these

7. Nonmetallic-sheathed cables can enter the top of surface-mounted cabinets, cutout boxes, and meter socket enclosures through nonflexible raceways not less than 18 in. and not more than _____ in length if all of the required conditions are met.

    (a) 3 ft
    (b) 10 ft
    (c) 25 ft
    (d) 100 ft

8. The wiring space within enclosures for _____ and overcurrent devices shall be permitted for other wiring and equipment subject to limitations for specific equipment in accordance with Article 312.

    (a) receptacles
    (b) luminaires
    (c) signs
    (d) switches

9. Enclosures for switches or overcurrent devices are allowed to have conductors feeding through where the wiring space at any cross section is not filled to more than _____ percent of the cross-sectional area of the space.

    (a) 20%
    (b) 30%
    (c) 40%
    (d) 60%

10. Cabinets, cutout boxes, and meter socket enclosures can be used for conductors feeding through, spliced, or tapping off to other enclosures, switches, or overcurrent devices where _____.

    (a) the total area of the conductors at any cross section does not exceed 40 percent of the cross-sectional area of that space
    (b) the total area of conductors, splices, and taps installed at any cross section does not exceed 75 percent of the cross-sectional area of that space
    (c) a warning label on the enclosure identifies the closest disconnecting means for any feed-through conductors
    (d) all of these

ARTICLE 314

OUTLET, PULL, AND JUNCTION BOXES; CONDUIT BODIES; AND HANDHOLE ENCLOSURES

Introduction to Article 314—Outlet, Pull, and Junction Boxes; Conduit Bodies; and Handhole Enclosures

Article 314 contains the installation requirements for outlet boxes, pull and junction boxes, conduit bodies, and handhole enclosures. As with the cabinets covered in Article 312, the conditions of use have a bearing on the type of material and equipment selected for the installation.

The information contained in this article will help you size an outlet box using the proper cubic-inch capacity as well as calculating the minimum dimensions for pull boxes. There are limits on the amount of weight that can be supported by an outlet box, and rules on how to support a device or outlet box to various surfaces. Article 314 will help you understand these rules so your installation will be compliant with the *NEC*.

Please use the 2020 *Code* book to answer the following questions.

1. The installation and use of all boxes and conduit bodies used as outlet, device, junction, or pull boxes, depending on their use, and handhole enclosures, are covered within _____.

   (a) Article 110
   (b) Article 200
   (c) Article 300
   (d) Article 314

2. Where internal _____ means are provided between all entries, nonmetallic boxes shall be permitted to be used with metal raceways or metal-armored cables.

   (a) grounding
   (b) bonding
   (c) connecting
   (d) splicing

3. Nonmetallic boxes can be used with _____.

   (a) nonmetallic sheaths
   (b) nonmetallic raceways
   (c) flexible cords
   (d) all of these

4. Metal boxes shall be _____ in accordance with Article 250.

   (a) grounded
   (b) bonded
   (c) secured
   (d) grounded and bonded

5. Boxes, conduit bodies, and fittings installed in wet locations shall be listed for use in wet locations.

   (a) True
   (b) False

6. _____ drainage openings not smaller than ⅛ in. and not larger than ¼ in. in diameter shall be permitted to be installed in the field in boxes or conduit bodies listed for use in damp or wet locations.

   (a) Listed
   (b) Approved
   (c) Labeled
   (d) Identified

7. Boxes and conduit bodies shall be of an approved size to provide free space for all enclosed _____.

   (a) conductors
   (b) splices
   (c) terminations
   (d) all of these

8. Where a box is provided with _____ or more securely installed barriers, the volume shall be apportioned to each of the resulting spaces; each barrier, if not marked with its volume, shall be considered to take up ½ cu in. if metal, and 1 cu in. if nonmetallic.

   (a) one
   (b) two
   (c) three
   (d) four

9. According to the *NEC*, the volume of a 3 in. × 2 in. × 2 in. device box is _____ cu in.

   (a) 8
   (b) 10
   (c) 12
   (d) 14

10. The total volume occupied by two internal cable clamps, six 12 AWG conductors, and a single-pole switch is _____ cu in.

    (a) 2.00
    (b) 4.50
    (c) 14.50
    (d) 20.25

11. When counting the number of conductors in a box, a conductor running through the box with an unbroken loop or coil not less than twice the minimum length required for free conductors shall be counted as _____ conductor(s).

    (a) one
    (b) two
    (c) three
    (d) four

12. Equipment grounding conductor(s), and not more than _____ fixture wires smaller than 14 AWG shall be permitted to be omitted from the calculations where they enter the box from a domed luminaire or similar canopy and terminate within that box.

    (a) one
    (b) two
    (c) three
    (d) four

13. Where one or more internal cable clamps are present in the box, a single volume allowance in accordance with Table 314.16(B) shall be made based on the largest conductor present in the box.

    (a) True
    (b) False

14. Where a luminaire stud or hickey is present in the box, _____ allowance in accordance with Table 314.16(B) shall be made for each type of fitting, based on the largest conductor present in the box.

    (a) a single volume
    (b) a double volume
    (c) a ¼ volume
    (d) no additional volume

15. For the purposes of determining box fill, each device or utilization equipment in the box which is wider than a single device box counts as two conductors for each _____ required for the mounting.

    (a) inch
    (b) kilometer
    (c) gang
    (d) box

16. Each strap containing one or more devices shall count as _____ allowance in accordance with Table 314.16(B), based on the largest conductor connected to a device(s) or equipment supported by the strap.

    (a) a single volume
    (b) a double volume
    (c) a ¼ volume
    (d) no additional volume

17. A device or utilization equipment wider than a single 2 in. device box shall have _____ allowance provided for each gang required for mounting.

    (a) a single volume
    (b) a double volume
    (c) a ¼ volume
    (d) no additional volume

18. Where one or more equipment grounding conductors enter a box, _____ allowance in accordance with Table 314.16(B) shall be made based on the largest equipment grounding conductor.

    (a) a single volume
    (b) a double volume
    (c) a ¼ volume
    (d) no additional volume

19. Conduit bodies that are durably and legibly marked by the manufacturer with their volume can contain splices, taps, or devices.

    (a) True
    (b) False

20. Short-radius conduit bodies such as capped elbows and service-entrance elbows that enclose conductors 6 AWG or smaller shall not contain _____.

    (a) splices
    (b) taps
    (c) devices
    (d) any of these

21. Where nonmetallic-sheathed cable or multiconductor Type UF cable is used, the sheath shall extend not less than _____ inside the box and beyond any cable clamp.

    (a) ¼ in.
    (b) ⅜ in.
    (c) ½ in.
    (d) ¾ in.

22. When Type NM cable is used with nonmetallic boxes not larger than 2¼ × 4 in., securing the cable to the box shall not be required if the cable is fastened within _____ in. of that box.

    (a) 6
    (b) 8
    (c) 10
    (d) 12

23. In installations within or behind noncombustible walls or ceilings, the front edge of a box, plaster ring, extension ring, or listed extender employing a flush-type cover, shall be set back not more than _____ from the finished surface.

    (a) ⅛ in.
    (b) ¼ in.
    (c) ⅜ in.
    (d) ½ in.

24. In installations within walls or ceilings constructed of wood or other combustible surface material, boxes, plaster rings, extension rings, or listed extenders shall _____.

    (a) extend to the finished surface or project therefrom
    (b) not be permitted
    (c) be fire rated
    (d) be set back no more than ¼ in.

25. Noncombustible surfaces that are broken or incomplete around boxes employing a flush-type cover or faceplate shall be repaired so there will be no gaps or open spaces larger than _____ at the edge of the box.

    (a) ¹⁄₁₆ in.
    (b) ⅛ in.
    (c) ¼ in.
    (d) ½ in.

26. Surface extensions shall be made by mounting and mechanically securing an extension ring over the box, unless otherwise permitted.

    (a) True
    (b) False

27. A surface extension can be made from the cover of a box where the cover is designed so it is unlikely to fall off or be removed if its securing means becomes loose. The wiring method shall be _____ for an approved length that permits removal of the cover and provides access to the box interior and arranged so that any grounding continuity is independent of the connection between the box and cover.

    (a) solid
    (b) flexible
    (c) rigid
    (d) cord

Understanding the 2020 National Electrical Code Workbook (Articles 90-480) | MikeHolt.com |

28. An outlet box or enclosure mounted on a building or other surface shall be _____.

    (a) rigidly and securely fastened in place
    (b) supported by cables that protrude from the box
    (c) supported by cable entries from the top and permitted to rest against the supporting surface
    (d) permitted to be supported by the raceway(s) terminating at the box

29. Metal braces used for the support of boxes shall be protected against corrosion.

    (a) True
    (b) False

30. Wood braces shall have a cross section not more than 1 in. × 2 in. nominal.

    (a) True
    (b) False

31. A wood brace used for supporting a box for structural mounting shall have a cross-section not less than nominal _____.

    (a) 1 in. × 2 in.
    (b) 2 in. × 2 in.
    (c) 2 in. × 3 in.
    (d) 2 in. × 4 in.

32. When mounting an enclosure in a finished surface, the enclosure shall be _____ secured to the surface by clamps, anchors, or fittings identified for the application.

    (a) temporarily
    (b) partially
    (c) never
    (d) rigidly

33. Support wire(s) used for enclosure support in suspended ceilings shall be fastened at _____ so as to be taut within the ceiling cavity.

    (a) each end
    (b) each corner
    (c) each ceiling support
    (d) the ceiling grid

34. Outlet boxes can be secured to suspended-ceiling framing members by mechanical means such as _____, or by other means identified for use with the suspended-ceiling framing member(s).

    (a) bolts
    (b) screws
    (c) rivets
    (d) any of these

35. Enclosures not over 100 cu in. having threaded entries and not containing a device shall be considered to be adequately supported where _____ or more conduits are threaded wrenchtight into the enclosure and each conduit is secured within 3 ft of the enclosure.

    (a) one
    (b) two
    (c) three
    (d) four

36. Two intermediate metal or rigid metal conduits threaded wrenchtight into an enclosure can be used to support an outlet box containing devices or luminaires, if each raceway is supported within _____ of the box.

    (a) 12 in.
    (b) 18 in.
    (c) 24 in.
    (d) 36 in.

37. Screws used for the purpose of attaching covers or other equipment to the box shall be either machine screws matching the thread gauge and size that is integral to the box or be in accordance with the manufacturer's instructions.

    (a) True
    (b) False

38. In completed installations, each outlet box shall have a _____.

    (a) cover
    (b) faceplate
    (c) canopy
    (d) any of these

39. Boxes used at luminaire outlets on a vertical surface shall be marked on the interior of the box to indicate the maximum weight of the luminaire that is permitted to be supported by the box if other than _____ lb.

    (a) 6 lb
    (b) 12 lb
    (c) 35 lb
    (d) 50 lb

40. A vertically mounted luminaire weighing not more than _____ can be supported to a device box or plaster ring with no fewer than two No. 6 or larger screws.

    (a) 4 lb
    (b) 6 lb
    (c) 8 lb
    (d) 10 lb

41. Boxes used at luminaire or lampholder outlets in a ceiling shall be designed so that a luminaire or lampholder can be attached and the boxes shall be required to support a luminaire weighing a minimum of _____.

    (a) 20 lb
    (b) 30 lb
    (c) 40 lb
    (d) 50 lb

42. A luminaire that weighs more than _____ can be supported by an outlet box that is listed for the weight of the luminaire to be supported.

    (a) 20 lb
    (b) 30 lb
    (c) 40 lb
    (d) 50 lb

43. Floor boxes _____ specifically for the application shall be used for receptacles located in the floor.

    (a) identified
    (b) listed
    (c) approved
    (d) designed

44. Listed outlet boxes to support ceiling-suspended fans that weigh more than _____ shall have the maximum allowable weight marked on the box.

    (a) 35 lb
    (b) 50 lb
    (c) 60 lb
    (d) 70 lb

45. Outlet boxes mounted in the ceilings of habitable rooms of _____, in a location acceptable for the future installation of a ceiling-suspended (paddle) fan, shall be listed for the sole support of ceiling-suspended paddle fans.

    (a) used for childcare
    (b) guest suites
    (c) dwelling occupancies
    (d) apartments

46. Utilization equipment weighing not more than 6 lb can be supported to any box or plaster ring secured to a box, provided the equipment is secured with at least two _____ or larger screws.

    (a) No. 6
    (b) No. 8
    (c) No. 10
    (d) any of these

47. Where splices, or, angle or U pulls are made, the distance between each raceway entry inside the box and the opposite wall of the box may not be less than _____ the trade size of the largest raceway in a row.

    (a) twice
    (b) 3 times
    (c) 6 times
    (d) 8 times

48. Where splices, or, angle or U pulls are made and the conductor enters and leaves from the same wall and row of the box, the distance to the opposite wall may not be less than _____ the trade size of the largest raceway in the row plus the sum of the remaining trade sizes in the same row.

    (a) twice
    (b) 3 times
    (c) 6 times
    (d) 8 times

49. Where _____ or, angle or "U" pulls are made, the calculated distance between raceways shall be increased for additional entries by the amount of the sum of the diameters of all other raceway entries in the same row on the same wall of the box. Each row shall be calculated individually, and the single row that provides the maximum distance shall be used.

    (a) junctions
    (b) transitions
    (c) taps
    (d) splices

50. Where angle or U pulls are made, the distance between each raceway entry inside the box or conduit body and the opposite wall of the box or conduit body shall not be less than _____ times the trade size of the largest raceway in a row plus the sum of the trade sizes of the remaining raceways in the same wall and row.

    (a) six
    (b) eight
    (c) ten
    (d) twelve

51. Pull boxes or junction boxes with any dimension over _____ ft shall have all conductors cabled or racked in an approved manner.

    (a) 3
    (b) 6
    (c) 9
    (d) 12

52. All _____ shall be provided with covers compatible with the box or conduit body construction and suitable for the conditions of use.

    (a) pull boxes
    (b) junction boxes
    (c) conduit bodies
    (d) all of these

53. Power distribution blocks shall be permitted in pull and junction boxes over _____ in³.

    (a) 90
    (b) 100
    (c) 120
    (d) 200

54. _____ shall be installed so that the wiring contained in them can be rendered accessible without removing any part of the building or structure or, in underground circuits, without excavating sidewalks, paving, or earth.

    (a) Boxes
    (b) Conduit bodies
    (c) Handhole enclosures
    (d) all of these

55. Handhole enclosures shall be designed and installed to withstand _____.

    (a) 600 lb
    (b) 3,000 lb
    (c) 6,000 lb
    (d) all loads likely to be imposed on them

56. Underground raceways and cable assemblies entering a handhole enclosure shall extend into the enclosure, but they are not required to be _____.

    (a) bonded
    (b) insulated
    (c) mechanically connected to the handhole enclosure
    (d) below minimum cover requirements after leaving the handhole

57. Conductors, splices, or terminations in a handhole enclosure shall be listed as suitable for _____.

    (a) wet locations
    (b) damp locations
    (c) direct burial in the earth
    (d) exterior use

58. Handhole enclosure covers shall have an identifying mark or logo that prominently identifies the function of the enclosure, such as "_____."

    (a) danger
    (b) utility
    (c) high voltage
    (d) electric

59. Metal handhole enclosure covers and other exposed conductive surfaces shall be _____.

    (a) listed
    (b) bonded to the equipment grounding conductor
    (c) grounded
    (d) installed

60. Handhole enclosure covers shall require the use of tools to open, or they shall weigh over _____.

(a) 45 lb
(b) 70 lb
(c) 100 lb
(d) 200 lb

ARTICLE 320

ARMORED CABLE (TYPE AC)

Introduction to Article 320—Armored Cable (Type AC)

Armored cable (Type AC) is an assembly of insulated conductors, 14 AWG through 1 AWG, individually wrapped in wax paper (jute) and contained within a flexible spiral metal sheath. To the casual observer the outside appearance of armored cable is like flexible metal conduit and metal-clad cable (Type MC). Type AC cable has been referred to as "BX®" cable over the years.

Please use the 2020 *Code* book to answer the following questions.

1. Article _____ covers the use, installation, and construction specifications for armored cable, Type AC.

   (a) 300
   (b) 310
   (c) 320
   (d) 334

2. Type _____ cable is a fabricated assembly of insulated conductors in a flexible interlocked metallic armor.

   (a) AC
   (b) TC
   (c) NM
   (d) MA

3. Type AC cable and associated fittings shall be _____.

   (a) identified
   (b) approved
   (c) listed
   (d) labeled

4. Type AC cable is permitted in _____.

   (a) wet locations
   (b) corrosive conditions
   (c) damp locations
   (d) cable trays

5. Armored cable shall not be installed _____.

   (a) in damp or wet locations
   (b) where subject to physical damage
   (c) where exposed to corrosive conditions
   (d) all of these

6. Exposed runs of Type AC cable can be installed on the underside of joists where supported at each joist and located so it is not subject to physical damage.

   (a) True
   (b) False

7. Type AC cable installed through, or parallel to, framing members shall be protected against physical damage from penetration by screws or nails.

   (a) True
   (b) False

8. When Type AC cable is run across the top of a floor joist in an attic without permanent ladders or stairs, guard strips within _____ of the scuttle hole or attic entrance shall protect the cable.

   (a) 3 ft
   (b) 4 ft
   (c) 5 ft
   (d) 6 ft

9. When armored cable is run parallel to the sides of rafters, studs, or floor joists in an accessible attic, the cable shall be protected with running boards.

   (a) True
   (b) False

10. The radius of the curve of the inner edge of any bend shall not be less than _____ for Type AC cable.

    (a) five times the largest conductor within the cable
    (b) three times the diameter of the cable
    (c) five times the diameter of the cable
    (d) six times the outside diameter of the conductors

11. Type AC cable shall be supported and secured by _____.

    (a) staples
    (b) cable ties listed and identified for securement and support
    (c) straps
    (d) any of these

12. Type AC cable shall be secured at intervals not exceeding 4½ ft and within _____ of every outlet box, cabinet, conduit body, or fitting.

    (a) 6 in.
    (b) 8 in.
    (c) 10 in.
    (d) 12 in.

13. Type AC cable installed horizontally through wooden or metal framing members is considered supported where support does not exceed _____ intervals.

    (a) 2 ft
    (b) 3 ft
    (c) 4½ ft
    (d) 6 ft

14. Armored cable used to connect recessed luminaires or equipment within an accessible ceiling can be unsupported and unsecured for lengths up to _____.

    (a) 2 ft
    (b) 3 ft
    (c) 4½ ft
    (d) 6 ft

15. At Type AC cable terminations, a(n) _____ shall be provided to protect wires from abrasion.

    (a) fitting
    (b) connector
    (c) electrical tape wrapped between the armor and the conductors
    (d) adapter

16. Type AC cable outer armor is permitted to act as an equipment grounding conductor.

    (a) True
    (b) False

17. Type AC cable installed in thermal insulation shall have conductors that are rated at 90 degrees C. The ampacity of the cable in this application shall not exceed that of a _____ rated conductor.

    (a) 60-degree C
    (b) 75-degree C
    (c) 90-degree C
    (d) 100-degree C

ARTICLE
330

METAL-CLAD CABLE (TYPE MC)

Introduction to Article 330—Metal-Clad Cable (Type MC)

Metal-clad cable (Type MC) is probably the most often used metal-protected wiring method. Type MC cable encloses insulated conductors in a metal sheath of either corrugated or smooth copper or aluminum tubing, or in spiral interlocked steel or aluminum. The physical characteristics of Type MC cable make it a versatile wiring method that can be used in almost any location, and for almost any application. The most commonly used Type MC cable is the interlocking kind, which looks like armored cable or flexible metal conduit. Traditional interlocked Type MC cable is not permitted to serve as an equipment grounding conductor; therefore, this cable must contain an equipment grounding conductor in accordance with 250.118(1). Another type of Type MC cable is called interlocked Type MC^AP® cable. It contains a bare aluminum grounding/bonding conductor running just below the metal armor, which allows the sheath to serve as an equipment grounding conductor [250.118(10)(b)].

Please use the 2020 *Code* book to answer the following questions.

1. The use, installation, and construction specifications of metal-clad cable, Type MC are covered within Article _____.

   (a) 300
   (b) 310
   (c) 320
   (d) 330

2. Type _____ cable is a factory assembly of insulated circuit conductors within an armor of interlocking metal tape, or a smooth or corrugated metallic sheath.

   (a) AC
   (b) MC
   (c) NM
   (d) CMS

3. Type MC cable shall be permitted for _____.

   (a) branch circuits
   (b) feeders
   (c) services
   (d) any of these

4. Type MC cable shall be listed and fittings used for connecting Type MC cable to boxes, cabinets, or other equipment shall _____.

   (a) be nonmetallic only
   (b) be listed and identified for such use
   (c) be listed and identified as weatherproof
   (d) include anti-shorting bushings

5. Type MC cable shall not be used under which of the following conditions?

   (a) Where subject to physical damage.
   (b) Direct buried in the earth or embedded in concrete unless identified for direct burial.
   (c) Exposed to cinder fills, strong chlorides, caustic alkalis, or vapors of chlorine or of hydrochloric acids.
   (d) all of these

6. Exposed runs of cable, except as provided in 300.11(A), shall closely follow the surface of the _____.

   (a) building finish
   (b) running boards
   (c) the underside of joists
   (d) any of these

7. Type MC cable installed through, or parallel to, framing members shall be protected against physical damage from penetration by screws or nails by 1¼ in. separation or protected by a suitable metal plate.

   (a) True
   (b) False

8. Smooth-sheath Type MC cable with an external diameter not greater than ¾ in. shall have a bending radius not less than _____ times the external diameter of the cable.

   (a) five
   (b) ten
   (c) twelve
   (d) thirteen

9. Bends made in interlocked or corrugated sheath Type MC cable shall have a radius of at least _____ times the external diameter of the metallic sheath.

   (a) five
   (b) seven
   (c) ten
   (d) twelve

10. Type MC cable shall be supported and secured by staples; cable ties _____ for securement and support; straps, hangers, or similar fittings; or other approved means designed and installed so as not to damage the cable.

    (a) listed and identified
    (b) marked or labeled
    (c) installed and approved
    (d) any of these

11. Type MC cable shall be secured at intervals not exceeding _____.

    (a) 3 ft
    (b) 4 ft
    (c) 6 ft
    (d) 8 ft

12. Type MC cable containing four or fewer conductors, sized no larger than 10 AWG, shall be secured within _____ of every box, cabinet, fitting, or other cable termination.

    (a) 8 in.
    (b) 12 in.
    (c) 18 in.
    (d) 24 in.

13. Type MC cable installed horizontally through wooden or metal framing members are considered secured and supported where such support does not exceed _____ intervals.

    (a) 3 ft
    (b) 4 ft
    (c) 6 ft
    (d) 8 ft

14. Type MC cable can be unsupported and unsecured where the cable is _____.

    (a) fished between access points through concealed spaces in finished buildings or structures
    (b) not more than 2 ft in length at terminals where flexibility is necessary
    (c) not more than 8 ft from the last point of support within an accessible ceiling
    (d) installed in attic spaces

ARTICLE
334

NONMETALLIC-SHEATHED CABLE (TYPE NM)

Introduction to Article 334—Nonmetallic-Sheathed Cable (Type NM)

Nonmetallic-sheathed cable (Type NM) provides very limited physical protection for the conductors inside, so the installation restrictions are stringent. Its low cost and relative ease of installation make it a common wiring method for residential and commercial branch circuits.

 Please use the 2020 *Code* book to answer the following questions.

1. The use, installation, and construction specifications of nonmetallic-sheathed cable are covered within Article _____.

   (a) 300
   (b) 334
   (c) 400
   (d) 410

2. Type _____ cable is a factory assembly that encloses two or more insulated conductors within a nonmetallic jacket.

   (a) AC
   (b) MC
   (c) NM
   (d) NMJ

3. Type NM cable and associated fittings shall be _____.

   (a) marked
   (b) approved
   (c) identified
   (d) listed

4. Type NM cables shall not be used in one- and two-family dwellings exceeding three floors above grade.

   (a) True
   (b) False

5. Type NM and Type NMC cables shall be permitted in _____, except as prohibited in 334.12.

   (a) one- and two-family dwellings and their attached/detached garages and storage buildings
   (b) multifamily dwellings permitted to be of Types III, IV, and V construction
   (c) other structures permitted to be of Types III, IV, and V construction
   (d) any of these

6. Type NM cable can be installed as open runs in dropped or suspended ceilings in other than one- and two-family and multi-family dwellings.

   (a) True
   (b) False

7. Type NM cable shall not be used _____.

   (a) in other than dwelling units
   (b) in the air void of masonry block not subject to excessive moisture
   (c) for exposed work
   (d) embedded in poured cement, concrete, or aggregate

8. Type NM cable shall closely follow the surface of the building finish or running boards when run exposed.

   (a) True
   (b) False

9. Type NM cable shall be protected from physical damage by _____.

   (a) EMT
   (b) Schedule 80 PVC conduit
   (c) RMC
   (d) any of these

10. Where Type NM cable is run at angles with joists in unfinished basements and crawl spaces, it is permissible to secure cables not smaller than _____ conductors directly to the lower edges of the joist.

    (a) three, 6 AWG
    (b) four, 8 AWG
    (c) four, 10 AWG
    (d) two, 6 AWG or three, 8 AWG

11. Type NM cable on a wall of an unfinished basement installed in a listed raceway shall have a _____ installed at the point where the cable enters the raceway.

    (a) suitable insulating bushing or adapter
    (b) sealing fitting
    (c) bonding bushing
    (d) junction box

12. The radius of the curve of the inner edge of any bend during or after installation of Type NM cable, shall not be less than _____ times the diameter of the cable.

    (a) 5
    (b) 6
    (c) 7
    (d) 8

13. Grommets or bushings for the protection of Type NM cable installed through or parallel to framing members shall be _____ for the purpose.

    (a) marked
    (b) approved
    (c) identified
    (d) listed

14. Type NM cable can be supported and secured by _____.

    (a) staples
    (b) cable ties listed and identified for securement and support
    (c) straps
    (d) any of these

15. Flat Type NM cables shall not be stapled on edge.

    (a) True
    (b) False

16. Type NM cable protected from physical damage by a raceway shall not be required to be _____ within the raceway.

    (a) covered
    (b) insulated
    (c) secured
    (d) unspliced

17. Nonmetallic-sheathed cable shall be permitted to be unsupported where the cable is _____.

    (a) fished between access points through concealed spaces in finished buildings or structures
    (b) not more than 6 ft from the last point of cable support to the point of connection to a luminaire within an accessible ceiling in one-, two-, or multifamily dwellings
    (c) between framing members and exterior masonry walls
    (d) where installed in attics

18. In addition to the insulated conductors, Type NM cable shall have an insulated equipment grounding conductor.

    (a) True
    (b) False

19. The _____ rating is permitted to be used for ampacity adjustment and correction calculations, provided the final calculated ampacity does not exceed that of a 60°C rated conductor.

    (a) 60°C
    (b) 75°C
    (c) 90°C
    (d) 104°C

20. Where more than two Type NM cables are installed through the same opening in wood framing that is to be sealed with thermal insulation, caulk, or sealing foam, the allowable ampacity of each conductor shall be _____.

    (a) no more than 20A
    (b) adjusted in accordance with Table 310.15(C)(1)
    (c) limited to 30A
    (d) calculated by an engineer

21. The 90°C rating is permitted to be used for ampacity adjustment and correction calculations, provided the final calculated ampacity does not exceed that of a _____ rated conductor.

    (a) 60°C
    (b) 75°C
    (c) 90°C
    (d) 104°C

22. Where more than two NM cables are installed through the same bored hole in wood framing that is to be sealed with _____, the ampacity of each conductor shall be adjusted.

    (a) thermal insulation
    (b) caulk
    (c) sealing foam
    (d) any of these

23. For Types NM and NMC cable, the conductor ampacity used for ambient temperature correction 310.15(B)(1), conductor bundling adjustment 310.15(C)(1), or both, is based on the 90-degree C conductor insulation rating 310.15(B)(2), provided the final calculated ampacity does not exceed that of a _____ rated conductor.

    (a) 60-degree C
    (b) 75-degree C
    (c) 90-degree C
    (d) 120-degree C

Notes

ARTICLE 336

POWER AND CONTROL TRAY CABLE (TYPE TC)

Introduction to Article 336—Power and Control Tray Cable (Type TC)

Power and control tray cable (Type TC) is flexible, inexpensive, and easily installed. It provides very limited physical protection for the conductors, so the installation restrictions are stringent. Its low cost and relative ease of installation make it a common wiring method for industrial applications.

Please use the 2020 *Code* book to answer the following questions.

1. Article _____ covers the use, installation, and construction specifications for power and control tray cable, Type TC.

   (a) 326
   (b) 330
   (c) 334
   (d) 336

2. Type _____ cable is a factory assembly of two or more insulated conductors, with or without associated bare or covered grounding conductors, under a nonmetallic jacket.

   (a) NM
   (b) TC
   (c) SE
   (d) UF

3. Type TC cable and associated fittings shall be _____.

   (a) identified
   (b) approved
   (c) listed
   (d) labeled

4. Type TC cable can be used _____.

   (a) for power, lighting, control, and signal circuits
   (b) in cable trays including those with mechanically discontinuous segments up to 1 ft
   (c) for Class 1 control circuits as permitted in Parts II and III of Article 725
   (d) all of these

5. In _____, type TC-ER-JP cable containing both power and control conductors shall be permitted for branch circuits and feeders.

   (a) multifamily dwellings
   (b) one- and two- family dwelling units
   (c) only duplexes
   (d) none of these

6. Where Type TC-ER-JP cable is used to connect a generator and associated equipment having terminals rated _____ or higher, the cable shall not be limited in ampacity by 334.80 or 340.80.

   (a) 60°C
   (b) 75°C
   (c) 90°C
   (d) 100°C

7. Type TC-ER-JP cable shall be permitted for branch circuits and feeders in one and two family dwelling units.

    (a) True
    (b) False

8. Where Type TC cable is installed in one- and two-family dwelling units, 725.136 provides rules for limitations on Class 2 or 3 circuits contained within the same cable with conductors of electric light, power, or Class 1 circuits.

    (a) True
    (b) False

9. Type TC cable shall be permitted to be direct buried, where _____ for such use.

    (a) identified
    (b) approved
    (c) listed
    (d) labeled

10. Type TC cable shall be permitted for use in hazardous (classified) locations where specifically _____ by other articles in this *Code*.

    (a) required
    (b) permitted
    (c) approved
    (d) identified

11. Type TC cable shall not be used where _____.

    (a) it will be exposed to physical damage
    (b) installed outside of a raceway or cable tray system, unless permitted in 336.10(4), 336.10(7), 336.10(9), and 336.10(10)
    (c) exposed to direct rays of the sun, unless identified as sunlight resistant
    (d) all of these

12. Bends in Type TC cable shall be made so as not to damage the cable. For TC Cable larger than 1 in and up to 2 in in diameter, without metal shielding, the minimum bending radius shall be at least _____ times the overall diameter of the cable.

    (a) 2 times
    (b) 3 times
    (c) 5 times
    (d) 7 times

ARTICLE 338

SERVICE-ENTRANCE CABLE (TYPES SE AND USE)

Introduction to Article 338—Service-Entrance Cable (Types SE and USE)

Service-entrance (SE) and underground service-entrance (USE) cables, can be a single conductor or a multiconductor assembly within an overall nonmetallic outer jacket or covering. This cable is used primarily for services but is permitted for feeders and branch circuits. When used as a service conductor(s) or service entrance conductor(s), Type SE cable assemblies will contain insulated phase conductors and a bare neutral conductor. For feeders or branch circuits, you must use Type SE cable that contains insulated phase and neutral conductors with an uninsulated equipment grounding conductor.

Please use the 2020 *Code* book to answer the following questions.

1. Type _____ cable is an assembly primarily used for services.

    (a) NM
    (b) UF
    (c) SE
    (d) SEC

2. Type _____ cable is a single conductor or multiconductor cable identified for use as underground service-entrance cable.

    (a) SE
    (b) NM
    (c) UF
    (d) USE

3. Types SE and USE cables and associated fittings shall be _____.

    (a) identified
    (b) approved
    (c) listed
    (d) labeled

4. Type SE cable shall be permitted to be used as _____.

    (a) branch circuits
    (b) feeders
    (c) underground service entrance conductors if in a raceway
    (d) branch circuits or feeders

5. Type SE cable can be used for interior wiring as long as it complies with the installation requirements of Part II of Article 334, excluding 334.80.

    (a) True
    (b) False

6. Where more than two Type SE cables are installed in contact with thermal insulations, caulk, or sealing foam without maintaining spacing between cables, the ampacity of each conductor shall be _____ in accordance with Table 310.15(C)(1).

    (a) increased
    (b) adjusted
    (c) corrected
    (d) multiplied

7. Where more than two Type SE cables are installed in contact with _____, the ampacity of each conductor shall be adjusted in accordance with Table 310.15(C)(1).

   (a) thermal insulation
   (b) caulk
   (c) sealing foam
   (d) any of these

8. For interior installations of Type SE cable with ungrounded conductor sizes _____ and smaller, where installed in thermal insulation, the ampacity shall be in accordance with 60 degree C (140 degree F) conductor temperature rating.

   (a) 14 AWG
   (b) 12 AWG
   (c) 10 AWG
   (d) 8 AWG

9. Type USE cable is permitted for _____ wiring.

   (a) underground
   (b) interior
   (c) aerial
   (d) above ground installations

10. Type USE cable used for service laterals shall be permitted to emerge from the ground if terminated in an enclosure at an outside location and protected in accordance with 300.5(D).

    (a) True
    (b) False

11. The radius of the curve of the inner edge of any bend, during or after installation, shall not be less than _____ times the diameter of Types USE or SE cable.

    (a) five
    (b) seven
    (c) ten
    (d) twelve

ARTICLE 340

UNDERGROUND FEEDER AND BRANCH-CIRCUIT CABLE (TYPE UF)

Introduction to Article 340—Underground Feeder and Branch-Circuit Cable (Type UF)

UF cable (Type UF) is a moisture-, fungus-, and corrosion-resistant cable suitable for direct burial in the Earth. It comes in sizes 14 AWG through 4/0 AWG [340.104]. The covering of multiconductor Type UF cable is molded plastic that encases the insulated conductors. Because the covering of Type UF cable encloses the insulated conductors, it is difficult to strip off the outer jacket to gain access to them, but this covering provides excellent corrosion protection. Be careful not to damage the conductor insulation or cut yourself when you remove the outer cover.

NFPA 70
National
Electrical
Code
2020

Please use the 2020 *Code* book to answer the following questions.

1. Article 340 covers the use, installation, and construction specifications for underground feeder and branch-circuit cable, Type _____.

    (a) USE
    (b) UF
    (c) UFC
    (d) NMC

2. Type _____ cable is a factory assembly of conductors with an overall covering of nonmetallic material suitable for direct burial in the earth.

    (a) NM
    (b) UF
    (c) SE
    (d) TC

3. Type UF cable and associated fittings shall be _____.

    (a) identified
    (b) approved
    (c) listed
    (d) labeled

4. Type UF cable is permitted to be used for inside wiring.

    (a) True
    (b) False

5. Type UF cable can be used for service conductors.

    (a) True
    (b) False

6. Type UF cable can be used in commercial garages.

    (a) True
    (b) False

7. Type UF cable shall not be used in _____.

    (a) motion picture studios
    (b) storage battery rooms
    (c) hoistways
    (d) all of these

8. Type UF cable shall not be used _____.

    (a) in any hazardous (classified) location except as otherwise permitted in this *Code*
    (b) embedded in poured cement, concrete, or aggregate
    (c) where exposed to direct rays of the sun, unless identified as sunlight resistant
    (d) all of these

9. Type UF cable shall not be used where subject to physical damage.

    (a) True
    (b) False

10. The ampacity of Type UF cable shall be that of _____ conductors in accordance with 310.14.

    (a) 60°C
    (b) 75°C
    (c) 90°C
    (d) 105°C

342 INTERMEDIATE METAL CONDUIT (TYPE IMC)

Introduction to Article 342—Intermediate Metal Conduit (Type IMC)

Intermediate metal conduit is a circular metal raceway with the same outside diameter as rigid metal conduit (Type RMC). The wall thickness of IMC is less than that of rigid metal conduit, so it has a larger interior cross-sectional area for holding conductors. IMC is lighter and less expensive than RMC and is approved by the *NEC* for use in the same applications. IMC also uses a different steel alloy, which makes it stronger than RMC even though the walls are thinner. Intermediate metal conduit is manufactured in both galvanized steel and aluminum; the steel type is much more common.

Please use the 2020 *Code* book to answer the following questions.

1. Article _____covers the use, installation, and construction specifications for intermediate metal conduit (IMC) and associated fittings.

   (a) 342
   (b) 348
   (c) 352
   (d) 356

2. IMC, elbows, couplings, and fittings shall be permitted to be installed in concrete, in direct contact with the earth, or in areas subject to severe corrosive influences where protected by corrosion protection _____ for the condition.

   (a) identified
   (b) approved
   (c) listed
   (d) suitable

3. Type IMC conduit shall be permitted to be installed where subject to severe physical damage.

   (a) True
   (b) False

4. Where practicable, contact of dissimilar metals shall be avoided in an IMC raceway installation to prevent the possibility of _____.

   (a) corrosion
   (b) galvanic action
   (c) short circuits
   (d) ground faults

5. A run of IMC shall not contain more than the equivalent of _____ quarter bend(s) between pull points such as conduit bodies and boxes.

   (a) one
   (b) two
   (c) three
   (d) four

6. When IMC is cut in the field, reaming is required to remove the burrs and rough edges.

   (a) True
   (b) False

7. IMC shall be secured _____.

   (a) by fastening within 3 ft of each outlet box, junction box, device box, cabinet, conduit body, or other conduit termination
   (b) within 5 ft of a box or termination fitting when structural members do not readily permit the raceway to be secured within 3 ft of the termination
   (c) except when the IMC is within 3 ft of the service head for an above-the-roof termination of a mast
   (d) any of these

8. Trade size 1 IMC run straight with threaded couplings shall be supported at intervals not exceeding 12 ft.

   (a) True
   (b) False

9. Horizontal runs of IMC supported by openings through framing members at intervals not exceeding 10 ft and securely fastened within 3 ft of terminations shall be permitted.

   (a) True
   (b) False

10. Threadless couplings and connectors used with intermediate metal conduit shall be made _____.

    (a) rainproof
    (b) tight
    (c) moistureproof
    (d) wrenchtight

11. Running threads shall not be used on IMC for connection at couplings.

    (a) True
    (b) False

12. Where IMC enters a box, fitting, or other enclosure, _____ shall be provided to protect the wire from abrasion unless the design of the box, fitting, or enclosure affords equivalent protection.

    (a) a bushing
    (b) duct seal
    (c) electrical tape
    (d) seal fittings

13. Where an intermediate metal conduit enters a box, fitting, or other enclosure, a bushing shall be provided to protect all wires regardless of size from abrasion unless the box, fitting, or enclosure is designed to provide such protection.

    (a) True
    (b) False

Introduction to Article 344—Rigid Metal Conduit (Type RMC)

Rigid metal conduit (Type RMC), commonly called "rigid," has long been the standard raceway used to protect conductors from physical damage and from difficult environments. The outside diameter of rigid metal conduit is the same as intermediate metal conduit. However, the wall thickness is greater than IMC so the interior cross-sectional area is smaller. RMC is heavier and more expensive than intermediate metal conduit, and it can be used in any location. It is manufactured in both galvanized steel and aluminum; the steel type is much more common.

NFPA 70 National Electrical Code 2020

Please use the 2020 *Code* book to answer the following questions.

1. Article 344 covers the use, installation, and construction specifications for _____ conduit and associated fittings.

   (a) intermediate metal
   (b) rigid metal
   (c) electrical metallic
   (d) aluminum metal

2. Galvanized steel, stainless steel, and red brass RMC elbows, couplings, and fittings shall be permitted to be installed in concrete, in direct contact with the earth, or in areas subject to severe corrosive influences when protected by _____ approved for the condition.

   (a) ceramic
   (b) corrosion protection
   (c) backfill
   (d) a natural barrier

3. Materials such as straps, bolts, and so forth, associated with the installation of RMC in wet locations shall be _____.

   (a) weatherproof
   (b) made of stainless steel
   (c) made of aluminum
   (d) protected against corrosion

4. Type RMC conduit shall be permitted to be installed where subject to severe physical damage.

   (a) True
   (b) False

5. Stainless steel and aluminum fittings and enclosures shall be permitted to be used with galvanized steel RMC, and galvanized steel fittings and enclosures shall be permitted to be used with aluminum RMC where not subject to _____.

   (a) physical damage
   (b) severe corrosive influences
   (c) excessive moisture
   (d) all of these

6. The minimum radius of a field bend on trade size 1¼ RMC is _____ in.

(a) 7
(b) 8
(c) 10
(d) 14

7. A run of RMC shall not contain more than the equivalent of _____ quarter bend(s) between pull points such as conduit bodies and boxes.

(a) one
(b) two
(c) three
(d) four

8. Cut ends of RMC shall be _____ or otherwise finished to remove rough edges.

(a) threaded
(b) reamed
(c) painted
(d) galvanized

9. Rigid metal conduit, (RMC), shall be securely fastened within _____ft of each outlet box, junction box, device box, cabinet, conduit body, or other conduit termination.

(a) 3 ft
(b) 4 ft
(c) 5 ft
(d) 6 ft

10. Where framing members do not readily permit fastening, rigid metal conduit, (RMC), may be fastened within _____ft of each outlet box, junction box, device box, cabinet, conduit body, or other conduit termination.

(a) 3 ft
(b) 4 ft
(c) 5 ft
(d) 6 ft

11. Where approved, rigid metal conduit, (RMC), shall not be required to be securely fastened within 3 ft of the service head for above-the-roof termination of a mast.

(a) True
(b) False

12. Horizontal runs of RMC supported by openings through _____ at intervals not exceeding 10 ft and securely fastened within 3 ft of termination points shall be permitted.

(a) walls
(b) trusses
(c) rafters
(d) framing members

13. Threadless couplings and connectors used with RMC buried in masonry or concrete shall be the _____ type.

(a) raintight
(b) wet and damp location
(c) nonabsorbent
(d) concrete tight

14. Threadless couplings and connectors used with RMC in wet locations shall be _____.

(a) listed for wet locations
(b) listed for damp locations
(c) nonabsorbent
(d) weatherproof

15. Running threads shall not be used on RMC for connection at _____.

(a) boxes
(b) cabinets
(c) couplings
(d) meter sockets

16. Where RMC enters a box, fitting, or other enclosure, _____ shall be provided to protect the wire from abrasion, unless the design of the box, fitting, or enclosure affords equivalent protection.

(a) a bushing
(b) duct seal
(c) electrical tape
(d) seal fittings

ARTICLE 348
FLEXIBLE METAL CONDUIT (TYPE FMC)

Introduction to Article 348—Flexible Metal Conduit (Type FMC)

Flexible metal conduit (Type FMC), commonly called "Greenfield" (after its inventor) or "flex," is an interlocked metal strip type of raceway made of either steel or aluminum. It is primarily used where flexibility is necessary or where equipment moves, shakes, or vibrates.

 Please use the 2020 *Code* book to answer the following questions.

1. Article 348 covers the use, installation, and construction specifications for flexible metal conduit (FMC) and associated _____.

   (a) fittings
   (b) connections
   (c) terminations
   (d) rating

2. _____ is a raceway of circular cross section made of a helically wound, formed, interlocked metal strip.

   (a) Type MC cable
   (b) Type AC cable
   (c) LFMC
   (d) FMC

3. FMC can be installed exposed or concealed where not subject to physical damage.

   (a) True
   (b) False

4. FMC shall not be installed _____.

   (a) in wet locations
   (b) embedded in poured concrete
   (c) where subject to physical damage
   (d) all of these

5. Bends in FMC shall be made so that the conduit is not damaged and the internal diameter of the conduit is _____.

   (a) larger than ⅜ in.
   (b) not effectively reduced
   (c) increased
   (d) larger than 1 in.

6. Bends in FMC _____ between pull points.

   (a) shall not be made
   (b) need not be limited (in degrees)
   (c) shall not exceed 360 degrees
   (d) shall not exceed 180 degrees

7. Cut ends of FMC shall be trimmed or otherwise finished to remove rough edges, except where fittings _____.

   (a) are the crimp-on type
   (b) thread into the convolutions
   (c) contain insulated throats
   (d) are listed for grounding

Article 348 | Flexible Metal Conduit (Type FMC)

8. Flexible metal conduit shall be securely fastened by a means approved by the authority having jurisdiction within _____ of termination.

   (a) 6 in.
   (b) 10 in.
   (c) 1 ft
   (d) 10 ft

9. Cable ties used to securely fasten flexible metal conduit shall be _____ for securement and support.

   (a) identified
   (b) labeled
   (c) marked
   (d) listed and identified

10. FMC shall be supported and secured _____.

    (a) at intervals not exceeding 4½ ft
    (b) within 8 in. on each side of a box where fished
    (c) where fished
    (d) at intervals not exceeding 6 ft

11. Flexible metal conduit shall not be required to be _____ where fished between access points through concealed spaces in finished buildings or structures and supporting is impracticable.

    (a) secured
    (b) supported
    (c) complete
    (d) secured and supported

12. For flexible metal conduit, if flexibility is necessary after installation, unsecured lengths from the last point the raceway is securely fastened shall not exceed _____.

    (a) 3 ft for trade sizes ½ through 1¼
    (b) 4 ft for trade sizes 1½ through 2
    (c) 5 ft for trade sizes 2½ and larger
    (d) all of these

13. FMC to a luminaire or electrical equipment within an accessible ceiling is permitted to be unsupported for not more than 6 ft from the last point where the raceway is securely fastened, including securement and support by listed FMC fittings.

    (a) True
    (b) False

14. When FMC is used where flexibility is necessary to minimize the transmission of vibration from equipment or to provide flexibility for equipment that requires movement after installation, _____ shall be installed.

    (a) an equipment grounding conductor
    (b) an expansion fitting
    (c) flexible nonmetallic connectors
    (d) adjustable supports

Introduction to Article 350—Liquidtight Flexible Metal Conduit (Type LFMC)

Liquidtight flexible metal conduit (Type LFMC), with its associated connectors and fittings, is a flexible raceway commonly used for connections to equipment that vibrates or must be occasionally moved. Liquidtight flexible metal conduit is commonly called "Sealtight®" or "liquidtight." It is similar in construction to flexible metal conduit, but it has an outer liquidtight thermoplastic covering. LFMC has the same primary purpose as flexible metal conduit, but also provides protection from liquids and some corrosive effects.

Please use the 2020 *Code* book to answer the following questions.

1. The use, installation, and construction specifications for liquidtight flexible metal conduit (LFMC) and associated fittings are covered within Article _____.

    (a) 300
    (b) 334
    (c) 350
    (d) 410

2. _____ is a raceway of circular cross section having an outer liquidtight, nonmetallic, sunlight-resistant jacket over an inner flexible metal core.

    (a) FMC
    (b) LFNMC
    (c) LFMC
    (d) Vinyl-clad Type MC

3. The use of LFMC shall be permitted for direct burial where listed and marked for the purpose.

    (a) True
    (b) False

4. All cut ends of LFMC conduit shall be _____ inside and outside to remove rough edges.

    (a) sanded
    (b) trimmed
    (c) brushed
    (d) any of these

5. Liquidtight flexible metal conduit shall be securely fastened by a means approved by the authority having jurisdiction within _____ of termination.

    (a) 6 in.
    (b) 10 in.
    (c) 1 ft
    (d) 10 ft

6. LFMC shall be supported and secured _____.

    (a) at intervals not exceeding 4½ ft
    (b) within 8 in. on each side of a box where fished
    (c) where fished
    (d) at intervals not exceeding 6 ft

7. Where used to securely fasten LFMC, cable ties shall be _____ for securement and support.

    (a) identified
    (b) labeled
    (c) marked
    (d) listed and identified

8. LFMC shall not be required to be secured or supported where fished between access points through _____ spaces in finished buildings or structures and supporting is impractical.

    (a) concealed
    (b) exposed
    (c) hazardous
    (d) completed

9. For liquidtight flexible metal conduit, if flexibility is necessary after installation, unsecured lengths from the last point the raceway is securely fastened shall not exceed _____.

    (a) 3 ft for trade sizes ½ through 1¼
    (b) 4 ft for trade sizes 1½ through 2
    (c) 5 ft for trade sizes 2½ and larger
    (d) all of these

10. For the purposes of the exceptions, _____ LFMC fittings shall be permitted as a means of securement and support.

    (a) identified
    (b) approved
    (c) listed
    (d) labeled

11. When LFMC is used to connect equipment where flexibility is necessary to minimize the transmission of vibration from equipment or for equipment requiring movement after installation, a(n) _____ conductor shall be installed.

    (a) main bonding
    (b) grounded
    (c) equipment grounding
    (d) grounding electrode

12. Where flexibility is not required after installation, liquidtight flexible metal conduit shall be permitted to be used as an equipment grounding conductor when installed in accordance with _____.

    (a) 250.102
    (b) 250.118(5)
    (c) 250.118(6)
    (d) 348.60

13. Article 352 covers the use, installation, and construction specifications for _____ and associated fittings.

    (a) ENT
    (b) RMC
    (c) IMC
    (d) PVC

ARTICLE
352

RIGID POLYVINYL CHLORIDE CONDUIT (TYPE PVC)

Introduction to Article 352—Rigid Polyvinyl Chloride Conduit (Type PVC)

Rigid polyvinyl chloride conduit (Type PVC) is a rigid nonmetallic conduit that provides many of the advantages of rigid metal conduit, while allowing installation in wet or corrosive areas. It is an inexpensive raceway and easily installed, lightweight, easily cut and glued together, and relatively strong. However, rigid polyvinyl chloride (PVC) is brittle when cold and will sag when hot. This type of conduit is commonly used as an underground raceway because of its low cost, ease of installation, and resistance to corrosion and decay.

Please use the 2020 *Code* book to answer the following questions.

1. A rigid nonmetallic raceway of circular cross section, with integral or associated couplings, connectors, and fittings for the installation of electrical conductors and cables describes _____.

   (a) ENT
   (b) RMC
   (c) IMC
   (d) PVC

2. PVC conduit is permitted in locations subject to severe corrosive influences and where subject to chemicals for which the materials are specifically _____.

   (a) approved
   (b) identified
   (c) listed
   (d) non-hazardous

3. Extreme _____ may cause PVC conduit to become brittle, and therefore more susceptible to damage from physical contact.

   (a) sunlight
   (b) corrosive conditions
   (c) heat
   (d) cold

4. PVC conduit shall be permitted for exposed work where subject to physical damage if identified for such use.

   (a) True
   (b) False

5. PVC conduit shall not be used _____, unless specifically permitted.

   (a) in hazardous (classified) locations
   (b) for the support of luminaires or other equipment
   (c) where subject to physical damage unless identified for such use
   (d) all of these

6. The number of conductors permitted in PVC conduit shall not exceed the percentage fill specified in _____.

   (a) Chapter 9, Table 1
   (b) Table 250.66
   (c) Table 310.16
   (d) 240.6

7. Field bends in PVC conduit shall be made only _____.

   (a) by hand forming the bend
   (b) with bending equipment identified for the purpose
   (c) with a truck exhaust pipe
   (d) by use of an open flame torch

8. Bends in PVC conduit shall _____ between pull points.

   (a) not be made
   (b) not be limited in degrees
   (c) be limited to 360 degrees
   (d) be limited to 180 degrees

9. The cut ends of PVC conduit shall be trimmed to remove the burrs and rough edges.

   (a) True
   (b) False

10. PVC conduit shall be securely fastened within _____ in. of each box.

    (a) 6
    (b) 12
    (c) 24
    (d) 36

11. PVC conduit trade size 1¼ to 2, shall be supported no greater than a maximum of _____ ft between supports.

    (a) 3
    (b) 4
    (c) 5
    (d) 6

12. Expansion fittings for PVC conduit shall be provided to compensate for thermal expansion and contraction where the length change is expected to be a _____ in. or greater.

    (a) ¹⁄₁₆
    (b) ⅛
    (c) ¼
    (d) ½

13. Where a PVC conduit enters a box, fitting, or other enclosure, a bushing or adapter shall be provided to protect the wire from abrasion unless the box, fitting, or enclosure design provides equivalent protection.

    (a) True
    (b) False

14. Where equipment grounding is required, a separate equipment grounding conductor shall be installed in the Type PVC conduit except where the _____ is used to ground equipment as permitted in 250.142.

    (a) grounding jumper
    (b) grounded conductor
    (c) bonding jumper
    (d) bonded conductor

15. Joints between PVC conduit, couplings, fittings, and boxes shall be made by _____.

    (a) the authority having jurisdiction
    (b) set screw fittings
    (c) an approved method
    (d) expansion fittings

ARTICLE 356

LIQUIDTIGHT FLEXIBLE NONMETALLIC CONDUIT (TYPE LFNC)

Introduction to Article 356—Liquidtight Flexible Nonmetallic Conduit (Type LFNC)

Liquidtight flexible nonmetallic conduit (Type LFNC) is a listed raceway of circular cross section with an outer liquidtight, nonmetallic, sunlight-resistant jacket over an inner flexible core with associated couplings, connectors, and fittings. It is commonly referred to as "Carflex®."

Please use the 2020 *Code* book to answer the following questions.

1. Article _____ covers the use, installation, and construction specifications for liquidtight flexible nonmetallic conduit (LFNC) and associated fittings.

   (a) 300
   (b) 334
   (c) 350
   (d) 356

2. Extreme cold can cause some types of nonmetallic conduits to become _____ and therefore more susceptible to damage from physical contact.

   (a) stiff
   (b) larger
   (c) weak
   (d) brittle

3. LFNC shall be permitted for _____.

   (a) direct burial where listed and marked for the purpose
   (b) exposed work
   (c) outdoors where listed and marked for this purpose
   (d) all of these

4. Liquidtight nonmetallic flexible conduit is not permitted to be used where _____.

   (a) subject to physical damage
   (b) ambient temperatures exceed its listing
   (c) in lengths greater than 6 ft unless approved
   (d) all of these

5. The number of conductors permitted in LFNC shall not exceed the percentage fill specified in _____.

   (a) Chapter 9, Table 1
   (b) Table 250.66
   (c) Table 310.16
   (d) 240.6

6. Bends in LFNC shall be made so that the conduit will not be damaged and the internal diameter of the conduit will not be effectively reduced. Bends can be made _____.

   (a) manually without auxiliary equipment
   (b) with bending equipment identified for the purpose
   (c) with any kind of conduit bending tool that will work
   (d) by the use of an open flame torch

7. Bends in LFNC shall _____ between pull points.

   (a) not be made
   (b) not be limited in degrees
   (c) be limited to 360 degrees
   (d) be limited to 180 degrees

8. Cable ties used to secure and support LFNC shall be _____ for the application and for securing and supporting.

   (a) identified
   (b) labeled
   (c) listed
   (d) marked

9. Where Type LFNC conduit is installed in lengths exceeding _____ ft, the conduit shall be securely fastened at intervals not exceeding 3 ft and within 12 in. on each side of every outlet box, junction box, cabinet, or fitting.

   (a) 2 ft
   (b) 3 ft
   (c) 6 ft
   (d) 10 ft

10. Where used to secure or support LFNC, cable ties shall be _____ for the application.

    (a) listed
    (b) labeled
    (c) marked
    (d) approved

11. Securing or supporting of LFNC is not required where installed in lengths not exceeding _____ from the last point where the raceway is securely fastened for connections within an accessible ceiling to a luminaire(s) or other equipment.

    (a) 3 ft
    (b) 6 ft
    (c) 8 ft
    (d) 10 ft

12. When LFNC is used, and equipment grounding is required, a separate _____ shall be installed in the conduit.

    (a) equipment grounding conductor
    (b) expansion fitting
    (c) flexible nonmetallic connector
    (d) grounded conductor

ARTICLE 358

ELECTRICAL METALLIC TUBING (TYPE EMT)

Introduction to Article 358—Electrical Metallic Tubing (Type EMT)

Electrical metallic tubing (Type EMT) is perhaps the most commonly used raceway in commercial and industrial installations. It is a lightweight raceway that is relatively easy to bend, cut, and ream. Because EMT is not threaded, all connectors and couplings are of the threadless type (either set screw or compression) and provide for quick, easy, and inexpensive installations as compared to other metallic raceway systems; all of which make it very popular. Electrical metallic tubing is manufactured in both galvanized steel and aluminum; the steel type is used most often.

Please use the 2020 *Code* book to answer the following questions.

1. Article _____ covers the use, installation, and construction specifications for electrical metallic tubing (EMT) and associated fittings.

    (a) 334
    (b) 350
    (c) 356
    (d) 358

2. _____ is an unthreaded thinwall metallic raceway of circular cross section designed for the routing and physical protection of electrical conductors and cables when joined together with listed fittings.

    (a) LFNC
    (b) EMT
    (c) NUCC
    (d) RTRC

3. The use of EMT shall be permitted for both exposed and concealed work in _____.

    (a) concrete, in direct contact with the earth, or in areas subject to severe corrosive influences where installed in accordance with 358.10(B)
    (b) dry, damp, and wet locations
    (c) any hazardous (classified) location as permitted by other articles in this *Code*
    (d) all of these

4. Galvanized steel and stainless steel EMT, elbows, couplings, and fittings can be installed in concrete, in direct contact with the earth, or in areas subject to severe corrosive influences where _____.

    (a) protected by corrosion protection
    (b) made of aluminum
    (c) made of stainless steel
    (d) listed for wet locations

5. When EMT is installed in wet locations, all supports, bolts, straps, and screws shall be _____.

   (a) made of aluminum
   (b) protected against corrosion
   (c) made of stainless steel
   (d) of nonmetallic materials only

6. EMT shall not be used where _____.

   (a) subject to severe physical damage or used for the support of luminaires except conduit bodies no larger than the largest trade size of the tubing
   (b) embedded in concrete
   (c) protected from corrosion only by enamel
   (d) installed in wet locations

7. EMT shall be securely fastened in place at intervals not to exceed _____ ft.

   (a) 4
   (b) 5
   (c) 8
   (d) 10

8. EMT run between termination points shall be securely fastened within _____ of each outlet box, junction box, device box, cabinet, conduit body, or other tubing termination.

   (a) 12 in.
   (b) 18 in.
   (c) 2 ft
   (d) 3 ft

9. EMT run in unbroken lengths between termination points, are permitted to be securely fastened within _____ ft of each outlet box, junction box, device box, cabinet, conduit body, or other tubing termination where structural members do not readily permit fastening.

   (a) 1
   (b) 3
   (c) 5
   (d) 10

10. EMT shall not be permitted as an equipment grounding conductor.

    (a) True
    (b) False

11. EMT couplings and connectors shall be made up _____.

    (a) of metal
    (b) in accordance with industry standards
    (c) tight
    (d) to be readily accessible

ARTICLE 362

ELECTRICAL NONMETALLIC TUBING (TYPE ENT)

Introduction to Article 362—Electrical Nonmetallic Tubing (Type ENT)

Electrical nonmetallic tubing is a pliable, corrugated, circular raceway. It resembles the flexible tubing you might see used at swimming pools and is often referred to as "Smurf Pipe" or "Smurf Tube" (as a reference to the children's cartoon characters "The Smurfs") because it was only available in blue when it first came out. It can now be purchased in additional colors such as red and yellow.

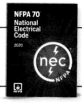 Please use the 2020 *Code* book to answer the following questions.

1. Article _____ covers the use, installation, and construction specifications for electrical nonmetallic tubing (ENT) and associated fittings.

    (a) 358
    (b) 362
    (c) 366
    (d) 392

2. ENT is composed of a material resistant to moisture and chemical atmospheres and is _____.

    (a) rigid
    (b) flame retardant
    (c) fireproof
    (d) flammable

3. When a building is supplied with a(n) _____ fire sprinkler system, ENT shall be permitted to be used within walls, floors, and ceilings, exposed or concealed, in buildings exceeding three floors above grade.

    (a) listed
    (b) identified
    (c) NFPA 13
    (d) NFPA 72

4. When a building is supplied with a fire sprinkler system, ENT can be installed above any suspended ceiling.

    (a) True
    (b) False

5. ENT and fittings can be _____, provided fittings identified for this purpose are used.

    (a) encased in poured concrete
    (b) embedded in a concrete slab on grade where the tubing is placed on sand or approved screenings
    (c) for wet locations indoors
    (d) any of these

6. ENT is not permitted in hazardous (classified) locations, unless permitted in other articles of the *Code*.

    (a) True
    (b) False

7. ENT shall be permitted for direct earth burial unless used with fittings listed for this purpose.

    (a) True
    (b) False

8. ENT shall not be used where exposed to the direct rays of the sun, unless identified as _____.

   (a) high-temperature rated
   (b) sunlight resistant
   (c) Schedule 80
   (d) suitable

9. The number of conductors permitted in ENT shall not exceed the percentage fill specified in _____.

   (a) Chapter 9, Table 1
   (b) Table 250.66
   (c) Table 310.16
   (d) 240.6

10. Cut ends of ENT shall be trimmed inside and _____ to remove rough edges.

    (a) outside
    (b) tapered
    (c) filed
    (d) beveled

11. ENT shall be installed as a complete system in accordance with 300.18 and shall be securely fastened in place by an approved means and supported in accordance with 362.30(A) and (B).

    (a) True
    (b) False

12. Cable ties used to securely fasten ENT shall be _____ for the application and for securing and supporting.

    (a) identified
    (b) labeled
    (c) listed
    (d) identified and listed

13. Unbroken lengths of electric nonmetallic tubing shall not be required to be secured where fished between access points for _____ work in finished buildings or structures and securing is impractical.

    (a) concealed
    (b) exposed
    (c) hazardous
    (d) completed

14. Bushings or adapters shall be provided at ENT terminations to protect the conductors from abrasion, unless the box, fitting, or enclosure design provides equivalent protection.

    (a) True
    (b) False

15. Where ENT is the wiring method and equipment grounding is required, a separate equipment grounding conductor shall be installed in the raceway.

    (a) True
    (b) False

16. Joints between lengths of ENT, couplings, fittings, and boxes shall be made by _____.

    (a) a qualified person
    (b) set screw fittings
    (c) an approved method
    (d) exothermic welding

ARTICLE 376

METAL WIREWAYS

Introduction to Article 376—Metal Wireways

Metal wireways are commonly used where access to conductors inside a raceway is required to make terminations, splices, or taps to several devices at a single location. High cost precludes their use for other than short distances, except in some commercial or industrial occupancies where the wiring is frequently revised.

They are often incorrectly called "troughs," "auxiliary gutters," "auxiliary wireways," or "gutters" in the field. Wireways and auxiliary gutters are similar in design but one of the main differences is in the application. A wireway is a raceway (Article 100) while an auxiliary gutter (Article 366) is a supplemental enclosure for wiring and is not considered a raceway.

 Please use the 2020 *Code* book to answer the following questions.

1. Metal wireways are sheet metal troughs with _____ for housing and protecting electric conductors and cable.

   (a) barriers
   (b) dividers
   (c) readily accessible sections
   (d) removable or hinged covers

2. Metal wireways shall not be permitted for _____.

   (a) exposed work
   (b) hazardous locations
   (c) wet locations
   (d) severe corrosive environments

3. Where a metal wireway houses and protects conductors, and where single conductor cables comprising each phase, neutral, or grounded conductor of an alternating-current circuit are connected in parallel as permitted in 310.10(G), the conductors shall be installed in groups consisting of not more than _____ conductor(s) per phase, neutral, or grounded conductor to prevent current imbalance in the paralleled conductors due to inductive reactance.

   (a) one
   (b) two
   (c) three
   (d) four

4. The purpose of having all parallel conductor sets installed in metal wireways within the same group, is to prevent _____ imbalance in the paralleled conductors due to inductive reactance.

   (a) current
   (b) voltage
   (c) inductive
   (d) all of these

5. The purpose of having all parallel conductor sets installed in metal wireways within the same group, is to prevent current imbalance in the paralleled conductors due to _____.

    (a) resistive reactance
    (b) mutual reactance
    (c) inductive reactance
    (d) excessive electromagnetic force

6. The sum of the cross-sectional areas of all contained conductors and cables at any cross section of a metal wireway shall not exceed _____ percent of the interior cross-sectional area of the wireway.

    (a) 50%
    (b) 20%
    (c) 25%
    (d) 80%

7. The ampacity adjustment factors in 310.15(C)(1) shall be applied to a metal wireway only where the number of current-carrying conductors in any cross section of the wireway exceeds _____.

    (a) 30
    (b) 40
    (c) 50
    (d) 60

8. The distance between horizontal supports of metal wireways shall not exceed _____.

    (a) 6 ft
    (b) 8 ft
    (c) 10 ft
    (d) 15 ft

9. Where insulated conductors are deflected within a metal wireway, the wireway shall be sized to meet the bending requirements corresponding to _____ wire per terminal in Table 312.6(A).

    (a) one
    (b) two
    (c) three
    (d) four

10. Power distribution blocks installed in metal wireways on the line side of the service equipment shall be marked "suitable for use on the line side of service equipment" or equivalent.

    (a) True
    (b) False

11. Power distribution blocks shall not have uninsulated live parts exposed within a _____.

    (a) trough
    (b) gutter
    (c) enclosure
    (d) wireway

12. Metal wireways shall be constructed and installed so that _____ continuity of the complete system are assured.

    (a) electrical
    (b) mechanical
    (c) structural
    (d) electrical and mechanical

ARTICLE
380
MULTIOUTLET ASSEMBLIES

Introduction to Article 380—Multioutlet Assemblies

A multioutlet assembly is a surface, flush, or freestanding raceway designed to hold conductors and receptacles, and is assembled in the field or at the factory [Article 100]. It is not limited to systems commonly referred to by the trade names "Plugtrak®" or "Plugmold®."

Please use the 2020 *Code* book to answer the following questions.

1. A multioutlet assembly can be installed in _____.

    (a) dry locations
    (b) damp locations
    (c) damp and wet locations
    (d) dry and damp locations

2. A multioutlet assembly shall not be installed _____.

    (a) in hoistways
    (b) where subject to severe physical damage
    (c) where subject to corrosive vapors
    (d) all of these

3. Metal multioutlet assemblies can pass through a dry partition, provided no receptacle is concealed in the partition and the cover of the exposed portion of the system can be removed.

    (a) True
    (b) False

ARTICLE 386 SURFACE METAL RACEWAYS

Introduction to Article 386—Surface Metal Raceways

Using a surface metal raceway is a common method of adding a raceway when exposed traditional raceway systems are not acceptable, and concealing the raceway is not economically feasible. They come in several colors and are available with colored or real wood inserts designed to make them look like molding rather than raceways. A surface metal raceway is commonly known as "Wiremold®" in the field.

Please use the 2020 *Code* book to answer the following questions.

1. Article 386 covers the use, installation, and construction specifications for surface _____ and associated fittings.

   (a) nonmetallic raceways
   (b) metal raceways
   (c) metal wire ways
   (d) enclosures

2. A surface metal raceway is a metal raceway that is intended to be mounted to the surface of a structure, with associated couplings, connectors, boxes, and fittings for the installation of electrical conductors.

   (a) True
   (b) False

3. Unbroken lengths of surface metal raceways can be run through dry _____.

   (a) walls
   (b) partitions
   (c) floors
   (d) all of these

4. Surface metal raceways shall not be used _____.

   (a) where subject to severe physical damage
   (b) where subject to corrosive vapors
   (c) in hoistways
   (d) all of these

5. The voltage between conductors in a surface metal raceway shall not exceed _____ unless the metal has a thickness of not less than 0.040 in. nominal.

   (a) 150V
   (b) 300V
   (c) 600V
   (d) 1,000V

6. The maximum size conductors permitted in a surface metal raceway shall not be larger than that for which the wireway is designed.

   (a) True
   (b) False

7. The maximum number of conductors permitted in any surface metal raceway shall be _____.

   (a) no more than 30 percent of the inside diameter
   (b) no greater than the number for which it was designed
   (c) no more than 75 percent of the cross-sectional area
   (d) that which is permitted in Table 312.6(A)

8. The ampacity adjustment factors of 310.15(C)(1) shall not apply to conductors installed in surface metal raceways where the _____.

   (a) cross-sectional area exceeds 4 sq in.
   (b) current-carrying conductors do not exceed 30 in number
   (c) total cross-sectional area of all conductors does not exceed 20 percent of the interior cross-sectional area of the raceway
   (d) all of these

9. Surface metal raceways and associated fittings shall be supported _____.

   (a) in accordance with the manufacturer's installation instructions
   (b) at intervals appropriate for the building design
   (c) at intervals not exceeding 4 ft
   (d) at intervals not exceeding 8 ft

10. The conductors, including splices and taps, in a metal surface raceway having a removable cover shall not fill the raceway to more than _____ percent of its cross-sectional area at the point of the splice or tap.

    (a) 38%
    (b) 40%
    (c) 53%
    (d) 75%

11. Surface metal raceway enclosures providing a transition from other wiring methods shall have a means for connecting a(n) _____ conductor.

    (a) grounded
    (b) ungrounded
    (c) equipment grounding
    (d) all of these

12. When combination surface metal raceways are used for both signaling and for lighting and power circuits, the different systems shall be run in separate compartments identified by _____ of the interior finish.

    (a) stamping
    (b) imprinting
    (c) color coding
    (d) any of these

ARTICLE 392

CABLE TRAYS

Introduction to Article 392—Cable Trays

A cable tray system is a unit or an assembly of units or sections with associated fittings that forms a structural system used to securely fasten or support cables and raceways. Cable tray systems include ladder, ventilated trough, ventilated channel, solid bottom, and other similar structures. They are manufactured in many forms—from a simple hanger or wire mesh to a substantial, rigid, steel support system. Cable trays are designed and manufactured to support specific wiring methods, as identified in 392.10(A).

Please use the 2020 *Code* book to answer the following questions.

1. Cable tray systems, including ladder, ventilated trough, ventilated channel, solid bottom, and other similar structures are covered within Article _____.

   (a) 358
   (b) 362
   (c) 366
   (d) 392

2. A cable tray is a unit or assembly of units or sections and associated fittings forming a _____ system used to securely fasten or support cables and raceways.

   (a) structural
   (b) flexible
   (c) movable
   (d) secure

3. Cable trays can be used as a support system for _____.

   (a) service conductors, feeders, and branch circuits
   (b) communications circuits
   (c) control and signaling circuits
   (d) all of these

4. _____ wiring methods can be installed in a cable tray.

   (a) Metal raceway
   (b) Nonmetallic raceway
   (c) Cable
   (d) all of these

5. Cable tray systems shall not be used _____.

   (a) in hoistways
   (b) where subject to severe physical damage
   (c) in hazardous (classified) locations
   (d) in hoistways or where subject to severe physical damage

6. Cable tray systems shall not have mechanically discontinuous segments between cable tray runs or between cable tray runs and equipment.

   (a) True
   (b) False

7. Each run of cable tray shall be _____ before the installation of cables.

   (a) tested for 25 ohms resistance
   (b) insulated
   (c) completed
   (d) all of these

8. Cable trays shall be _____ except as permitted by 392.18(D).

   (a) exposed
   (b) accessible
   (c) readily accessible
   (d) exposed and accessible

9. In industrial facilities where conditions of maintenance and supervision ensure that only qualified persons will service the installation, cable tray systems can be used to support _____.

   (a) raceways
   (b) cables
   (c) boxes and conduit bodies
   (d) all of these

10. For raceways terminating at a cable tray, a(n) _____ cable tray clamp or adapter shall be used to securely fasten the raceway to the cable tray system.

    (a) listed
    (b) approved
    (c) identified
    (d) marked

11. Where single conductor cables comprising each phase, neutral, or grounded conductor of a circuit are connected in parallel in a cable tray, the conductors shall be installed _____, to prevent current imbalance in the paralleled conductors due to inductive reactance.

    (a) in groups consisting of not more than three conductors per phase or neutral, or grounded conductor
    (b) in groups consisting of not more than one conductor per phase, neutral, or grounded conductor
    (c) as individual conductors securely bound to the cable tray
    (d) in separate groups

12. Cable trays shall be supported at intervals in accordance with the installation instructions.

    (a) True
    (b) False

13. A box is not required where conductors or cables in cable tray transition to a raceway wiring method from a cable tray.

    (a) True
    (b) False

14. Cable _____ made and insulated by approved methods can be located within a cable tray provided they are accessible, and do not project above the side rails where the splices are subject to physical damage.

    (a) connections
    (b) jumpers
    (c) splices
    (d) conductors

15. Metal cable trays containing only nonpower conductors (such as communications, data, and signaling conductors and cables) shall be electrically continuous through approved connections or the use of a(n) _____.

    (a) grounding electrode conductor
    (b) bonding jumper
    (c) equipment grounding conductor
    (d) grounded conductor

16. Steel or aluminum cable tray systems shall be permitted to be used as an equipment grounding conductor, provided the cable tray sections and fittings are identified as _____, among other requirements.

    (a) an equipment grounding conductor
    (b) special
    (c) industrial
    (d) all of these

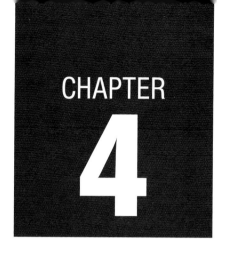

CHAPTER 4

EQUIPMENT FOR GENERAL USE

Introduction to Chapter 4—Equipment for General Use

With the first three chapters of the *NEC* behind you, this fourth one is necessary for building a solid foundation in general equipment installations. It helps you apply the first three chapters to installations involving general equipment. You need to understand the first four chapters of the *Code* to properly apply the requirements to Chapters 5, 6, and 7, and at times to Chapter 8.

Chapter 4 is arranged in the following manner:

▶ **Article 400—Flexible Cords and Flexible Cables.** Article 400 covers the general requirements, applications, and construction specifications for flexible cords and flexible cables.

▶ **Article 402—Fixture Wires.** This article covers the general requirements and construction specifications for fixture wires.

▶ **Article 404—Switches.** The requirements of Article 404 apply to switches of all types. These include snap (toggle) switches, dimmer switches, fan switches, knife switches, circuit breakers, and automatic switches such as time clocks, timers, and switches and circuit breakers used for a disconnecting means.

▶ **Article 406—Receptacles and Attachment Plugs (Caps).** This article covers the rating, type, and installation of receptacles and attachment plugs. It also covers flanged surface inlets.

▶ **Article 408—Switchboards and Panelboards.** Article 408 covers specific requirements for switchboards, panelboards, and distribution boards that supply lighting and power circuits.

> **Author's Comment:**
>
> ▶ See Article 100 for the definitions of "Panelboard" and "Switchboard."

▶ **Article 410—Luminaires and Lamps.** This article contains the requirements for luminaires, lampholders, and lamps. Because of the many types and applications of luminaires, manufacturer's instructions are very important and helpful for proper installation. Underwriters Laboratories produces a pamphlet called the *Luminaire Marking Guide*, which provides information for properly installing common types of incandescent, fluorescent, and high-intensity discharge (HID) luminaires. Spaces dedicated to the cultivation and growth of agricultural products, ("hot houses" etc.), that reproduce the natural effects of sunlight and seasonal temperatures may present unique conditions. Additional requirements are addressed in the Horticultural Part XVI.

▶ **Article 411—Low-Voltage Lighting.** Article 411 covers lighting systems, and their associated components, that operate at no more than 30V alternating current, or 60V direct current.

▶ **Article 422—Appliances.** This article covers electric appliances used in any occupancy.

• • •

▶ **Article 424—Fixed Electric Space-Heating Equipment.** Article 424 covers fixed electric equipment used for space heating. For the purpose of this article, heating equipment includes heating cable, unit heaters, boilers, central systems, and other fixed electric space-heating equipment. Article 424 does not apply to process heating and room air-conditioning.

▶ **Article 430—Motors, Motor Circuits, and Controllers.** This article contains the specific requirements for conductor sizing, overcurrent protection, control circuit conductors, motor controllers, and disconnecting means. The installation requirements for motor control centers are covered in Article 430, Part VIII.

▶ **Article 440—Air-Conditioning and Refrigeration Equipment.** Article 440 applies to electrically driven air-conditioning and refrigeration equipment with a motorized hermetic refrigerant compressor. The requirements in this article are in addition to, or amend, the requirements in Article 430 and others.

▶ **Article 445—Generators.** Article 445 contains the electrical installation requirements for generators and other requirements, such as where they can be installed, nameplate markings, conductor ampacity, and disconnecting means.

▶ **Article 450—Transformers.** This article covers the installation of transformers.

▶ **Article 480—Storage Batteries.** Article 480 covers stationary installations of storage batteries.

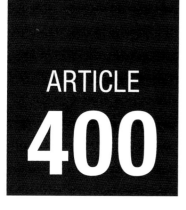

ARTICLE 400

FLEXIBLE CORDS AND FLEXIBLE CABLES

Introduction to Article 400—Flexible Cords and Flexible Cables

This article covers the general requirements, applications, and construction specifications for flexible cords and flexible cables. The *NEC* does not consider flexible cords to be a wiring method like those addressed in Chapter 3.

Always use a flexible cord (and fittings) identified for the application. Table 400.4 will help you in that regard. For example, use cords listed for a wet location if you are using them outdoors. The jacket material of any flexible cord is tested to maintain its insulation properties and other characteristics in the environments for which it has been listed. Tables 400.5(A)(1) and 400.5(A)(2) are also important tables to turn to when looking for the ampacity of flexible cords. Flexible cords and flexible cables may include the various types of wire which are used for lamps, appliances, extension cords, drop and pendant lights, pool pumps, and so on.

Please use the 2020 *Code* book to answer the following questions.

1. Article 400 covers general requirements, applications, and construction specifications for flexible cords and flexible cables.

   (a) True
   (b) False

2. HPD cord shall be permitted for _____.

   (a) not hard usage
   (b) hard usage
   (c) extra-hard usage
   (d) all of these

3. The ampacities of flexible cords and flexible cables are found in _____.

   (a) Table 310.16
   (b) Tables 400.5(A)(1) and (A)(2)
   (c) Chapter 9, Table 1
   (d) Table 430.52

4. Where flexible cords are used in ambient temperatures other than _____ degrees C the temperature correction factors from Table 310.15(B)(1) shall be applied to the ampacity in Table 400.5(A)(1) and Table 400.5(A)(2).

   (a) 30
   (b) 60
   (c) 75
   (d) 90

5. Flexible cords and flexible cables can be used for _____.

   (a) wiring of luminaires
   (b) connection of portable luminaires or appliances
   (c) connection of utilization equipment to facilitate frequent interchange
   (d) all of these

6. Unless specifically permitted in 400.10, flexible cords, flexible cables, and cord sets, and power-supply cords shall not be used where subject to physical damage.

   (a) True
   (b) False

7. Flexible cord sets and power-supply cords shall not be used as a substitute for _____ wiring of a structure.

   (a) temporary
   (b) fixed
   (c) concealed
   (d) permanent

8. Flexible cord sets and power-supply cords shall not be used where they are _____.

   (a) run through holes in walls, ceilings, or floors
   (b) run through doorways, windows, or similar openings
   (c) as a substitute for the fixed wiring of a structure
   (d) all of these

9. Flexible cords and power-supply cords shall not be concealed behind building _____, or run through doorways, windows, or similar openings.

   (a) structural ceilings
   (b) suspended or dropped ceilings
   (c) floors or walls
   (d) all of these

10. Flexible cords and flexible cables shall be connected to fittings so that tension will not be transmitted to joints or terminals by _____.

    (a) knotting the cord
    (b) winding the cord with tape
    (c) fittings designed for the purpose
    (d) any of these

11. Flexible cords and flexible cables shall be protected by _____ where passing through holes in covers, outlet boxes, or similar enclosures.

    (a) sleeves
    (b) grommets
    (c) raceways
    (d) bushing or fittings

ARTICLE
402 FIXTURE WIRES

Introduction to Article 402—Fixture Wires

This article covers the general requirements and construction specifications for fixture wires. One such requirement is that fixture wires can be no smaller than 18 AWG. Another is that they must be of a type listed in Table 402.3. That table makes up the bulk of Article 402. Table 402.5 lists the ampacity for fixture wires.

Please use the 2020 *Code* book to answer the following questions.

1. The ampacity of 18 TFFN is _____.

    (a) 6A
    (b) 8A
    (c) 10A
    (d) 14A

2. The smallest size fixture wire permitted by the *NEC* is _____ AWG.

    (a) 22
    (b) 20
    (c) 18
    (d) 16

3. The number of fixture wires in a single conduit or tubing shall not exceed the percentage fill specified in _____.

    (a) Chapter 9, Table 1
    (b) Table 250.66
    (c) Table 310.16
    (d) 240.6

4. Fixture wires shall not be used for branch-circuit wiring, except as permitted in other articles of the *Code*.

    (a) True
    (b) False

ARTICLE
404 SWITCHES

Introduction to Article 404—Switches

The requirements of Article 404 address switches of all types including snap (toggle) switches, dimmer switches, fan switches, knife switches, circuit breakers, and automatic switches such as time clocks and timers.

Please use the 2020 *Code* book to answer the following questions.

---

1. Article 404 covers all _____ used as switches operating at 1000 volts and below, unless specifically referenced elsewhere in this *Code* for higher voltages.

   (a) switches
   (b) switching devices
   (c) circuit breakers
   (d) all of these

2. Three-way and four-way switches shall be wired so that all switching is done only in the _____ circuit conductor.

   (a) ungrounded
   (b) grounded
   (c) equipment ground
   (d) neutral

3. The grounded circuit conductor for the controlled lighting circuit shall be installed at the location where switches control lighting loads that are supplied by a grounded general-purpose branch circuit serving _____.

   (a) habitable rooms or occupiable spaces
   (b) attics
   (c) crawlspaces
   (d) basements

4. Where multiple switch locations control the same lighting load such that the entire floor area of the room or space is visible from the single or combined switch locations, the grounded circuit conductor shall be required at all locations.

   (a) True
   (b) False

5. Switches controlling line-to-neutral lighting loads shall not be required to have a grounded conductor provided at the switch location where a switch controls a _____.

   (a) ceiling fan
   (b) bathroom exhaust fan
   (c) lighting load consists of all fluorescent fixtures with integral disconnects for the ballasts
   (d) receptacle load

6. Switch enclosures shall not be used as _____ for conductors feeding through or tapping off to other switches or overcurrent devices, unless the enclosure complies with 312.8.

   (a) junction boxes
   (b) raceways
   (c) auxiliary gutters
   (d) any of these

---

7. Surface-mounted switches or circuit breakers in a damp or wet location shall be enclosed in a _____ enclosure or cabinet that complies with 312.2.

    (a) weatherproof
    (b) rainproof
    (c) watertight
    (d) raintight

8. Switches shall not be installed within tubs or shower spaces unless installed as part of a listed tub or shower assembly.

    (a) True
    (b) False

9. Which of the following switches shall indicate whether they are in the open (off) or closed (on) position?

    (a) General-use switches.
    (b) Motor-circuit switches.
    (c) Circuit breakers.
    (d) all of these

10. Switches and circuit breakers used as switches shall be installed so that they may be operated from a readily accessible place.

    (a) True
    (b) False

11. Switches and circuit breakers used as switches can be mounted _____ if they are installed adjacent to motors, appliances, or other equipment that they supply and are accessible by portable means.

    (a) not higher than 6 ft 7 in.
    (b) higher than 6 ft 7 in.
    (c) in the mechanical equipment room
    (d) up to 8 ft high

12. Snap switches shall not be grouped or ganged in enclosures unless the voltage between adjacent devices does not exceed _____.

    (a) 100V
    (b) 200V
    (c) 300V
    (d) 400V

13. Metal faceplates for snap switches, including dimmer and similar control switches, shall be _____.

    (a) bonded to the grounded electrode
    (b) bonded to the equipment grounding conductor
    (c) counted as one box fill volume allowance
    (d) replaced with nonmetallic switch cover plates

14. Snap switches, dimmers, and control switches are considered to be part of the effective ground-fault current path when _____.

    (a) the switch is connected to the intersystem bonding termination
    (b) the switch is mounted with metal screws to a metal box or a metal cover that is connected to an equipment grounding conductor
    (c) an equipment grounding conductor or equipment bonding jumper is connected to the equipment grounding termination of the snap switch
    (d) the switch is mounted with metal screws to a metal box or a metal cover that is connected to an equipment grounding conductor or an equipment grounding conductor or equipment bonding jumper is connected to the equipment grounding termination of the snap switch

15. Where no means exists within the enclosure for bonding a snap switch to an equipment grounding conductor, it shall be permitted for replacement purposes only where the wiring method does not include an equipment grounding conductor and the switch is _____.

    (a) located within 6 ft vertically from ground
    (b) GFCI protected
    (c) AFCI protected
    (d) located within 3 ft horizontally from ground

16. The metal mounting yoke of a replacement switch is not required to be connected to an equipment grounding conductor if the wiring at the existing switch does not contain an equipment grounding conductor, and the _____.

    (a) switch faceplate is metallic and installed with nonmetallic screws
    (b) circuit is GFCI protected
    (c) the switch is mounted to a nonmetallic box
    (d) circuit is AFCI protected

17. Snap switches in listed assemblies are not required to be connected to an equipment grounding conductor if _____.

    (a) the device is provided with a nonmetallic faceplate and the device is designed such that no metallic faceplate replaces the one provided
    (b) the device is equipped with a nonmetallic yoke
    (c) all parts of the device that are accessible after installation of the faceplate are manufactured of nonmetallic material
    (d) all of these

18. A snap switch with an integral nonmetallic enclosure complying with 300.15(E) is required to be connected to an equipment grounding conductor.

    (a) True
    (b) False

19. Snap switches installed in boxes that are set back of the finished surface shall have the _____ seated against the finished wall surface.

    (a) extension plaster ears
    (b) body
    (c) toggle
    (d) all of these

20. Metal enclosures for switches or circuit breakers shall be connected to the circuit _____ conductor.

    (a) grounded
    (b) grounding
    (c) equipment grounding
    (d) any of these

21. Where nonmetallic enclosures for switches are used with metal raceways or metal armored cables, they shall _____.

    (a) provide an internal bonding means between all entries
    (b) have and integral bonding means if entries are threaded
    (c) have an external bonding jumper from raceway to raceway
    (d) provide an internal bonding means between all entries and have and integral bonding means if entries are threaded

22. General-use _____ switches shall be used only to control permanently installed incandescent luminaires unless listed for control of other loads and installed accordingly.

    (a) dimmer
    (b) fan speed control
    (c) timer
    (d) all of these

23. Switches shall be marked with the _____.

    (a) current
    (b) voltage
    (c) maximum horsepower, if horsepower rated
    (d) all of these

24. Where in the off position, a switching device with a marked OFF position shall completely disconnect all _____ conductors of the load it controls.

    (a) grounded
    (b) ungrounded
    (c) grounding
    (d) all of these

25. Electronic control switches shall not introduce _____ on the equipment grounding conductor during normal operation.

    (a) current
    (b) voltage
    (c) impedance
    (d) resistance

Notes

RECEPTACLES, ATTACHMENT PLUGS, AND CORD CONNECTORS

Introduction to Article 406—Receptacles, Attachment Plugs, and Cord Connectors

This article covers the rating, type, and installation of receptacles and attachment plugs. It also covers flanged surface inlets.

Please use the 2020 *Code* book to answer the following questions.

1. Article _____ covers the rating, type, and installation of receptacles, cord connectors, and attachment plugs (cord caps).

   (a) 400
   (b) 404
   (c) 406
   (d) 408

2. A childcare facility is a building or structure, or portion thereof, used for educational, supervision, or personal care services for more than _____ children seven years in age or less.

   (a) two
   (b) three
   (c) four
   (d) six

3. A housing shield intended to fit over a faceplate for flush-mounted wiring devices, or an integral component of an outlet box or of a faceplate for flush-mounted wiring devices is an "outlet box _____."

   (a) in-use cover
   (b) protector
   (c) shield
   (d) hood

4. Receptacles incorporating an isolated grounding conductor connection intended for the reduction of electromagnetic interference shall be identified by _____ on the face of the receptacle.

   (a) an orange triangle
   (b) a green triangle
   (c) the color orange
   (d) the engraved word "ISOLATED"

5. Except as permitted for two-wire replacements, receptacles installed on _____ branch circuits shall be of the grounding type.

   (a) 15 and 20A
   (b) up to 30A
   (c) 125V
   (d) 250V

6. All nonlocking-type, 125V, 15A and 20A receptacles that are controlled by _____, or that incorporate control features that remove power from the receptacle for the purpose of energy management or building automation, shall be permanently marked with the word "controlled."

   (a) wall switches
   (b) remote control
   (c) wireless communication
   (d) an automatic control device

7. Where a grounding means exists in the receptacle enclosure a(n) _____-type receptacle shall be used.

   (a) isolated ground
   (b) grounding
   (c) GFCI
   (d) dedicated

8. When replacing a nongrounding-type receptacle where attachment to an equipment grounding conductor does not exist in the receptacle enclosure, a _____ can be used as the replacement.

   (a) nongrounding-type receptacle
   (b) grounding receptacle
   (c) GFCI-type receptacle marked "No Equipment Ground"
   (d) nongrounding-type receptacle or a GFCI-type receptacle marked "No Equipment Ground"

9. When nongrounding-type receptacles are replaced by GFCI-type receptacles where attachment to an equipment grounding conductor does not exist in the receptacle enclosure, _____ shall be marked "No Equipment Ground."

   (a) the receptacle
   (b) the protective device
   (c) the branch circuit
   (d) these receptacles or their cover plates

10. Where attachment to an equipment grounding conductor does not exist in the receptacle enclosure, a nongrounding-type receptacle(s) shall be permitted to be replaced with a grounding-type receptacle(s) where supplied through a ground-fault circuit interrupter and _____ shall be marked "GFCI Protected" and "No Equipment Ground," visible after installation.

    (a) the receptacle(s)
    (b) their cover plates
    (c) the branch circuit
    (d) the receptacle(s) or their cover plates

11. Where attachment to an equipment grounding conductor does not exist in the receptacle enclosure, a nongrounding-type receptacle shall be permitted to be replaced with a GFCI-type receptacle; however, some equipment or appliance manufacturers require that the _____ to the equipment or appliance includes an equipment grounding conductor.

    (a) feeder
    (b) branch circuit
    (c) small-appliance circuit
    (d) power cord

12. Where attachment to an equipment grounding conductor does not exist in the receptacle enclosure, a non-grounding-type receptacle(s) shall be permitted to be replaced with a GFCI-type receptacle(s) where supplied through a ground-fault circuit interrupter; however, some cord-and-plug-connected equipment or appliances require an equipment grounding conductor and are listed in 250.114.

    (a) True
    (b) False

13. When replacing receptacles in locations that would require GFCI protection under the current *NEC*, _____ receptacles shall be installed.

    (a) dedicated
    (b) isolated ground
    (c) GFCI-protected
    (d) grounding

14. Where a receptacle outlet is supplied by a branch circuit that requires arc-fault circuit-interrupter protection [210.12(A) or 210.12(B)], a replacement receptacle at this outlet shall be a _____.

    (a) listed (receptacle) outlet branch-circuit type arc-fault circuit-interrupter receptacle
    (b) receptacle protected by a listed (receptacle) outlet branch-circuit type arc-fault circuit-interrupter type receptacle
    (c) receptacle protected by a listed combination type arc-fault circuit-interrupter type circuit breaker
    (d) any of these

15. Listed tamper-resistant receptacles shall be provided where replacements are made at receptacle outlets that are required to be tamper-resistant elsewhere in this *Code* except where a non-grounding receptacle is replaced with _____ receptacle.

    (a) an isolated
    (b) a GFCI-type
    (c) another non-grounding
    (d) any of these

16. Weather-resistant receptacles _____ where replacements are made at receptacle outlets that are required to be so protected elsewhere in the *Code*.

    (a) shall be provided
    (b) are not required
    (c) are optional
    (d) are not allowed

17. Automatically controlled receptacles shall be replaced with _____ controlled receptacles.

    (a) listed
    (b) suitably
    (c) equivalently
    (d) identified

18. When replacing automatically controlled receptacles, if automatic control is no longer required, the receptacle and any associated receptacles marked in accordance with 406.3(E) shall be replaced with a receptacle and faceplate marked in accordance with 406.3(E).

    (a) True
    (b) False

19. Receptacles mounted in boxes set back from the finished surface shall be installed so that the mounting _____ of the receptacle is held rigidly at the finished surface.

    (a) screws
    (b) yoke or strap
    (c) cover plate
    (d) grounding clip

20. Receptacles mounted in boxes flush with the finished surface or projecting beyond it shall be installed so that the mounting yoke or strap of the receptacle is held rigidly against the _____.

    (a) box or box cover
    (b) faceplate
    (c) the finished surface
    (d) bonding connection

21. Receptacles mounted to and supported by a cover shall be secured by more than one screw unless listed and identified for securing by a single screw.

    (a) True
    (b) False

22. Receptacle assemblies for installation in countertop surfaces shall be _____ for countertop applications.

    (a) identified
    (b) labeled
    (c) listed
    (d) approved

23. Receptacle assemblies and _____ receptacle assemblies listed for work surface or countertop applications shall be permitted to be installed in work surfaces.

    (a) AFCI
    (b) GFCI
    (c) current-limiting
    (d) all of these

24. Receptacles in or on countertop surfaces or work surfaces shall not be installed _____, unless listed for countertop or work surface applications.

    (a) in the sides of cabinets
    (b) in a face-up position
    (c) on GFCI circuits
    (d) on the kitchen small-appliance circuit

25. Receptacles shall not be grouped or ganged in enclosures unless the voltage between adjacent devices does not exceed _____.

    (a) 100V
    (b) 200V
    (c) 300V
    (d) 400V

26. Metal faceplates for receptacles shall be grounded.

    (a) True
    (b) False

27. Attachment plugs and cord connectors shall be listed and marked with the _____.

    (a) manufacturer's name or identification
    (b) voltage rating
    (c) amperage rating
    (d) all of these

28. An outdoor receptacle in a location protected from the weather, or in another damp location, shall be installed in an enclosure that is weatherproof when the receptacle is _____.

    (a) covered
    (b) enclosed
    (c) protected
    (d) recessed in the finished surface

29. A receptacle is considered to be in a location protected from the weather when located under roofed open porches, canopies, marquees, and the like, where it will not be subjected to _____.

    (a) spray from a hose
    (b) a direct lightning hit
    (c) beating rain or water runoff
    (d) falling or wind-blown debris

30. Nonlocking 15A and 20A, 125V and 250V receptacles installed in damp locations shall be listed as _____.

    (a) raintight
    (b) watertight
    (c) weatherproof
    (d) weather resistant

31. Receptacles _____, 125V and 250V installed in a wet location shall have an enclosure that is weatherproof whether or not the attachment plug cap is inserted.

    (a) 15A and 20A
    (b) 30A and less
    (c) up to 50A
    (d) up to 100A

32. When 15A and 20A receptacles are installed in a wet location, the outlet box _____ shall be listed for extra-duty use.

    (a) sleeve
    (b) hood
    (c) threaded entry
    (d) mounting

33. Where installed in a wet location, all _____ receptacle(s) shall be listed and identified as weather resistant.

    (a) 125V, 30A nonlocking
    (b) 250V, 15A nonlocking
    (c) 125V, 30A locking
    (d) 250V, 15A locking

34. A 30A, 208V receptacle installed in a wet location, where the product intended to be plugged into it is not attended while in use, shall have an enclosure that is weatherproof with the attachment plug cap inserted or removed.

    (a) True
    (b) False

35. Receptacles shall not be installed within a zone measured _____ horizontally and 8 ft vertically from the top of the bathtub rim or shower stall threshold.

    (a) 3 ft
    (b) 4 ft
    (c) 5 ft
    (d) 6 ft

36. Receptacles shall not be installed within a zone measured 3 ft horizontally and _____ vertically from the top of the bathtub rim or shower stall threshold.

    (a) 6 ft
    (b) 6 ft 7 in.
    (c) 7 ft
    (d) 8 ft

37. A receptacle shall not be installed within, or directly over, a bathtub or shower space.

    (a) True
    (b) False

38. In bathrooms with less than the required zone required by 406.9(C), the receptacle(s) can be installed opposite the bathtub rim or shower stall threshold on the farthest wall within the room.

    (a) True
    (b) False

39. Where tamper resistance receptacles are required, receptacles located more than _____ above the floor shall not be required to be tamper resistant.

    (a) 4 ft
    (b) 5 ft
    (c) 5 ½ ft
    (d) 6 ft 7 in.

40. In dwelling units, all nonlocking type 125V and 250V, 15A and 20A receptacles installed _____ shall be listed as tamper resistant.

    (a) in bedrooms
    (b) outdoors, at grade level
    (c) above counter tops
    (d) in all areas specified in 210.52 and 550.13

41. Nonlocking-type 125V and 250V, 15A and 20A receptacles installed in _____ shall be listed as tamper resistant.

    (a) guest rooms and guest suites of hotels and motels
    (b) childcare facilities
    (c) preschools and education facilities
    (d) all of these

42. Nonlocking-type 125V and 250V, 15A and 20A receptacles installed _____ shall be listed as tamper resistant.

    (a) in business offices, corridors, waiting rooms and the like in clinics, medical and dental offices, and outpatient facilities
    (b) as a subset of assembly occupancies described in 518.2 to include places of awaiting transportation, gymnasiums, skating rinks, and auditoriums
    (c) in dormitory units
    (d) all of these

43. Nonlocking-type 15A and 20A, 125V and 250V receptacles in a dwelling unit shall be listed as tamper resistant except _____.

    (a) receptacles located more than 5½ ft above the floor
    (b) receptacles that are part of a luminaire or appliance
    (c) a receptacle located within the dedicated space for an appliance that, in normal use, is not easily moved from one place to another
    (d) all of these

44. Nongrounding, nonlocking-type, 15A and 20A, 125V and 250V receptacles used for replacements in a dwelling unit shall not be required to be listed as tamper resistant.

    (a) True
    (b) False

ARTICLE 408

SWITCHBOARDS AND PANELBOARDS

Introduction to Article 408—Switchboards and Panelboards

Article 408 covers the specific requirements for switchboards and panelboards that control power and lighting circuits. As you study this article, keep these key points in mind:

▸ Perhaps the most important objective of Article 408 is to ensure that the installation will prevent contact between current-carrying conductors and people or equipment.

▸ The circuit directory of a panelboard must clearly identify the purpose or use of each circuit that originates in the panelboard.

▸ You must understand the detailed grounding and overcurrent protection requirements for panelboards.

 Please use the 2020 *Code* book to answer the following questions.

---

1. Article 408 covers _____.

   (a) switchboards
   (b) switchgear
   (c) panelboards
   (d) all of these

2. Panelboards supplied by a three-phase, 4-wire, delta-connected system shall have the phase with the higher voltage-to-ground (high-leg) connected to the _____ phase.

   (a) A
   (b) B
   (c) C
   (d) any of these

3. A switchboard, switchgear, or panelboard containing a 4-wire, _____ system where the midpoint of one phase winding is grounded, shall be legibly and permanently field-marked to caution that one phase has a higher voltage-to-ground.

   (a) wye-connected
   (b) delta-connected
   (c) solidly grounded
   (d) ungrounded

4. For panelboards, every circuit and circuit _____, including spare positions, shall be legibly identified on a circuit directory located on the face, inside of, or in an approved location adjacent to the panel door, and at each switch or circuit breaker in a switchboard or switchgear.

   (a) manufacturer
   (b) conductor
   (c) feeder
   (d) modification

5. Panelboard circuit directories can include labels that depend on transient conditions of occupancy.

   (a) True
   (b) False

6. All switchboards, switchgear, and panelboards supplied by a feeder(s) in _____ shall be permanently marked to indicate each device or equipment where the power supply originates.

   (a) other than one- or two-family dwellings
   (b) all dwelling units
   (c) all nondwelling units
   (d) b and c

---

7. The label required for switchboards, switchgear, and panelboards [408.4(B)] shall be permanently affixed, of sufficient durability to withstand the environment involved, and handwritten.

    (a) True
    (b) False

8. Conduits and raceways, including end fittings, shall not rise more than _____ in. above the bottom of a switchboard enclosure.

    (a) 3
    (b) 4
    (c) 5
    (d) 6

9. Panelboards for one- and two-family dwellings shall have a short-circuit current rating not less than the _____.

    (a) equipment rated current
    (b) available fault current
    (c) overcurrent protection rated current
    (d) ground-fault protection current

10. Unused openings for circuit breakers and switches in switchboards and panelboards shall be closed using _____, or other approved means that provide protection substantially equivalent to the wall of the enclosure.

    (a) duct seal and tape
    (b) identified closures
    (c) exothermic welding
    (d) sheet metal

11. Reconditioned switchboards and switchgear that have been damaged by fire, products of combustion, or water, shall be specifically evaluated by _____ prior to being returned to service.

    (a) the installer
    (b) its manufacturer
    (c) a qualified testing laboratory
    (d) its manufacturer or a qualified testing laboratory

12. Panelboards are not permitted to be reconditioned.

    (a) True
    (b) False

13. Switchboards and switchgear, or sections of switchboards or switchgear, shall be permitted to be reconditioned. Reconditioned switchgear shall be listed or field labeled as _____.

    (a) used
    (b) repurposed
    (c) redesigned
    (d) reconditioned

14. Each section of switchboard or switchgear equipment that requires rear or side access to make field connections shall be so marked by _____ on the front.

    (a) the installer
    (b) the manufacturer
    (c) field evaluation
    (d) a or b

15. Where a panelboard is supplied through a transformer, the overcurrent protection shall be located _____.

    (a) at the main distribution panel
    (b) on the primary side of the transformer
    (c) on the secondary side of the transformer
    (d) on either the primary or secondary side of the transformer

16. A panelboard shall be protected by an overcurrent device within the panelboard, or at any point on the _____ side of the panelboard.

    (a) load
    (b) supply
    (c) branch circuit
    (d) any of these

17. Plug-in-type back-fed circuit breakers used to terminate field-installed ungrounded supply conductors shall be _____ by an additional fastener that requires more than a pull to release.

    (a) grounded
    (b) secured in place
    (c) shunt tripped
    (d) current-limited

18. Panelboard cabinets and panelboard frames, if of metal, shall be in physical contact with each other and shall be connected to an _____.

    (a) equipment grounding conductor
    (b) grounding electrode conductor
    (c) steel building structure
    (d) separate ground rod

19. When separate equipment grounding conductors are provided in panelboards, a _____ shall be secured inside the cabinet.

    (a) grounded conductor
    (b) terminal lug
    (c) terminal bar
    (d) bonding jumper

20. Each _____ conductor shall terminate within the panelboard at an individual terminal that is not used for another conductor.

    (a) grounded
    (b) ungrounded
    (c) grounding
    (d) all of these

21. Panelboards _____ installed in the face-up position.

    (a) shall not be
    (b) are permitted to be
    (c) listed for such purpose, may be
    (d) approved for such use, may be

22. Panelboards are permitted to be installed in the face-up position.

    (a) True
    (b) False

ARTICLE
410

LUMINAIRES, LAMPHOLDERS, AND LAMPS

Introduction to Article 410—Luminaires, Lampholders, and Lamps

This article covers luminaires, lampholders, lamps, decorative lighting products, and lighting for temporary seasonal and holiday use. Even though Article 410 is highly detailed, it is broken down into 16 parts. The first five are sequential, and apply to all luminaires, lampholders, and lamps:

▶ Part I. General

▶ Part II. Locations

▶ Part III. Outlet Boxes and Covers

▶ Part IV. Supports

▶ Part V. Equipment Grounding Conductors

The first five parts contain mostly mechanical information and are not hard to follow or absorb. Part VI, Wiring, ends the sequence. The seventh, ninth, and tenth parts provide requirements for manufacturers to follow—use only equipment that conforms to these requirements. Part VIII provides requirements for installing lampholders. The rest of Article 410 addresses specific types of lighting. Spaces dedicated to the cultivation and growth of agricultural products (such as "hot houses") that reproduce the natural effects of sunlight and seasonal temperature may present unique conditions. Additional requirements are addressed in the Horticultural Part XVI.

Author's Comment:

▶ Article 411 addresses "Low-Voltage Lighting" which are lighting systems and their associated components that operate at no more than 30V alternating current or 60V direct current.

Please use the 2020 *Code* book to answer the following questions.

1. Article 410 covers luminaires, portable luminaires, lampholders, pendants, incandescent filament lamps, arc lamps, electric-discharge lamps, and _____, and the wiring and equipment forming part of such products and lighting installations.

    (a) decorative lighting products
    (b) lighting accessories for temporary seasonal and holiday use
    (c) portable flexible lighting products
    (d) all of these

2. Closet storage space is defined as a volume bounded by the sides and back closet walls extending from the closet floor vertically to a height of _____ ft or the highest clothes-hanging rod at a horizontal distance of 2 ft from the sides and back of the closet walls.

    (a) 6
    (b) 7
    (c) 8
    (d) 9

3. All luminaires, lampholders, and retrofit kits shall be _____.

   (a) listed
   (b) approved
   (c) labeled
   (d) a or c

4. If a retrofit kit is installed in a luminaire in accordance with the installation instructions, the retrofitted luminaire shall be considered reconditioned and field marked or labeled as such.

   (a) True
   (b) False

5. A luminaire marked "Suitable for Wet Locations" _____ be permitted to be used in a damp location.

   (a) shall
   (b) shall not
   (c) a or b
   (d) none of these

6. Luminaires _____ "Suitable for Wet Locations" shall be permitted to be used in a damp location.

   (a) marked
   (b) listed
   (c) identified
   (d) approved for

7. Luminaires can be installed in a commercial cooking hood if the luminaire is _____.

   (a) identified
   (b) vapor tight
   (c) corrosion resistant
   (d) all of these

8. No parts of cord-connected luminaires, chain-, cable-, or cord-suspended luminaires, lighting track, pendants, or paddle fans shall be located within a zone measured 3 ft horizontally and _____ ft vertically from the top of the bathtub rim or shower stall threshold.

   (a) 4
   (b) 6
   (c) 8
   (d) 10

9. Luminaires located where subject to bathroom shower spray shall be marked suitable for _____ locations.

   (a) damp
   (b) wet
   (c) outdoor
   (d) wet or outdoor

10. Luminaires located within the actual outside dimension of a bathtub and shower shall be marked for damp locations or marked for wet locations where they are _____.

    (a) below 7 ft in height
    (b) below 6 ft 7 in. in height
    (c) subject to shower spray
    (d) not GFCI protected

11. Which of the following types of luminaires can be installed in a clothes closet?

    (a) A surface-mounted or recessed incandescent luminaire with completely enclosed light source.
    (b) A surface-mounted or recessed fluorescent luminaire.
    (c) A surface-mounted or recessed LED luminaire with a completely enclosed light source.
    (d) all of these

12. Incandescent luminaires that have open lamps, and pendant-type luminaires, shall be permitted in clothes closets where proper clearance is maintained from combustible products.

    (a) True
    (b) False

13. Surface-mounted fluorescent luminaires in clothes closets shall be permitted on the wall above the door, or on the ceiling, provided there is a minimum clearance of _____ between the luminaire and the nearest point of a storage space.

    (a) 3 in.
    (b) 6 in.
    (c) 9 in.
    (d) 12 in.

14. In clothes closets, recessed incandescent or LED luminaires with a completely enclosed light source can be installed in the wall or the ceiling, provided there is a minimum clearance of _____ between the luminaire and the nearest point of a storage space.

    (a) 3 in.
    (b) 6 in.
    (c) 9 in.
    (d) 12 in.

15. Luminaires shall maintain a minimum clearance from the closet storage space of _____.

    (a) 12 in. for surface-mounted incandescent or LED luminaires with a completely enclosed light source
    (b) 6 in. for surface-mounted fluorescent luminaires
    (c) 6 in. for recessed fluorescent luminaires or recessed incandescent or LED luminaires with a completely enclosed light source
    (d) all of these

16. The *NEC* allows a lighting outlet on the wall in a clothes closet when it is at least 6 in. away from storage space.

    (a) True
    (b) False

17. Surface-mounted fluorescent or LED luminaires are permitted within the closet storage space if identified for this use.

    (a) True
    (b) False

18. Luminaires installed under metal-corrugated sheet roof decking shall be installed and supported so there is not less than _____ in. measured from the lowest surface of the roof decking to the top of the luminaire.

    (a) 1
    (b) 1¼
    (c) 1½
    (d) 2

19. Electric-discharge and LED luminaires supported independently of the outlet box shall be connected to the branch circuit through _____.

    (a) raceways
    (b) Type MC, AC, MI, or NM cable
    (c) flexible cords
    (d) any of these

20. When electric-discharge and LED luminaires that are designed not to be supported solely by the outlet box are surface mounted over a concealed outlet box, the luminaire shall provide access to the wiring within the outlet box by means of suitable openings in the back of the luminaire.

    (a) True
    (b) False

21. Metal raceways shall be bonded to the metal pole with a(n) _____.

    (a) grounding electrode
    (b) grounded conductor
    (c) equipment grounding conductor
    (d) any of these

22. Luminaires attached to the framing members of a suspended ceiling shall be secured to the framing member(s) by mechanical means such as _____.

    (a) bolts
    (b) screws
    (c) rivets
    (d) any of these

23. _____ clips identified for use with the type of ceiling framing member(s) and luminaires shall be permitted to be used to secure luminaires to the ceiling framing members.

    (a) Marked
    (b) Labeled
    (c) Identified
    (d) Listed

24. Luminaires and lighting equipment shall be connected to a(an) _____.

    (a) grounding electrode conductor
    (b) grounded conductor
    (c) equipment grounding conductor
    (d) any of these

25. Luminaires and equipment shall be mechanically connected to an equipment grounding conductor as specified in 250.118 and shall be sized in accordance with _____.

    (a) 250.66
    (b) 250.102
    (c) 250.122
    (d) 310.16

26. Replacement luminaires shall be permitted to connect an equipment grounding conductor in the same manner as replacement receptacles.

    (a) True
    (b) False

27. Replacement luminaires are not required to be connected to an equipment grounding conductor if no equipment grounding conductor exists at the outlet box and the luminaire is _____.

    (a) more than 20 years old
    (b) mounted to the box using nonmetallic fittings and screws
    (c) mounted more than 6 ft above the floor
    (d) GFCI protected

28. An electric-discharge or LED luminaire or listed assembly can be cord connected if the luminaire is located _____ the outlet, the cord is visible for its entire length except at terminations, and the cord is not subject to strain or physical damage.

    (a) within
    (b) directly below
    (c) directly above
    (d) adjacent to

29. A recessed luminaire that is not identified for contact with insulation shall have all recessed parts spaced not less than _____ from combustible materials.

    (a) ½ in.
    (b) ¾ in.
    (c) 1 in.
    (d) 3 in.

30. Thermal insulation shall not be installed above a recessed luminaire or within _____ in. of the recessed luminaire's enclosure, wiring compartment unless the luminaire is identified as Type IC for insulation contact.

    (a) 1 in.
    (b) 2 in.
    (c) 3 in.
    (d) 6 in.

31. In indoor locations other than dwellings and associated accessory buildings, fluorescent luminaires that utilize double-ended lamps and contain a ballast(s) that can be serviced in place shall have a disconnecting means either internal or external to each luminaire.

    (a) True
    (b) False

32. For existing installed luminaires without disconnecting means in indoor locations, other than dwellings and associated accessory structures, a disconnecting means _____ in fluorescent luminaires that utilize double-ended lamps (typical fluorescent lamps) at the time a ballast is replaced.

    (a) shall be installed
    (b) is not required to be added
    (c) shall not be installed
    (d) can be a screw terminal

33. Lighting track fittings can be equipped with general-purpose receptacles.

    (a) True
    (b) False

34. The connected load on lighting track is permitted to exceed the rating of the track under some conditions.

    (a) True
    (b) False

35. A 120V section of lighting track that is continuously loaded shall not exceed 12 ft in length, in accordance with 220.43(B).

    (a) True
    (b) False

36. Track lighting shall not be installed _____.

    (a) where likely to be subjected to physical damage
    (b) in wet or damp locations
    (c) where concealed
    (d) all of these

37. Lighting track shall not be installed less than _____ ft above the finished floor except where protected from physical damage or where the track operates at less than 30V rms, open-circuit voltage.

    (a) 4
    (b) 5
    (c) 5½
    (d) 6

38. Lighting track shall not be installed within the zone measured 3 ft horizontally and _____ vertically from the top of the bathtub rim or shower stall threshold.

    (a) 2 ft
    (b) 3 ft
    (c) 4 ft
    (d) 8 ft

39. Lighting track shall have two supports for a single section of _____ or shorter in length and each individual section of not more than 4 ft attached to it shall have one additional support, unless the track is identified for supports at greater intervals.

    (a) 2 ft
    (b) 4 ft
    (c) 6 ft
    (d) 8 ft

40. Lighting equipment identified for horticultural use is designed to provide a spectral characteristic needed for the growth of plants and can also provide supplemental general illumination within the growing environment.

    (a) True
    (b) False

41. Lighting equipment _____ for horticultural use shall be installed and used in accordance with the manufacturer's installation instructions and installation markings on the equipment as required by that listing.

    (a) labeled
    (b) designed
    (c) identified
    (d) suitable

42. Flexible cord shall only be permitted when provided as part of listed lighting equipment identified for horticultural use for _____.

    (a) connecting a horticultural lighting luminaire directly to a branch circuit outlet
    (b) interconnecting horticultural lighting luminaires
    (c) connecting a horticultural lighting luminaire to a remote power source
    (d) any of these

43. Lighting equipment identified for horticultural use employing flexible cord(s) with one or more conductors shall be supplied by lighting outlets protected by a listed _____.

    (a) AFCI
    (b) GFPE
    (c) GFCI
    (d) a and c

ARTICLE 411

LOW-VOLTAGE LIGHTING

Introduction to Article 411—Low-Voltage Lighting

Article 411 provides the requirements for indoor or outdoor low-voltage lighting systems and their components. They are often found in such applications as landscaping, lighting under kitchen cabinets, commercial display lighting, and in museums. Do not let the half-page size of Article 411 give you the impression that low-voltage lighting is not something you need to be concerned about. These systems are limited in their voltage, but the current rating can be as high as 25A which means they are still a potential source of fire and electrical shock. Installation of these systems is widespread and becoming more so.

Please use the 2020 *Code* book to answer the following questions.

1. Article 411 covers lighting systems and their associated components operating at no more than _____ ac or _____ dc.

    (a) 15V, 30V
    (b) 30V, 60V
    (c) 60V, 125V
    (d) 125V, 250V

2. Article 411 covers lighting systems and their associated components operating at no more than _____ ac or _____ dc where wet contact is likely to occur.

    (a) 15V, 30V
    (b) 30V, 60V
    (c) 60V, 125V
    (d) 125V, 250V

3. Listed low-voltage lighting systems or a lighting system assembled from listed parts shall be permitted to be reconditioned.

    (a) True
    (b) False

4. Low-voltage lighting systems shall be listed or assembled with listed components.

    (a) True
    (b) False

5. Low-voltage lighting systems can be concealed or extended through a building wall, floor, or ceiling without regard to the wiring method used.

    (a) True
    (b) False

6. Low-voltage lighting systems shall be installed not less than _____ horizontally from the nearest edge of the water in pools, spas, fountains, or similar locations, unless permitted by Article 680.

    (a) 5 ft
    (b) 6 ft
    (c) 10 ft
    (d) 20 ft

ARTICLE 422 APPLIANCES

Please use the 2020 *Code* book to answer the following questions.

1. Appliances such as _____ rated 150V or less to ground and 60A or less, single- or three-phase, shall be provided with Class A GFCI protection for personnel.

   (a) automotive vacuum machines
   (b) drinking water coolers and bottle fill stations
   (c) cord-and-plug-connected high-pressure spray washing machines
   (d) all of these

2. Appliances such as _____ rated 150V or less to ground and 60A or less, single- or three-phase, shall be provided with Class A GFCI protection for personnel.

   (a) tire inflation machines
   (b) vending machines
   (c) sump pumps
   (d) all of these

3. The GFCI required for appliances shall be readily accessible, listed, and located _____.

   (a) within the branch circuit overcurrent device
   (b) in a device or outlet within the supply circuit
   (c) in an integral part of the attachment plug
   (d) any of these

4. Where the GFCI protection required for appliances is an integral part of the appliance cord, it shall be installed not more than _____ from the attachment plug.

   (a) 12 in.
   (b) 18 in.
   (c) 24 in.
   (d) 30 in.

5. The ampacities of branch circuit conductors for appliances shall not be less than the marked rating of the _____.

   (a) receptacle outlet
   (b) appliance
   (c) over-current protection device
   (d) power cord

6. The branch circuit rating for a nonmotor-operated appliances that are continuously loaded shall have the branch-circuit rating sized not less than _____ percent of the appliance marked ampere rating, unless otherwise listed.

   (a) 80
   (b) 100
   (c) 125
   (d) 150

7. If a branch circuit supplies a single nonmotor-operated appliance, the rating of overcurrent protection shall not exceed _____ if the overcurrent protection rating is not marked and the appliance is rated 13.30A or less.

   (a) 15A
   (b) 20A
   (c) 25A
   (d) 30A

8. If a branch circuit supplies a single nonmotor-operated appliance, the rating of overcurrent protection shall not exceed _____ percent of the appliance rated current if the overcurrent protection rating is not marked and the appliance is rated over 13.30A.

   (a) 100
   (b) 125
   (c) 150
   (d) 160

9. Central heating equipment, other than fixed electric space-heating equipment, shall be supplied by a(n) _____ branch circuit.

   (a) multiwire
   (b) individual
   (c) multipurpose
   (d) small-appliance

10. The branch-circuit overcurrent device and conductors for fixed storage-type water heater having a capacity of _____ gallons or less shall be sized not smaller than 125 percent of the rating of the water heater.

    (a) 60
    (b) 75
    (c) 90
    (d) 120

11. The branch-circuit overcurrent device and conductors for fixed storage-type water heaters that have a capacity of 120 gal or less shall be sized not smaller than _____ percent of the rating of the water heater.

    (a) 80%
    (b) 115%
    (c) 125%
    (d) 150%

12. The branch-circuit overcurrent device and conductors for fixed storage-type water heater having a capacity of 120 gallons or less shall be sized not smaller than 125 percent of the rating of the _____.

    (a) overcurrent device
    (b) water heater
    (c) branch-circuit conductors
    (d) UL listing

13. Flexible cord for appliances are permitted _____.

    (a) to connect appliances to facilitate their frequent interchange
    (b) to prevent the transmission of noise
    (c) to facilitate the removal or disconnection of appliances that are fastened in place for maintenance or repair and the appliance is intended or identified for flexible cord connection.
    (d) any of these

14. An in-sink waste disposer can be cord-and-plug-connected, but the cord shall not be less than 18 in. or more than _____ in length.

    (a) 30 in.
    (b) 36 in.
    (c) 42 in.
    (d) 48 in.

15. An in-sink waste disposer can be cord-and-plug-connected, but receptacles shall be _____ to protect against physical damage to the flexible cord.

    (a) located
    (b) shielded
    (c) guarded
    (d) any of these

16. The flexible appliance cord for a _____ shall have an equipment grounding conductor and be terminated with a grounding-type attachment plug

    (a) dishwasher
    (b) in-sink waste disposer
    (c) range hood
    (d) all of these

17. The length of the cord for a trash compactor shall not be longer than _____ ft, measured from the face of the attachment plug to the plane of the rear of the appliance.

    (a) 2 ft
    (b) 4 ft
    (c) 6 ft
    (d) 8 ft

18. The length of the cord for a built-in dishwasher shall not be longer than _____ ft, measured from the face of the attachment plug to the plane of the rear of the appliance.

    (a) 6.50 ft
    (b) 7 ft
    (c) 7.50 ft
    (d) 8 ft

19. Receptacles for built-in dishwashers and trash compactors shall be located to protect against physical damage to the _____.

    (a) flexible cord
    (b) cord cap
    (c) appliance
    (d) receptacle

20. The receptacle for a trash compactor shall be located _____ occupied by the appliance.

    (a) in the space
    (b) adjacent to the space
    (c) directly above
    (d) in the space or adjacent to the space

21. Where the flexible cord for a built in dishwasher passes through an opening, it shall be protected against damage by a(an) _____.

    (a) bushing
    (b) grommet
    (c) approved means
    (d) any of these

22. The receptacle for a built-in dishwasher shall be located _____ adjacent to the space occupied by the dishwasher.

    (a) in the space
    (b) to the left of and
    (c) directly above and
    (d) no less than 6 in. from and

23. Wall-mounted ovens and counter-mounted cooking units shall be permitted to be connected with a flexible cord identified as _____ for the purpose.

    (a) listed
    (b) manufactured
    (c) suitable
    (d) sufficient

24. The receptacle for a cord connected range hood is permitted to be supplied by _____.

    (a) one of the small appliance branch circuits
    (b) an individual branch circuit
    (c) the refrigerator branch circuit if dedicated
    (d) all of these

25. Range hoods shall be permitted to be cord-and-plug-connected with a flexible cord identified as suitable for use on range hoods in the installation instructions of the appliance manufacturer provided _____.

    (a) the length of the cord is not less than 18 in. and not over 4 ft
    (b) receptacles are located to protect against physical damage to the flexible cord
    (c) the receptacle is supplied by an individual branch circuit
    (d) all of these

26. Range hoods shall be permitted to be cord-and-plug-connected with a flexible cord identified as suitable for use on range hoods in the installation instructions of the appliance manufacturer provided the range hood is part of a microwave oven assembly.

    (a) True
    (b) False

27. Ceiling-suspended (paddle) fans shall be supported independently of an outlet box or by a listed _____.

    (a) outlet box or listed outlet box system identified for the use and installed in accordance with 314.27(C)
    (b) outlet box system, a listed locking support and mounting receptacle, and a compatible factory installed attachment fitting designed for support, identified for the use and installed in accordance with 314.27(E)
    (c) mounting means directly to the structural member for use without an outlet box
    (d) outlet box or listed outlet box system identified for the use and installed in accordance with 314.27(C) or outlet box system, a listed locking support and mounting receptacle, and a compatible factory installed attachment fitting designed for support, identified for the use and installed in accordance with 314.27(E)

28. Each appliance shall have a means that _____ disconnects all ungrounded circuit conductors.

    (a) sequentially
    (b) automatically
    (c) simultaneously
    (d) all of these

29. For permanently connected appliances rated at not over _____ or 1/8 hp, the branch-circuit overcurrent device shall be permitted to serve as the disconnecting means where the switch or circuit breaker is within sight from the appliance or is capable of being locked in the open position in accordance with 110.25.

    (a) 75 VA
    (b) 150 VA
    (c) 225 VA
    (d) 300 VA

30. For permanently connected appliances rated over _____, the branch-circuit switch or circuit breaker can serve as the disconnecting means where the switch or circuit breaker is within sight from the appliance or is capable of being locked in the open position in accordance with 110.25.

    (a) 200 VA
    (b) 300 VA
    (c) 400 VA
    (d) 500 VA

31. For permanently connected motor-operated appliances with motors rated over _____, a switch or circuit breaker located within sight from the motor-operated appliance or be capable of being locked in the open position in compliance with 110.25, can serve as the appliance disconnect.

    (a) 1/8 hp
    (b) 1/4 hp
    (c) 15A
    (d) 1 kW

32. For cord-and-plug-(or attachment fitting-) connected appliances, a(n) _____ plug (or attachment fitting) and receptacle combination shall be permitted to serve as the disconnecting means.

    (a) labeled
    (b) accessible
    (c) metal enclosed
    (d) none of these

ARTICLE 424

FIXED ELECTRIC SPACE-HEATING EQUIPMENT

Introduction to Article 424—Fixed Electric Space-Heating Equipment

Many people are surprised to see how many pages there are in Article 424. This is a nine-part article on fixed electric space heaters. Why is there so much text for what seems to be a simple application? The answer is that this article covers a variety of applications—heaters come in various configurations for various uses. Not all these parts are for the electrician in the field—the requirements in Part IV are for manufacturers.

Fixed space heaters (wall-mounted, ceiling-mounted, or free-standing) are common in many utility buildings and other small structures, as well as in some larger structures. When used to heat floors, space-heating cables address the thermal layering problem typical of forced-air systems—so it is likely you will encounter them. Duct heaters are very common in large office and educational buildings since they provide a distributed heating scheme. Locating the heater in the ductwork, but close to the occupied space, eliminates the waste of transporting heated air through sheet metal routed in unheated spaces, so it is likely you will encounter those as well.

Please use the 2020 *Code* book to answer the following questions.

1. Article _____ covers fixed electric equipment used for space heating including heating cables, unit heaters, boilers, central heating systems, or other fixed electric space-heating equipment.

   (a) 410
   (b) 422
   (c) 424
   (d) 440

2. Branch-circuit conductors for fixed electric space-heating equipment and any associated motors shall be sized not smaller than _____ percent of the load.

   (a) 80
   (b) 110
   (c) 125
   (d) 150

3. Branch-circuit conductors for fixed electric space-heating equipment and any associated motors shall be sized not smaller than 150 percent of the load.

   (a) True
   (b) False

4. Means shall be provided to simultaneously disconnect the _____ of all fixed electric space-heating equipment from all ungrounded conductors.

   (a) heater
   (b) motor controller(s)
   (c) supplementary overcurrent device(s)
   (d) all of these

5. A unit switch with a marked "_____" position that is part of a fixed space heater, and disconnects all ungrounded conductors, shall be permitted to serve as the required disconnecting means.

    (a) on
    (b) closed
    (c) off
    (d) none of these

6. Ground-fault circuit-interrupter protection for personnel shall be provided for cables installed in electrically heated floors of _____.

    (a) bathrooms
    (b) hydromassage bathtub locations
    (c) kitchens
    (d) all of these

7. Duct heater controller equipment shall have a disconnecting means installed within _____ the controller except as allowed by 424.19(A).

    (a) 25 ft of
    (b) sight from
    (c) the side of
    (d) none of these

ARTICLE 430

MOTORS, MOTOR CIRCUITS, AND CONTROLLERS

Introduction to Article 430—Motors, Motor Circuits, and Controllers

Article 430 contains the specific rules for conductor sizing, overcurrent protection, control circuit conductors, controllers, and disconnects for electric motors. The installation requirements for motor control centers are covered in Part VIII, and air-conditioning and refrigeration equipment are covered in Article 440.

This is one of the longest articles in the *NEC*. It is also one of the most complex, but motors are complex equipment. They are electrical and mechanical devices, but what makes motor applications complex is the fact that they are inductive loads with a high-current demand at start-up that is typically six (or more) times the running current. This makes overcurrent protection for motor applications necessarily different from the overcurrent protection employed for other types of equipment. So, do not confuse general overcurrent protection with motor protection—you must calculate and apply them differently using the rules in Article 430.

You might be uncomfortable with the allowances for overcurrent protection found in this article, such as protecting a 10 AWG conductor with a 60A overcurrent protective device. As you progress through Article 430, you will learn to understand how motor overcurrent protection works and realize just why these allowances are not only safe, but necessary.

Please use the 2020 *Code* book to answer the following questions.

1. Article _____ covers motors, motor branch-circuit and feeder conductors and their protection, motor overload protection, motor control circuits, motor controllers, and motor control centers.

   (a) 410
   (b) 430
   (c) 440
   (d) 450

2. For general motor applications, the motor branch-circuit short-circuit and ground-fault protection device shall be sized based on the _____ values.

   (a) motor nameplate
   (b) NEMA standard
   (c) *NEC* Table
   (d) Factory Mutual

3. The motor _____ currents listed in Tables 430.247 through 430.250 shall be used to determine the ampacity of motor circuit conductors and short-circuit and ground-fault protection devices.

   (a) nameplate
   (b) full-load
   (c) power factor
   (d) service factor

4. Motors shall be located so that adequate _____ is provided and so that maintenance, such as lubrication of bearings and replacing of brushes, can be readily accomplished.

   (a) space
   (b) ventilation
   (c) protection
   (d) all of these

5. In determining the highest rated motor for purposes of complying with 430.24, 430.53(B), and 430.53(C), the highest rated motor shall be based on the rated full-load current as selected _____.

   (a) from the motor nameplate
   (b) from Tables 430.247, 430.248, 430.249, and 430.250
   (c) by multiplying the horsepower by 746 watts
   (d) using the largest horsepower motor

6. Branch-circuit conductors supplying a single continuous-duty motor shall have an ampacity not less than _____ rating.

   (a) 125 percent of the motor's nameplate current
   (b) 125 percent of the motor's full-load current rating as determined by 430.6(A)(1)
   (c) 125 percent of the motor's full locked-rotor
   (d) 80 percent of the motor's full-load current

7. Conductors supplying several motors shall not be sized smaller than _____ percent of the full-load current rating of the highest rated motor, plus the sum of the full-load current ratings of all other motors in the group, plus the ampacity of other loads.

   (a) 80%
   (b) 100%
   (c) 125%
   (d) 150%

8. Conductors supplying several motors, or a motor(s) and other load(s), shall have an ampacity not less than the sum of 125% of the full-load current rating of the highest rated motor plus the sum of the full-load current ratings of all the other motors in the group and 100% of the remaining noncontinuous and continuous non-motor loads.

   (a) True
   (b) False

9. Each motor used in a continuous duty application and rated more than 1 hp shall be protected against overload by a separate overload device that is responsive to motor current. The overload device for motors with a marked temperature rise 40°C or less, shall be rated at no more than _____ percent of the motor nameplate full-load current rating.

   (a) 80
   (b) 115
   (c) 125
   (d) 175

10. Overload devices are intended to protect motors, motor control apparatus, and motor branch-circuit conductors against _____.

    (a) excessive heating due to motor overloads
    (b) excessive heating due to failure to start
    (c) short circuits and ground faults
    (d) excessive heating due to motor overloads and excessive heating due to failure to start

11. A separate overload device used to protect continuous-duty motors rated more than 1 hp shall be selected to trip at no more than _____ percent of the motor nameplate full-load current rating if marked with a service factor of 1.15 or greater.

    (a) 110%
    (b) 115%
    (c) 120%
    (d) 125%

12. Part IV of Article 430 specifies devices intended to protect _____ against overcurrent due to short circuits or ground faults.

    (a) motor branch-circuit conductors
    (b) motor control apparatus
    (c) motors
    (d) all of these

13. The maximum dual-element time-delay fuse branch circuit protection for a single-phase motor is _____ percent of the appropriate current rating found in Table 430.248.

    (a) 125
    (b) 150
    (c) 175
    (d) 225

14. The maximum instantaneous trip breaker branch circuit protection for a single-phase motor is _____ percent of the appropriate current rating found in Table 430.52.

    (a) 175
    (b) 225
    (c) 300
    (d) 800

15. The maximum rating or setting of an inverse time breaker used as the motor branch-circuit short-circuit and ground-fault protective device for a single-phase motor is _____ percent of the full-load current given in Table 430.248.

    (a) 125
    (b) 175
    (c) 250
    (d) 300

16. Where the motor short-circuit and ground-fault protection devices determined by Table 430.52 do not correspond to the standard sizes or ratings, a higher rating that does not exceed the next higher standard ampere rating shall be permitted.

    (a) True
    (b) False

17. A motor can be provided with combined overcurrent protection using a single protective device to provide branch-circuit _____ protection where the rating of the device provides the overload protection specified in 430.32.

    (a) short-circuit
    (b) ground-fault
    (c) motor overload
    (d) all of these

18. A feeder supplying fixed motor load(s) shall have a protective device with a rating or setting _____ branch-circuit short-circuit and ground-fault protective device for any motor in the group, plus the sum of the full-load currents of the other motors of the group.

    (a) not greater than the largest rating or setting of the
    (b) 125 percent of the largest rating of any
    (c) equal to the largest rating of any
    (d) at least 80 percent of the

19. Overcurrent protection for motor control circuits shall not exceed _____ percent if the conductor is based on Table 310.17 and does not extend beyond the motor control equipment enclosure.

    (a) 100
    (b) 150
    (c) 300
    (d) 400

20. Motor control circuit conductors that extend beyond the motor control equipment enclosure shall have short-circuit and ground-fault protection sized not greater than _____ percent of the value specified in Table 310.16 for 60°C conductors.

    (a) 100
    (b) 150
    (c) 300
    (d) 400

21. Motor control circuits shall be arranged so they will be disconnected from all sources of supply when the disconnecting means is in the open position.

    (a) True
    (b) False

22. The motor controller shall have horsepower ratings at the application voltage _____ the horsepower rating of the motor.

    (a) not lower than
    (b) not higher than
    (c) equal to
    (d) six times

23. A _____ rated in amperes shall be permitted as a controller for all motors.

    (a) branch-circuit inverse time circuit breaker or molded case switch
    (b) dual-element time-delay fuse
    (c) snap switch
    (d) GFCI protected device

24. For stationary motors of 2 hp or less and 300V or less on ac circuits, the controller can be an ac-rated only general-use snap switch where the motor full-load current rating is not more than _____ percent of the rating of the switch.

    (a) 50%
    (b) 60%
    (c) 70%
    (d) 80%

25. An individual disconnecting means shall be provided for each motor controller and be located _____ from the controller location.

    (a) in sight
    (b) within 3 ft
    (c) within 10 ft
    (d) within 25 ft

26. A _____ shall be located in sight from the motor location and the driven machinery location.

    (a) controller
    (b) protection device
    (c) disconnecting means
    (d) all of these

27. Where more than one motor disconnecting means is provided in the same motor branch circuit, at least one of the disconnecting means shall be readily accessible.

    (a) True
    (b) False

28. A motor disconnecting means can be a listed _____.

    (a) molded case circuit breaker
    (b) motor-circuit switch rated in horsepower
    (c) molded case switch
    (d) any of these

29. If a motor disconnecting means is a motor-circuit switch, it shall be rated in _____.

    (a) horsepower
    (b) watts
    (c) amperes
    (d) locked-rotor current

30. A branch-circuit overcurrent device can serve as the disconnecting means for a stationary motor of 1/8 hp or less.

    (a) True
    (b) False

31. A horsepower-rated _____ having a horsepower rating not less than the motor rating shall be permitted to serve as the disconnecting means.

    (a) attachment plug and receptacle
    (b) flanged surface inlet and cord connector
    (c) automatic controller
    (d) attachment plug and receptacle or flanged surface inlet and cord connector

32. Circuit conductors on the output of an adjustable-speed drive system are susceptible to breakdown under certain conditions due to the characteristics of the output waveform of the drive.

    (a) True
    (b) False

33. Circuit conductors on the output of an adjustable-speed drive system are susceptible to breakdown under certain conditions. Factors affecting the conductors include but are not limited to the output _____.

    (a) voltage
    (b) frequency
    (c) current
    (d) any of these

ARTICLE 440

AIR-CONDITIONING AND REFRIGERATION EQUIPMENT

Introduction to Article 440—Air-Conditioning and Refrigeration Equipment

This article applies to electrically driven air-conditioning and refrigeration equipment. Each equipment manufacturer has the motor for a given air-conditioning unit built to its own specifications. Cooling and other characteristics are different from those of nonhermetic motors. For each motor, the manufacturer has worked out all the details and typically identifies the conductor and protection size (and other information) on the nameplate. So, when wiring an air conditioner, trust the information on the nameplate and do not try to over-complicate the situation. The math for sizing the overcurrent protection and conductor minimum ampacity has already been done for you.

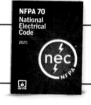

Please use the 2020 *Code* book to answer the following questions.

---

1. Article 440 applies to electric motor-driven air-conditioning and refrigerating equipment that has a hermetic refrigerant motor-compressor.

   (a) True
   (b) False

2. The rules of _____, as applicable, shall apply to air-conditioning and refrigerating equipment that does not incorporate a hermetic refrigerant motor-compressor.

   (a) Article 422
   (b) Article 424
   (c) Article 430
   (d) any of these

3. Multimotor and combination-load air-conditioning equipment shall be provided with a visible nameplate marked with the minimum supply circuit conductor ampacity, the maximum rating of the branch-circuit short-circuit and ground-fault protective device.

   (a) True
   (b) False

4. Where air-conditioning and refrigeration equipment is installed outdoors on a roof, a(n) _____ conductor of the wire type shall be installed in outdoor portions of metallic raceway systems that use compression-type fittings.

   (a) equipment grounding
   (b) grounding
   (c) equipment bonding
   (d) bonding

5. The disconnecting means for air-conditioning and refrigerating equipment shall be readily accessible and not more than _____ from the air-conditioning or refrigerating equipment.

   (a) 3 ft
   (b) 10 ft
   (c) 25 ft
   (d) 50 ft

6. Disconnecting means for air-conditioning or refrigerating equipment can be installed _____ the air-conditioning or refrigerating equipment, but not on panels that are designed to allow access to the equipment, and not over the equipment nameplate.

    (a) on or within
    (b) on top of
    (c) within 100 ft of
    (d) any of these

ARTICLE
445 GENERATORS

Introduction to Article 445—Generators

This article contains the electrical installation and other requirements for generators. These rules include such things as where generators can be installed, nameplate markings, conductor ampacity, transference of power, and disconnect requirements.

Please use the 2020 *Code* book to answer the following questions.

---

1. Article 445 contains installation and other requirements for generators.

   (a) True
   (b) False

2. Stationary generators _____ and less shall be listed.

   (a) 250V
   (b) 300V
   (c) 600V
   (d) 1000V

3. The ampacity of the conductors from the generator output terminals to the first distribution device(s) containing overcurrent protection shall not be less than _____ percent of the nameplate current rating of the generator.

   (a) 75
   (b) 115
   (c) 125
   (d) 140

4. Generators shall have the _____ conductor sized not smaller than required to carry the maximum unbalanced current as determined by 220.61.

   (a) neutral
   (b) grounding
   (c) bonding
   (d) all of these

5. Generators with greater than _____ rating shall be provided with a remote emergency stop switch to shut down the prime mover.

   (a) 12.50 kW
   (b) 15 kW
   (c) 25 kW
   (d) 35 kW

6. For other than cord-and-plug-connected portable generators, an emergency shutdown device for a dwelling unit shall be located _____ at a readily accessible location.

   (a) inside the dwelling unit
   (b) outside the dwelling unit
   (c) within sight of the generator
   (d) inside or outside the dwelling unit

---

7. Article 450 covers the installation of all _____.

    (a) motors and motor control centers
    (b) refrigeration and air-conditioning
    (c) transformers
    (d) generators

ARTICLE 450 TRANSFORMERS

Introduction to Article 450—Transformers

Article 450 opens by saying, "This article covers the installation of all transformers." Then it lists eight exceptions. So, what does it really cover? Essentially, this article covers transformers supplying power and lighting loads. For the purposes of Article 450 only, a transformer is an individual power transformer, single- or poly-phase, identified by a single nameplate—unless otherwise indicated.

A major concern with transformers is preventing overheating. The *Code* does not completely address this issue. Article 90 explains that the *NEC* is not a design manual, and it assumes that anyone using the *Code* has a certain level of expertise. Proper transformer selection is an important part of preventing them from overheating. The *NEC* assumes you have already selected a transformer suitable for the load characteristics. For the *Code* to tell you how to do that would push it into the realm of a design manual. Article 450 then takes you to the next logical step—providing overcurrent protection and the proper connections. But this article does not stop there; 450.9 provides ventilation requirements, and 450.13 contains accessibility requirements.

Part I contains the general requirements such as guarding, marking, and accessibility; Part II contains those for different types of transformers; and Part III covers transformer vaults.

Please use the 2020 *Code* book to answer the following questions.

1. The equipment grounding conductor terminal bar of a dry-type transformer shall be bonded to the enclosure in accordance with 250.12 and shall not be installed on or over any _____.

    (a) ungrounded conductor terminations
    (b) transformer coils or windings
    (c) vented portion of the enclosure
    (d) all of these

2. The primary overcurrent protection for a transformer rated 1,000V, nominal, or less, with no secondary protection and having a primary current rating of over 9A shall be set at not more than _____ percent.

    (a) 125
    (b) 167
    (c) 200
    (d) 300

3. Transformer top surfaces that are horizontal and readily accessible shall be marked _____.

    (a) to warn of high surface temperature(s)
    (b) for arc flash boundary
    (c) to prohibit storage
    (d) all of these

4. Transformers with ventilating openings shall be installed so that the ventilating openings are _____.

    (a) a minimum 18 in. above the floor
    (b) not blocked by walls or obstructions
    (c) aesthetically located
    (d) vented to the exterior of the building

5. Dry-type transformers 1000 volts nominal or less and not exceeding _____ kVA that are installed in hollow spaces of buildings and not permanently closed in by the structure, shall not be required to be readily accessible.

(a) 10 kVA
(b) 25 kVA
(c) 50 kVA
(d) 112.5 kVA

6. For transformers, other than Class 2 and Class 3, a means is required to disconnect all transformer ungrounded primary conductors. The disconnecting means shall be located within sight of the transformer unless the disconnect _____.

(a) location is field marked on the transformer
(b) is lockable open in accordance with 110.25
(c) is nonfusible
(d) location is field marked on the transformer and is lockable open in accordance with 110.25

ARTICLE
480

STORAGE BATTERIES

Introduction to Article 480—Storage Batteries

The stationary battery is the heart of any uninterruptible power supply. Article 480 addresses stationary batteries for commercial and industrial grade power supplies; not the small, "point of use," UPS boxes.

Stationary batteries are also used in other applications, such as emergency power systems. Regardless of the application, if it uses stationary batteries, this article applies.

Lead-acid stationary batteries fall into two general categories; flooded and valve regulated (VRLA). These differ markedly in such ways as maintainability, total cost of ownership, and scalability. The *NEC* does not address these differences since they are engineering issues rather than fire safety or electrical safety matters [90.1].

The *Code* does not address such design issues as optimum tier height, distance between tiers, determination of charging voltage, or string configuration. Nor does it address battery testing, monitoring, or maintenance. All of these involve highly specialized areas of knowledge and are required for optimizing operational efficiency. Standards other than the *NEC* address these topics.

What the *Code* does address in Article 480, are issues related to preventing electrocution and the ignition of the gases that all stationary batteries (even "sealed" ones) emit.

Please use the 2020 *Code* book to answer the following questions.

1. The provisions of Article _____ apply to stationary installations of storage battery installations.

   (a) 450
   (b) 460
   (c) 470
   (d) 480

2. Nominal battery voltage, as it relates to storage batteries, is the value of a(n) _____ of a given voltage class for convenient designation.

   (a) cell or battery
   (b) container
   (c) electrolyte
   (d) intertier connector

3. Nominal battery voltage is typically _____.

   (a) 2V per cell for lead-acid systems
   (b) 1.20V for per cell for alkali systems
   (c) 3.60 to 3.80V per cell for Li-ion systems
   (d) all of these

4. A storage battery is a single or group of _____ cells connected together electrically in series, in parallel, or a combination of both, and comprised of lead-acid, nickel-cadmium, or other rechargeable electrochemical types.

   (a) disposable
   (b) reusable
   (c) rechargeable
   (d) recyclable

5. Where mating dissimilar metals, antioxidant material suitable for the battery connection shall be used where _____ by the battery manufacturer.

   (a) documented
   (b) required
   (c) recommended
   (d) the antioxidant is supplied

6. Electrical _____ to a storage battery, and the cable(s) between cells on separate levels or racks, shall not put mechanical strain on the battery terminals.

   (a) connections
   (b) continuity
   (c) conductivity
   (d) accessibility

7. Conductors are commonly _____ to eliminate stress on storage battery terminations.

   (a) pre-fabricated
   (b) pre-insulated
   (c) pre-formed
   (d) pre-evaluated

8. The terminals of all storage battery cells or multicell units shall be readily accessible for _____ where required by the equipment design.

   (a) readings
   (b) inspections
   (c) cleaning
   (d) all of these

9. Wiring and equipment supplied from storage batteries shall be in accordance with Chapters 1 through 4 of the *NEC* unless otherwise permitted by 480.6.

   (a) True
   (b) False

10. A disconnecting means is required within sight of the storage battery for all ungrounded stationary battery system conductors operating at over _____ dc.

    (a) 30V
    (b) 40V
    (c) 50V
    (d) 60V

11. A(n) _____ disconnecting means is required within sight of the storage battery for all ungrounded stationary battery system conductors operating at over 60V dc.

    (a) accessible
    (b) readily accessible
    (c) safety
    (d) all of these

12. For one-family and two-family dwellings, a disconnecting means or its remote control for a stationary battery system shall be located at a readily accessible location _____ for emergency use.

    (a) outside the building
    (b) inside the building
    (c) within sight
    (d) outside or inside the building

13. The emergency disconnect required for one and two-family dwelling storage battery systems, shall be labeled _____.

    (a) "DANGER HIGH VOLTAGE"
    (b) "CAUTION MAY BE ENERGIZED"
    (c) "EMERGENCY DISCONNECT"
    (d) "FIRST RESPONDER USE ONLY"

14. Metallic structures for the support of storage batteries shall be provided with nonconducting support members for the cells or shall be constructed with a continuous insulating material and paint alone shall not be considered as an insulating material.

    (a) True
    (b) False

15. Provisions appropriate to the storage battery technology shall be made for sufficient diffusion and ventilation of gases from the battery, if present, to prevent the accumulation of a(an) _____ mixture.

    (a) explosive
    (b) noxious
    (c) toxic
    (d) chemical

16. For battery racks, there shall be a minimum clearance of _____ between a cell container and any wall or structure on the side not requiring access for maintenance.

    (a) 1 in.
    (b) 6 in.
    (c) 12 in.
    (d) 24 in.

17. Battery stands are permitted to contact adjacent walls or structures, provided that the battery shelf has a free air space for not less than _____ percent of its length.

    (a) 50
    (b) 75
    (c) 90
    (d) 100

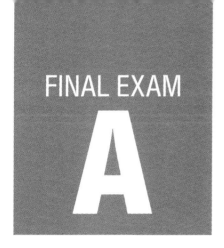

FINAL EXAM A

STRAIGHT ORDER

Please use the 2020 *Code* book to answer the following questions.

1. The *NEC* is _____.

   (a) intended to be a design manual
   (b) meant to be used as an instruction guide for untrained persons
   (c) for the practical safeguarding of persons and property
   (d) published by the Bureau of Standards

2. The *NEC* does not cover electrical installations in ships, watercraft, railway rolling stock, aircraft, or automotive vehicles.

   (a) True
   (b) False

3. The *Code* covers underground mine installations and self-propelled mobile surface mining machinery and its attendant electrical trailing cable.

   (a) True
   (b) False

4. Chapters 5, 6, and 7 apply to special occupancies, special equipment, or other special conditions and may supplement or modify the requirements in Chapters 1 through 7.

   (a) True
   (b) False

5. Nonmandatory Informative Annexes contained in the back of the *Code* book are _____.

   (a) for information only
   (b) not enforceable as a requirement of the *Code*
   (c) enforceable as a requirement of the *Code*
   (d) for information only and not enforceable as a requirement of the *Code*

6. A battery system includes storage batteries and battery chargers, and can include inverters, converters, and associated electrical equipment.

   (a) True
   (b) False

7. A load is considered to be continuous if the maximum current is expected to continue for _____ hour(s) or more.

   (a) ½
   (b) 1
   (c) 2
   (d) 3

8. An effective ground-fault current path is an intentionally constructed, low-impedance electrically conductive path designed and intended to carry current during a ground-fault condition from the point of a ground fault on a wiring system to _____.

   (a) ground
   (b) earth
   (c) the electrical supply source
   (d) the grounding electrode

9. A system intended to provide protection of equipment from damaging line-to-ground fault currents by causing a disconnecting means to open all ungrounded conductors of the faulted circuit at current levels less than the supply circuit overcurrent device defines "_____."

    (a) ground-fault protection of equipment
    (b) guarded
    (c) personal protection
    (d) automatic protection

10. Connected (connecting) to ground or to a conductive body that extends the ground connection is called "_____."

    (a) equipment grounding
    (b) bonded
    (c) grounded
    (d) all of these

11. A conductor used to connect the system grounded conductor, or the equipment to a grounding electrode or to a point on the grounding electrode system, is called the "_____ conductor."

    (a) main grounding
    (b) common main
    (c) equipment grounding
    (d) grounding electrode

12. A hybrid system is comprised of multiple power sources, such as _____, but not the utility power system.

    (a) photovoltaic
    (b) wind
    (c) micro-hydro generators
    (d) all of these

13. An overload is the same as a short circuit or ground fault.

    (a) True
    (b) False

14. NFPA 70E, *Standard for Electrical Safety in the Workplace*, provides information to help determine the electrical safety training requirements expected of a qualified person.

    (a) True
    (b) False

15. Any electrical circuit that controls any other circuit through a relay or an equivalent device is called a "_____."

    (a) primary circuit
    (b) remote-control circuit
    (c) signal circuit
    (d) controller

16. Each disconnecting means shall be legibly marked to indicate its purpose unless located and arranged so _____.

    (a) that it can be locked out and tagged
    (b) it is not readily accessible
    (c) the purpose is evident
    (d) that it operates at less than 300 volts-to-ground

17. Electrical equipment rooms or enclosures housing electrical apparatus that are controlled by a lock(s) shall be considered _____ to qualified persons.

    (a) readily accessible
    (b) accessible
    (c) available
    (d) secured

18. An insulated grounded conductor _____ or smaller shall be identified by a continuous white or gray outer finish, or by three continuous white or gray stripes along its entire length on other than green insulation.

    (a) 8 AWG
    (b) 6 AWG
    (c) 4 AWG
    (d) 3 AWG

19. Each multiwire branch circuit shall be provided with a means that will simultaneously disconnect all _____ conductors at the point where the branch circuit originates.

    (a) circuit
    (b) grounded
    (c) grounding
    (d) ungrounded

20. GFCI protection shall be provided for all 15A and 20A, 125V, single-phase receptacles _____ in dwelling unit kitchens.

    (a) installed to serve the countertop surfaces
    (b) within 6 ft from the top inside edge of the bowl of the sink
    (c) for all receptacles
    (d) installed to serve the countertop surfaces and within 6 ft from the top inside edge of the bowl of the sink

21. In other than dwelling units, GFCI protection shall be provided for all 125V through 250V receptacles supplied by single-phase branch circuits rated 150V or less to ground, 50A or less, where receptacles are installed within _____ ft from the top inside edge of the bowl of a sink.

    (a) 3
    (b) 4
    (c) 5
    (d) 6

22. 120V, single-phase, 15A and 20A branch circuits supplying outlets and devices installed in _____ of hotels and motels shall be protected by any of the means described in 210.12(A)(1) through (6).

    (a) guest rooms
    (b) conference rooms
    (c) lobbies and common hallways
    (d) game rooms

23. The total rating of utilization equipment fastened in place, other than luminaires, shall not exceed _____ percent of a multiple outlet branch circuit rating.

    (a) 25
    (b) 50
    (c) 80
    (d) 100

24. The required receptacle outlet for heating, air-conditioning, and refrigeration equipment shall not be connected to the load side of the equipment's branch-circuit disconnecting means.

    (a) True
    (b) False

25. For attics and underfloor spaces, utility rooms, and basements in all occupancies, at least _____ lighting outlet(s) containing a switch or controlled by a wall switch shall be installed where these spaces are used for storage or contain equipment requiring servicing.

    (a) one
    (b) two
    (c) three
    (d) four

26. Feeder grounded conductors that are not connected to an overcurrent device shall be permitted to be sized at _____ percent of the continuous and noncontinuous load.

    (a) 80
    (b) 100
    (c) 115
    (d) 125

27. Each feeder disconnect rated 1,000A or more and installed on solidly grounded wye electrical systems of more than 150V to ground, but not exceeding _____ phase-to-phase, shall be provided with ground-fault protection of equipment in accordance with 230.95.

    (a) 50V
    (b) 100V
    (c) 150V
    (d) 600V

28. Where a premises wiring system contains feeders supplied from more than one nominal voltage system, each ungrounded conductor of a feeder shall be identified by phase or line and system by _____, or other approved means.

    (a) color coding
    (b) marking tape
    (c) tagging
    (d) any of these

29. The 125 percent multiplier for a continuous load as specified in 210.20(A) _____ included when using the unit loads in table 220.12 for calculating the minimum lighting load for a specified occupancy.

    (a) is
    (b) is not
    (c) is permitted to be
    (d) shall not be

30. Where the lighting load for a nondwelling building is designed and constructed to comply with an energy code adopted by the local authority, the lighting load shall be permitted to be calculated using the unit values specified in the _____.

    (a) energy code
    (b) manufacturer's instructions
    (c) *NEC*
    (d) lighting design manual

31. The vertical clearance of final spans of overhead service conductors above, or within _____ ft measured horizontally of platforms, projections, or surfaces that will permit personal contact shall be maintained in accordance with 230.24(B).

    (a) 3
    (b) 6
    (c) 8
    (d) 10

32. Overhead service conductors shall have a minimum clearance from final grade of _____ above areas or sidewalks accessible only to pedestrians, measured from final grade or other accessible surface where the voltage does not exceed 150 volts to ground.

    (a) 8 ft
    (b) 10 ft
    (c) 12 ft
    (d) 15 ft

33. Overhead service conductors shall have a minimum vertical clearance of _____ ft from final grade over residential property and driveways, as well as over commercial areas not subject to truck traffic where the voltage does not exceed 300 volts-to-ground.

    (a) 10
    (b) 12
    (c) 15
    (d) 18

34. Where exposed to the weather, raceways enclosing service-entrance conductors shall be _____ for use in wet locations and arranged to drain.

    (a) approved or listed
    (b) listed and identified
    (c) suitable
    (d) listed and labeled

35. Service-entrance and overhead service conductors shall be arranged so that _____ will not enter the service raceway or equipment.

    (a) dust
    (b) vapor
    (c) water
    (d) lightning

36. A service disconnecting means shall be installed at a(n) _____ location.

    (a) dry
    (b) readily accessible
    (c) outdoor
    (d) indoor

37. For installations that supply only limited loads of a single branch circuit, the service disconnecting means shall have a rating not less than _____.

    (a) 15A
    (b) 20A
    (c) 25A
    (d) 30A

38. Outside feeder tap conductors can be of unlimited length without overcurrent protection at the point they receive their supply if the tap conductors _____.

    (a) are protected from physical damage
    (b) terminate at a single circuit breaker or a single set of fuses that limits the load to the ampacity of the tap conductors
    (c) the overcurrent device is part of the building feeder disconnect
    (d) all of these

39. Where a method to reduce clearing time for fuses rated 1200A or greater is required in accordance with 240.67(B), the _____ reduction system shall be performance tested when first installed on site.

    (a) ground-fault
    (b) short-circuit
    (c) arc-fault
    (d) arc-energy

40. Grounded electrical systems shall be connected to earth in a manner that will _____.

    (a) limit voltages due to lightning, line surges, or unintentional contact with higher-voltage lines
    (b) stabilize the voltage-to-ground during normal operation
    (c) facilitate overcurrent device operation in case of ground faults
    (d) limit voltages due to lightning, line surges, or unintentional contact with higher-voltage lines and stabilize the voltage-to-ground during normal operation

41. For grounded systems, normally noncurrent-carrying conductive materials enclosing electrical conductors or equipment shall be connected to earth so as to limit the voltage-to-ground on these materials.

    (a) True
    (b) False

42. In grounded systems, normally noncurrent-carrying electrically conductive materials that are likely to become energized shall be connected _____ in a manner that establishes an effective ground-fault current path.

    (a) together
    (b) to the electrical supply source
    (c) to the closest grounded conductor
    (d) together and to the electrical supply source

43. For a separate building or structure supplied by a feeder or branch circuit, the grounded conductor can serve as the ground-fault return path for the building/structure disconnecting means for existing installations made in compliance with previous editions of the *Code* as long as the installation continues to meet the condition(s) that _____.

    (a) there are no continuous metallic paths between buildings and structures
    (b) ground-fault protection of equipment is not installed on the supply side of the feeder
    (c) the neutral conductor is sized no smaller than the larger required by 220.61 or 250.122
    (d) all of these

44. The size of the grounding electrode conductor for a building or structure supplied by a feeder shall not be smaller than that identified in _____, based on the largest ungrounded supply conductor.

    (a) 250.66
    (b) 250.102
    (c) 250.122
    (d) Table 310.16

45. Concrete-encased electrodes of _____ shall not be required to be part of the grounding electrode system where the steel reinforcing bars or rods aren't accessible for use without disturbing the concrete.

    (a) hazardous (classified) locations
    (b) health care facilities
    (c) existing buildings or structures
    (d) agricultural buildings with equipotential planes

46. Grounding electrodes of the rod type less than _____ in. in diameter shall be listed.

    (a) ½
    (b) ⅝
    (c) ¾
    (d) 1

47. Where rock bottom is encountered at an angle up to 45 degrees when driving a rod or pipe electrode, the electrode shall be permitted to be buried in a trench _____ deep.

    (a) 30 in
    (b) 6 ft
    (c) 8 ft
    (d) 10 ft

48. Grounding electrode conductors of the wire type shall be _____.

    (a) solid
    (b) stranded
    (c) insulated or bare
    (d) any of these

49. If a building or structure is supplied by a service or feeder with _____ or more disconnecting means in separate enclosures, the grounding electrode connections shall be made in accordance with 250.64(D)(1), 250.64(D)(2), or 250.64(D)(3).

    (a) one
    (b) two
    (c) three
    (d) four

50. An encased or buried connection to a concrete-encased, driven, or buried grounding electrode shall be accessible.

    (a) True
    (b) False

51. The normally noncurrent-carrying metal parts of service equipment, such as service _____, shall be bonded together.

    (a) raceways or service cable armor
    (b) equipment enclosures containing service conductors, including meter fittings, boxes, or the like, interposed in the service raceway or armor
    (c) cable trays
    (d) all of these

52. When bonding enclosures, metal raceways, frames, and fittings, any nonconductive paint, enamel, or similar coating shall be removed at _____.

    (a) contact surfaces
    (b) threads
    (c) contact points
    (d) all of these

53. What is the minimum size copper equipment bonding jumper for a 40A rated circuit?

    (a) 14 AWG
    (b) 12 AWG
    (c) 10 AWG
    (d) 8 AWG

54. The metal water piping system(s) installed in or attached to a building or structure [250.104(A)(3)] shall be bonded to _____.

    (a) the building or structure disconnecting means enclosure where located at the building or structure
    (b) the equipment grounding conductor run with the supply conductors
    (c) one or more grounding electrodes used
    (d) any of these

55. The grounded conductor of each separately derived system shall be bonded to the nearest available point of the metal water piping system(s) in the area served by each separately derived system and each bonding jumper shall be sized in accordance with Table 250.102(C)(1) based on the largest ungrounded conductor of the separately derived system.

    (a) True
    (b) False

56. A separate water piping bonding jumper shall be required if the metal frame of a building or structure is used as the grounding electrode for a separately derived system and is bonded to the metal water piping in the area served by the separately derived system.

    (a) True
    (b) False

57. Listed FMC can be used as the equipment grounding conductor if the conduit does not exceed trade size _____.

    (a) 1¼
    (b) 1½
    (c) 2
    (d) 2¼

58. The armor of Type AC cable is recognized by the *NEC* as an equipment grounding conductor.

    (a) True
    (b) False

59. A(n) _____ shall be used to connect the grounding terminal of a grounding-type receptacle to a metal box that is connected to an equipment grounding conductor.

    (a) equipment bonding jumper
    (b) grounded conductor jumper
    (c) equipment bonding jumper or grounded conductor jumper
    (d) equipment bonding jumper and grounded conductor jumper

60. A listed expansion/deflection fitting or other approved means shall be used where a raceway crosses a _____ intended for expansion, contraction or deflection used in buildings, bridges, parking garages, or other structures.

    (a) junction box
    (b) structural joint
    (c) cable tray
    (d) unistrut hanger

61. The interior of underground raceways shall be considered a _____ location.

    (a) wet
    (b) dry
    (c) damp
    (d) corrosive

62. Raceways, cable assemblies, boxes, cabinets, and fittings shall be securely fastened in place.

    (a) True
    (b) False

63. Where independent support wires of a suspended ceiling assembly are used to support raceways, cable assemblies, or boxes above a ceiling, they shall be secured at _____ end(s).

    (a) one
    (b) both
    (c) the line and load
    (d) at the attachment to the structural member

64. In general, where installed in raceways, conductors _____ and larger shall be stranded.

    (a) 2 AWG
    (b) 4 AWG
    (c) 6 AWG
    (d) 8 AWG

65. Parallel conductors shall have the same _____.

    (a) length
    (b) material
    (c) size in circular mil area
    (d) all of these

66. Article _____ covers the installation and construction specifications of cabinets, cutout boxes, and meter socket enclosures.

    (a) 300
    (b) 310
    (c) 312
    (d) 314

67. Nonmetallic-sheathed cables can enter the top of surface-mounted cabinets, cutout boxes, and meter socket enclosures through nonflexible raceways not less than 18 in. and not more than _____ in length if all of the required conditions are met.

    (a) 3 ft
    (b) 10 ft
    (c) 25 ft
    (d) 100 ft

68. Where internal _____ means are provided between all entries, nonmetallic boxes shall be permitted to be used with metal raceways or metal-armored cables.

    (a) grounding
    (b) bonding
    (c) connecting
    (d) splicing

69. Type MC cable installed through, or parallel to, framing members shall be protected against physical damage from penetration by screws or nails by 1¼ in. separation or protected by a suitable metal plate.

    (a) True
    (b) False

70. Type MC cable containing four or fewer conductors, sized no larger than 10 AWG, shall be secured within _____ of every box, cabinet, fitting, or other cable termination.

    (a) 8 in.
    (b) 12 in.
    (c) 18 in.
    (d) 24 in.

71. Type NM cable on a wall of an unfinished basement installed in a listed raceway shall have a _____ installed at the point where the cable enters the raceway.

    (a) suitable insulating bushing or adapter
    (b) sealing fitting
    (c) bonding bushing
    (d) junction box

72. Type _____ cable is a single conductor or multiconductor cable identified for use as underground service-entrance cable.

    (a) SE
    (b) NM
    (c) UF
    (d) USE

73. Types SE and USE cables and associated fittings shall be _____.

    (a) identified
    (b) approved
    (c) listed
    (d) labeled

74. Running threads shall not be used on IMC for connection at couplings.

    (a) True
    (b) False

75. Horizontal runs of RMC supported by openings through _____ at intervals not exceeding 10 ft and securely fastened within 3 ft of termination points shall be permitted.

    (a) walls
    (b) trusses
    (c) rafters
    (d) framing members

76. Where RMC enters a box, fitting, or other enclosure, _____ shall be provided to protect the wire from abrasion, unless the design of the box, fitting, or enclosure affords equivalent protection.

    (a) a bushing
    (b) duct seal
    (c) electrical tape
    (d) seal fittings

77. Flexible metal conduit shall be securely fastened by a means approved by the authority having jurisdiction within _____ of termination.

    (a) 6 in.
    (b) 10 in.
    (c) 1 ft
    (d) 10 ft

78. Where used to secure or support LFNC, cable ties shall be _____ for the application.

    (a) listed
    (b) labeled
    (c) marked
    (d) approved

79. EMT run between termination points shall be securely fastened within _____ of each outlet box, junction box, device box, cabinet, conduit body, or other tubing termination.

    (a) 12 in
    (b) 18 in
    (c) 2 ft
    (d) 3 ft

80. When a building is supplied with a fire sprinkler system, ENT can be installed above any suspended ceiling.

    (a) True
    (b) False

81. Unbroken lengths of electric nonmetallic tubing shall not be required to be secured where fished between access points for _____ work in finished buildings or structures and securing is impractical.

    (a) concealed
    (b) exposed
    (c) hazardous
    (d) completed

82. A box is not required where conductors or cables in cable tray transition to a raceway wiring method from a cable tray.

    (a) True
    (b) False

83. Article 400 covers general requirements, applications, and construction specifications for flexible cords and flexible cables.

    (a) True
    (b) False

84. The ampacities of flexible cords and flexible cables are found in _____.

    (a) Table 310.16
    (b) Tables 400.5(A)(1) and (A)(2)
    (c) Chapter 9, Table 1
    (d) Table 430.52

85. Switches shall not be installed within tubs or shower spaces unless installed as part of a listed tub or shower assembly.

    (a) True
    (b) False

86. When replacing a nongrounding-type receptacle where attachment to an equipment grounding conductor does not exist in the receptacle enclosure, a _____ can be used as the replacement.

    (a) nongrounding-type receptacle
    (b) grounding receptacle
    (c) GFCI-type receptacle marked "No Equipment Ground"
    (d) nongrounding-type receptacle or a GFCI-type receptacle marked "No Equipment Ground"

87. Receptacles mounted in boxes set back from the finished surface shall be installed so that the mounting _____ of the receptacle is held rigidly at the finished surface.

    (a) screws
    (b) yoke or strap
    (c) cover plate
    (d) grounding clip

88. In dwelling units, all nonlocking type 125V and 250V, 15A and 20A receptacles installed _____ shall be listed as tamper resistant.

    (a) in bedrooms
    (b) outdoors, at grade level
    (c) above counter tops
    (d) in all areas specified in 210.52 and 550.13

89. The *NEC* allows a lighting outlet on the wall in a clothes closet when it is at least 6 in. away from storage space.

    (a) True
    (b) False

90. Luminaires attached to the framing members of a suspended ceiling shall be secured to the framing member(s) by mechanical means such as _____.

    (a) bolts
    (b) screws
    (c) rivets
    (d) any of these

91. For existing installed luminaires without disconnecting means in indoor locations, other than dwellings and associated accessory structures, a disconnecting means _____ in fluorescent luminaires that utilize double-ended lamps (typical fluorescent lamps) at the time a ballast is replaced.

    (a) shall be installed
    (b) is not required to be added
    (c) shall not be installed
    (d) can be a screw terminal

92. Article 411 covers lighting systems and their associated components operating at no more than _____ ac or _____ dc.

    (a) 15V, 30V
    (b) 30V, 60V
    (c) 60V, 125V
    (d) 125V, 250V

93. If a branch circuit supplies a single nonmotor-operated appliance, the rating of overcurrent protection shall not exceed _____ percent of the appliance rated current if the overcurrent protection rating is not marked and the appliance is rated over 13.30A.

    (a) 100
    (b) 125
    (c) 150
    (d) 160

94. The branch-circuit overcurrent device and conductors for fixed storage-type water heaters that have a capacity of 120 gal or less shall be sized not smaller than _____ percent of the rating of the water heater.

    (a) 80%
    (b) 115%
    (c) 125%
    (d) 150%

95. Wall-mounted ovens and counter-mounted cooking units shall be permitted to be connected with a flexible cord identified as _____ for the purpose.

    (a) listed
    (b) manufactured
    (c) suitable
    (d) sufficient

96. Article _____ covers fixed electric equipment used for space heating including heating cables, unit heaters, boilers, central heating systems, or other fixed electric space-heating equipment.

    (a) 410
    (b) 422
    (c) 424
    (d) 440

97. Ground-fault circuit-interrupter protection for personnel shall be provided for cables installed in electrically heated floors of _____.

    (a) bathrooms
    (b) hydromassage bathtub locations
    (c) kitchens
    (d) all of these

98. Where the motor short-circuit and ground-fault protection devices determined by Table 430.52 do not correspond to the standard sizes or ratings, a higher rating that does not exceed the next higher standard ampere rating shall be permitted.

    (a) True
    (b) False

99. The ampacity of the conductors from the generator output terminals to the first distribution device(s) containing overcurrent protection shall not be less than _____ percent of the nameplate current rating of the generator.

    (a) 75
    (b) 115
    (c) 125
    (d) 140

100. Conductors are commonly _____ to eliminate stress on storage battery terminations.

    (a) prefabricated
    (b) pre-insulated
    (c) preformed
    (d) pre-evaluated

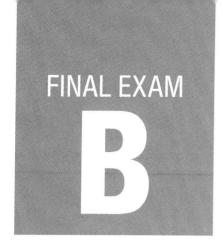

RANDOM ORDER

1. A run of IMC shall not contain more than the equivalent of _____ quarter bend(s) between pull points such as conduit bodies and boxes.

   (a) one
   (b) two
   (c) three
   (d) four

2. Electrical equipment secured to and in _____ contact with a metal rack or structure provided for its support shall be permitted to be considered as being connected to an equipment grounding conductor if the metal rack or structure is connected to an equipment grounding conductor by one of the means indicated in 250.134.

   (a) electrical
   (b) direct
   (c) metal to metal
   (d) mechanical

3. Exposed structural metal interconnected to form a metal building frame that is not intentionally grounded or bonded and is likely to become energized, shall be bonded to the _____.

   (a) service equipment enclosure or building disconnecting means
   (b) grounded conductor at the service
   (c) grounding electrode conductor where of sufficient size
   (d) any of these

4. A branch-circuit overcurrent device can serve as the disconnecting means for a stationary motor of ⅛ hp or less.

   (a) True
   (b) False

5. Rod and pipe grounding electrodes shall not be less than _____ in length.

   (a) 6 ft
   (b) 8 ft
   (c) 10 ft
   (d) 20 ft

6. The required number of receptacle outlets on fixed walls in meeting rooms shall be determined in accordance with _____.

   (a) 210.52(A)(1)
   (b) 210.52(A)(1) and (A)(2)
   (c) 210.52(A)(1) through (A)(3)
   (d) 210.52(A)(1) through (A)(4)

7. Overhead service-entrance cables shall be equipped with a _____.

   (a) raceway
   (b) service head
   (c) cover
   (d) all of these

8. Unless specifically permitted in 400.10, flexible cords, flexible cables, and cord sets, and power-supply cords shall not be used where subject to physical damage.

   (a) True
   (b) False

9. Outside secondary conductors can be of unlimited length without overcurrent protection at the point they receive their supply if the conductors _____.

   (a) are protected from physical damage
   (b) terminate at a single overcurrent device equal to or less than their ampacity
   (c) the overcurrent device is part of the building disconnect
   (d) all of these

10. One or more 120-volt, 15-ampere branch circuit shall be provided to supply bathroom(s) receptacle outlet(s) required by 210.52(D).

    (a) True
    (b) False

11. The grounding of electrical systems, circuit conductors, surge arresters, surge-protective devices, and conductive normally noncurrent-carrying metal parts of equipment shall be installed and arranged in a manner that will prevent objectionable current.

    (a) True
    (b) False

12. Where Type LFNC conduit is installed in lengths exceeding _____ ft, the conduit shall be securely fastened at intervals not exceeding 3 ft and within 12 in. on each side of every outlet box, junction box, cabinet, or fitting.

    (a) 2 ft
    (b) 3 ft
    (c) 6 ft
    (d) 10 ft

13. The number of conductors permitted in LFNC shall not exceed the percentage fill specified in _____.

    (a) Chapter 9, Table 1
    (b) Table 250.66
    (c) Table 310.16
    (d) 240.6

14. Type MC cable shall not be used under which of the following conditions?

    (a) Where subject to physical damage.
    (b) Direct buried in the earth or embedded in concrete unless identified for direct burial.
    (c) Exposed to cinder fills, strong chlorides, caustic alkalis, or vapors of chlorine or of hydrochloric acids.
    (d) all of these

15. Type AC cable installed horizontally through wooden or metal framing members is considered supported where support does not exceed _____ intervals.

    (a) 2 ft.
    (b) 3 ft.
    (c) 4½ ft.
    (d) 6 ft.

16. A branch circuit that supplies only one utilization equipment is a(n) _____ branch circuit.

    (a) individual
    (b) general-purpose
    (c) isolated
    (d) special-purpose

17. Bends in PVC conduit shall _____ between pull points.

    (a) not be made
    (b) not be limited in degrees
    (c) be limited to 360 degrees
    (d) be limited to 180 degrees

18. Unused openings other than those intended for the operation of equipment, intended for mounting purposes, or permitted as part of the design for listed equipment shall be _____.

    (a) filled with cable clamps or connectors only
    (b) taped over with electrical tape
    (c) repaired only by welding or brazing in a metal slug
    (d) closed to afford protection substantially equivalent to the wall of the equipment

19. Raceways shall be provided with expansion, expansion-deflection, or deflection fittings where necessary to compensate for thermal expansion, deflection, and contraction.

    (a) True
    (b) False

20. Flexible cord shall only be permitted when provided as part of listed lighting equipment identified for horticultural use for _____.

    (a) connecting a horticultural lighting luminaire directly to a branch circuit outlet
    (b) interconnecting horticultural lighting luminaires
    (c) connecting a horticultural lighting luminaire to a remote power source
    (d) any of these

21. As applied to electrical equipment, the term reconditioned may be interchangeable with the term_____.

    (a) rebuilt
    (b) refurbished
    (c) remanufactured
    (d) any of these

22. PVC conduit shall be securely fastened within _____ in. of each box.

    (a) 6
    (b) 12
    (c) 24
    (d) 36

23. Cable tray systems shall not have mechanically discontinuous segments between cable tray runs or between cable tray runs and equipment.

    (a) True
    (b) False

24. When armored cable is run parallel to the sides of rafters, studs, or floor joists in an accessible attic, the cable shall be protected with running boards.

    (a) True
    (b) False

25. Where practicable, rod, pipe, and plate electrodes shall be installed _____.

    (a) directly below the electrical meter
    (b) on the north side of the building
    (c) below permanent moisture level
    (d) all of these

26. A system or circuit conductor that is intentionally grounded is called a(an) "_____."

    (a) grounding conductor
    (b) unidentified conductor
    (c) grounded conductor
    (d) grounding electrode conductor

27. In an ac system, if the size of the grounding electrode conductor or bonding jumper connected to a concrete-encased electrode does not extend on to other types of electrodes that require a larger size of conductor, the grounding electrode conductor shall not be required to be larger than _____ AWG copper.

    (a) 10
    (b) 8
    (c) 6
    (d) 4

28. An outlet box or enclosure mounted on a building or other surface shall be _____.

    (a) rigidly and securely fastened in place
    (b) supported by cables that protrude from the box
    (c) supported by cable entries from the top and permitted to rest against the supporting surface
    (d) permitted to be supported by the raceway(s) terminating at the box

29. Where bonding jumper(s) are used to connect the grounding electrodes together to form the grounding electrode system, rebar is permitted to be used as a conductor to interconnect the electrodes.

    (a) True
    (b) False

30. A permanently connected surge-protective device (SPD) intended for installation on the load side of the service disconnect overcurrent device, including SPDs located at the branch panel, is a Type _____ SPD.

    (a) 1
    (b) 2
    (c) 3
    (d) 4

31. The working space in front of the electric equipment shall not be less than _____ in. wide, or the width of the equipment, whichever is greater.

    (a) 15
    (b) 30
    (c) 40
    (d) 60

32. Where practicable, contact of dissimilar metals shall be avoided in an IMC raceway installation to prevent the possibility of _____.

    (a) corrosion
    (b) galvanic action
    (c) short circuits
    (d) ground faults

33. A service disconnecting means shall not be installed in bathrooms.

    (a) True
    (b) False

34. Product testing, evaluation, and listing (product certification) shall be performed by _____.

    (a) recognized qualified electrical testing laboratories
    (b) the manufacturer
    (c) qualified person
    (d) electrical engineer

35. A feeder supplying fixed motor load(s) shall have a protective device with a rating or setting _____ branch-circuit short-circuit and ground-fault protective device for any motor in the group, plus the sum of the full-load currents of the other motors of the group.

    (a) not greater than the largest rating or setting of the
    (b) 125 percent of the largest rating of any
    (c) equal to the largest rating of any
    (d) at least 80% of the

36. Molded-case circuit breakers are permitted to be reconditioned.

    (a) True
    (b) False

37. Where direct-buried conductors and cables emerge from grade, they shall be protected by enclosures or raceways to a point at least _____ above finished grade.

    (a) 3 ft
    (b) 6 ft
    (c) 8 ft
    (d) 10 ft

38. Each direct-buried single conductor cable shall be located _____ in the trench to the other single conductor cables in the same parallel set of conductors, including equipment grounding conductors.

    (a) perpendicular
    (b) bundled together
    (c) in close proximity
    (d) spaced apart

39. Snap switches, dimmers, and control switches are considered to be part of the effective ground-fault current path when _____.

    (a) the switch is connected to the intersystem bonding termination
    (b) the switch is mounted with metal screws to a metal box or a metal cover that is connected to an equipment grounding conductor
    (c) an equipment grounding conductor or equipment bonding jumper is connected to the equipment grounding termination of the snap switch
    (d) the switch is mounted with metal screws to a metal box or a metal cover that is connected to an equipment grounding conductor or an equipment grounding conductor or equipment bonding jumper is connected to the equipment grounding termination of the snap switch

40. Raceways shall be _____ between outlet, junction, or splicing points prior to the installation of conductors.

    (a) installed complete
    (b) tested for ground faults
    (c) a minimum of 80 percent complete
    (d) torqued

41. The radius of the curve of the inner edge of any bend during or after installation of Type NM cable, shall not be less than _____ times the diameter of the cable.

    (a) 5
    (b) 6
    (c) 7
    (d) 8

42. Where a panelboard is supplied through a transformer, the overcurrent protection shall be located _____.

    (a) at the main distribution panel
    (b) on the primary side of the transformer
    (c) on the secondary side of the transformer
    (d) on either the primary or secondary side of the transformer

43. Two or more _____ small-appliance branch circuits shall be provided to supply power for receptacle outlets in the dwelling unit kitchen, dining room, breakfast room, pantry, or similar dining areas.

    (a) 15A
    (b) 20A
    (c) auxiliary
    (d) supplemental

44. All _____ shall be provided with covers compatible with the box or conduit body construction and suitable for the conditions of use.

    (a) pull boxes
    (b) junction boxes
    (c) conduit bodies
    (d) all of these

45. Direct-buried conductors, cables, or raceways, which are subject to movement by settlement or frost, shall be arranged to prevent damage to the _____ or to equipment connected to the raceways.

    (a) siding of the building mounted on
    (b) landscaping around the cable or raceway
    (c) enclosed conductors
    (d) expansion fitting

46. A _____ rated in amperes shall be permitted as a controller for all motors.

    (a) branch-circuit inverse time circuit breaker or molded case switch
    (b) dual-element time-delay fuse
    (c) snap switch
    (d) GFCI protected device

47. Where portions of a cable raceway or sleeve are subjected to different temperatures and condensation is known to be a problem, the _____ shall be sealed to prevent the circulation of warm air to a colder section of the raceway or sleeve.

    (a) opening
    (b) cable
    (c) space
    (d) raceway or sleeve

48. The ampacities of branch circuit conductors for appliances shall not be less than the marked rating of the _____.

    (a) receptacle outlet
    (b) appliance
    (c) over-current protection device
    (d) power cord

49. A "service drop" is defined as the overhead conductors between the utility electric supply system and the _____.

    (a) service equipment
    (b) service point
    (c) grounding electrode
    (d) equipment grounding conductor

50. The primary overcurrent protection for a transformer rated 1,000V, nominal, or less, with no secondary protection and having a primary current rating of over 9A shall be set at not more than _____ percent.

    (a) 125%
    (b) 167%
    (c) 200%
    (d) 300%

51. Luminaires installed under metal-corrugated sheet roof decking shall be installed and supported so there is not less than _____ in. measured from the lowest surface of the roof decking to the top of the luminaire.

    (a) 1 in
    (b) 1¼ in
    (c) 1½ in
    (d) 2 in

52. Surface metal raceway enclosures providing a transition from other wiring methods shall have a means for connecting a(n) _____ conductor.

    (a) grounded
    (b) ungrounded
    (c) equipment grounding
    (d) all of these

53. Information and technology equipment and systems are used for creation and manipulation of _____.

    (a) data
    (b) voice
    (c) video
    (d) all of these

54. Where fuses are used as the service overcurrent device, the disconnecting means shall be located ahead of the supply side of the fuses in accordance with 230.91.

    (a) True
    (b) False

55. A surface metal raceway is a metal raceway that is intended to be mounted to the surface of a structure, with associated couplings, connectors, boxes, and fittings for the installation of electrical conductors.

(a) True
(b) False

56. Lighting track is a manufactured assembly designed to support and _____ luminaires that are capable of being readily repositioned on the track.

(a) connect
(b) protect
(c) energize
(d) all of these

57. Where a lighting outlet(s) is installed for interior stairways, there shall be a listed wall-mounted control device at each floor level and landing level that includes an entryway to control the lighting outlet(s) where the stairway between floor levels has six risers or more unless remote, central, or automatic control is used.

(a) True
(b) False

58. The *Code* does not cover installations under the exclusive control of an electrical utility such as _____.

(a) service drops and laterals
(b) electric utility office buildings
(c) electric utility warehouses
(d) electric utility garages

59. A multiwire branch circuit consists of _____.

(a) two or more ungrounded conductors that have a voltage between them
(b) a grounded conductor that has equal voltage between it and each ungrounded conductor of the circuit
(c) a grounded conductor connected to the neutral or grounded conductor of the system
(d) all of these

60. Conductors, splices, or terminations in a handhole enclosure shall be listed as suitable for _____.

(a) wet locations
(b) damp locations
(c) direct burial in the earth
(d) exterior use

61. Underground service conductors shall have _____.

(a) adequate mechanical strength
(b) sufficient ampacity for the loads calculated
(c) 90°C insulation rating
(d) adequate mechanical strength and sufficient ampacity for the loads calculated

62. As defined by 230.95, the rating of the service disconnect shall be considered to be the rating of the largest _____ that can be installed or the highest continuous current trip setting for which the actual overcurrent device installed in a circuit breaker is rated or can be adjusted.

(a) fuse
(b) circuit
(c) conductor
(d) all of these

63. Where conductors in parallel are run in separate raceways, the raceways shall have the same electrical characteristics.

(a) True
(b) False

64. The distance between horizontal supports of metal wireways shall not exceed _____.

(a) 6 ft
(b) 8 ft
(c) 10 ft
(d) 15 ft

65. A single receptacle is a single contact device with no other contact device on the same _____.

(a) circuit
(b) yoke
(c) run
(d) equipment

66. At the time of installation, grounded conductors _____ or larger can be identified by distinctive white or gray markings at their terminations.

(a) 10 AWG
(b) 8 AWG
(c) 6 AWG
(d) 4 AWG

67. For circuits rated 100A or less, when the equipment terminals are listed for use with 75°C conductors, the _____ column of Table 310.16 shall be used to determine the ampacity of THHN conductors.

    (a) 30°C
    (b) 60°C
    (c) 75°C
    (d) 90°C

68. By definition, an attachment fitting is different from an attachment plug because no _____ is associated with the fitting.

    (a) cable
    (b) fixture wire
    (c) cord
    (d) wiring compartment

69. Securing or supporting of LFNC is not required where installed in lengths not exceeding _____ from the last point where the raceway is securely fastened for connections within an accessible ceiling to a luminaire(s) or other equipment.

    (a) 3 ft
    (b) 6 ft
    (c) 8 ft
    (d) 10 ft

70. Three-way and four-way switches shall be wired so that all switching is done only in the _____ circuit conductor.

    (a) ungrounded
    (b) grounded
    (c) equipment ground
    (d) neutral

71. Article _____ covers the rating, type, and installation of receptacles, cord connectors, and attachment plugs (cord caps).

    (a) 400
    (b) 404
    (c) 406
    (d) 408

72. At least one receptacle outlet shall be located within _____ of the outer end of a peninsular countertop or work surface.

    (a) 1 ft
    (b) 2 ft
    (c) 3 ft
    (d) 4 ft

73. Grounding electrode conductors or supply-side bonding jumpers or conductors shall not be permitted within raceways containing service conductors.

    (a) True
    (b) False

74. FMC shall be supported and secured _____.

    (a) at intervals not exceeding 4½ ft
    (b) within 8 in. on each side of a box where fished
    (c) where fished
    (d) at intervals not exceeding 6 ft

75. A "_____" is a device or group of devices that govern, in some predetermined manner, the electric power delivered to the apparatus to which it is connected.

    (a) relay
    (b) breaker
    (c) transformer
    (d) controller

76. At least one lighting outlet controlled by a listed wall-mounted control device shall be installed in every habitable room, kitchen, and bathroom of a dwelling unit.

    (a) True
    (b) False

77. For one- and two-family dwelling units, all service conductors shall terminate in an emergency disconnecting means having a short-circuit current rating equal to or greater than the _____, installed in a readily accessible outdoor location.

    (a) demand load
    (b) peak demand load
    (c) available fault current
    (d) service conductor rating

78. Closet storage space is defined as a volume bounded by the sides and back closet walls extending from the closet floor vertically to a height of _____ ft or the highest clothes-hanging rod at a horizontal distance of 2 ft from the sides and back of the closet walls.

    (a) 6
    (b) 7
    (c) 8
    (d) 9

79. For a separate building or structure supplied by a separately derived system when overcurrent protection is not provided for the supply conductors to the building/structure as permitted by 240.21(C)(4), the installation shall be _____ in accordance with 250.30(A).

    (a) AFCI protected
    (b) grounded and bonded
    (c) isolated
    (d) all of these

80. A motor can be provided with combined overcurrent protection using a single protective device to provide branch-circuit _____ protection where the rating of the device provides the overload protection specified in 430.32.

    (a) short-circuit
    (b) ground-fault
    (c) motor overload
    (d) all of these

81. NFPA 70E, *Standard for Electrical Safety in the Workplace*, provides guidance, such as determining severity of potential exposure, planning safe work practices, arc-flash labeling, and selecting _____.

    (a) personal protective equipment
    (b) coordinated overcurrent protective devices
    (c) emergency egress plans
    (d) fire suppression systems

82. The minimum working space on a circuit for equipment operating at 750 volts-to-ground, with exposed live parts on one side and grounded parts on the other side of the working space, is _____.

    (a) 1 ft
    (b) 3 ft
    (c) 4 ft
    (d) 6 ft

83. Nonlocking 15A and 20A, 125V and 250V receptacles installed in damp locations shall be listed as _____.

    (a) raintight
    (b) watertight
    (c) weatherproof
    (d) weather resistant

84. "Within sight from" means visible and not more than _____ ft distant from the equipment.

    (a) 10
    (b) 20
    (c) 25
    (d) 50

85. Each motor used in a continuous duty application and rated more than 1 hp shall be protected against overload by a separate overload device that is responsive to motor current. The overload device for motors with a marked temperature rise 40°C or less, shall be rated at no more than _____ percent of the motor nameplate full-load current rating.

    (a) 80
    (b) 115
    (c) 125
    (d) 175

86. Wiring shall be installed so that the completed system will be free from _____, other than as required or permitted elsewhere in the *Code*.

    (a) short circuits
    (b) ground faults
    (c) connections to the earth
    (d) all of these

87. The minimum clearance for overhead service conductors not exceeding 1,000V that pass over parking areas subject to truck traffic is _____ ft.

    (a) 10
    (b) 12
    (c) 15
    (d) 18

88. "Nonautomatic" is defined as requiring _____ to perform a function.

    (a) protection from damage
    (b) human intervention
    (c) mechanical linkage
    (d) all of these

89. Alternating-current circuits of less than 50V shall be grounded if supplied by a transformer whose supply system exceeds 150 volts-to-ground.

    (a) True
    (b) False

90. A Type 2 surge protective device is permitted to be connected on either the line or load side of the service equipment.

    (a) True
    (b) False

91. Article 411 covers lighting systems and their associated components operating at no more than _____ ac or _____ dc where wet contact is likely to occur.

    (a) 15V, 30V
    (b) 30V, 60V
    (c) 60V, 125V
    (d) 125V, 250V

92. The bonding jumper(s) required for the metal water piping system(s) installed in or attached to a building or structure supplied by a feeder(s) or branch circuit(s) shall be sized in accordance with _____.

    (a) 250.66
    (b) 250.102(D)
    (c) 250.122
    (d) 310.16

93. If a 20A branch circuit supplies multiple receptacles, the receptacles shall have an ampere rating of no less than _____.

    (a) 10A
    (b) 15A
    (c) 20A
    (d) 30A

94. Two or more common grounding electrodes that are bonded together shall be considered as a single grounding electrode system in this sense.

    (a) True
    (b) False

95. Where nails or screws are likely to penetrate nonmetallic-sheathed cable or ENT installed through metal framing members, a steel sleeve, steel plate, or steel clip not less than _____ in thickness shall be used to protect the cable or tubing.

    (a) $\frac{1}{16}$ in.
    (b) $\frac{1}{8}$ in.
    (c) $\frac{1}{2}$ in.
    (d) $\frac{3}{4}$ in.

96. Type NM cables shall not be used in one- and two-family dwellings exceeding three floors above grade.

    (a) True
    (b) False

97. The conductors connected to the alternating-current output of an inverter are known as the _____.

    (a) bipolar photovoltaic array
    (b) monopole subarray
    (c) emergency standby power
    (d) inverter output circuit

98. Swimming pool structures and structural _____ [680.26(B)(1) and (B)(2)] shall not be used as a grounding electrode.

    (a) reinforcing steel
    (b) equipotential planes
    (c) pool shells
    (d) pool pump houses

99. For permanently connected motor-operated appliances with motors rated over _____, a switch or circuit breaker located within sight from the motor-operated appliance or be capable of being locked in the open position in compliance with 110.25, can serve as the appliance disconnect.

    (a) $\frac{1}{8}$ hp
    (b) $\frac{1}{4}$ hp
    (c) 15A
    (d) 1 kW

100. Equipment and devices shall only be permitted within ducts or plenum chambers specifically fabricated to transport environmental air if necessary for their direct action upon, or sensing of, the _____.

    (a) contained air
    (b) air quality
    (c) air temperature
    (d) humidity

ABOUT THE AUTHOR

Mike Holt—Author

Founder and President
Mike Holt Enterprises
Groveland, Florida

Mike Holt is an author, businessman, educator, speaker, publisher and *National Electrical Code* expert. He has written hundreds of electrical training books and articles, founded three successful businesses, and has taught thousands of electrical *Code* seminars across the US and internationally. His company, Mike Holt Enterprises, has been serving the electrical industry for over 40 years, creating and publishing books, videos, online training, and curriculum support for electrical trainers, students, organizations, and electrical professionals. His devotion to the trade, coupled with the lessons he learned at the University of Miami's MBA program, have helped him build one of the largest electrical training and publishing companies in the United States.

Mike is committed to changing lives and helping people take their careers to the next level. He has always felt a responsibility to provide education beyond the scope of just passing an exam. He draws on his previous experience as an electrician, inspector, contractor and instructor, to guide him in developing powerful training solutions that electricians understand and enjoy. He is always mindful of how hard learning can be for students who are intimidated by school, by their feelings towards learning, or by the complexity of the *NEC*. He's mastered the art of simplifying and clarifying complicated technical concepts and his extensive use of illustrations helps students apply the content and relate the material to their work in the field. His ability to take the intimidation out of learning is reflected in the successful careers of his students.

Mike has dedicated his career to studying and understanding the *National Electrical Code* and finding the easiest way to share that knowledge with others. He has taught over 1,000 classes on over 40 different electrical related subjects to hundreds of thousands of students. His dynamic presentation style, deep understanding of the trade, and ability to connect with students explains his unique position as one of the top educators in the country.

Mike's commitment to pushing boundaries and setting high standards extends into his personal life as well. He's an eight-time Overall National Barefoot Waterski Champion. Mike has more than 20 gold medals, many national records, and has competed in three World Barefoot Tournaments. In 2015, at the tender age of 64, he started a new adventure—competitive mountain bike racing. Every day he continues to find ways to motivate himself, both mentally and physically.

Mike and his wife, Linda, reside in New Mexico and Florida, and are the parents of seven children and six grandchildren. As his life has changed over the years, a few things have remained constant: his commitment to God, his love for his family, and doing what he can to change the lives of others through his products and seminars.

Special Acknowledgments

My Family. First, I want to thank God for my godly wife who's always by my side and also for my children.

My Staff. A personal thank you goes to my team at Mike Holt Enterprises for all the work they do to help me with my mission of changing peoples' lives through education. They work tirelessly to ensure that in addition to our products meet and exceed the educational needs of our customers, we stay committed to building life-long relationships throughout their electrical careers.

The National Fire Protection Association. A special thank you must be given to the staff at the National Fire Protection Association (NFPA), publishers of the *NEC*—in particular, Jeff Sargent for his assistance in answering my many *Code* questions over the years. Jeff, you're a "first class" guy, and I admire your dedication and commitment to helping others understand the *NEC*. Other former NFPA staff members I would like to thank include John Caloggero, Joe Ross, and Dick Murray for their help in the past.

ABOUT THE ILLUSTRATOR

Mike Culbreath—Illustrator

Mike Culbreath
Graphic Illustrator
Alden, Michigan

Mike Culbreath has devoted his career to the electrical industry and worked his way up from apprentice electrician to master electrician. He started working in the electrical field doing residential and light commercial construction, and later did service work and custom electrical installations. While working as a journeyman electrician, he suffered a serious on-the-job knee injury. As part of his rehabilitation, Mike completed courses at Mike Holt Enterprises, and then passed the exam to receive his Master Electrician's license. In 1986, with a keen interest in continuing education for electricians, he joined the staff to update material and began illustrating Mike Holt's textbooks and magazine articles.

Mike started with simple hand-drawn diagrams and cut-and-paste graphics. Frustrated by the limitations of that style of illustrating, he took a company computer home to learn how to operate some basic computer graphics software. Realizing that computer graphics offered a lot of flexibility for creating illustrations, Mike took every computer graphics class and seminar he could to help develop his skills. He's worked as an illustrator and editor with the company for over 30 years and, as Mike Holt has proudly acknowledged, has helped to transform his words and visions into lifelike graphics.

Originally from south Florida, Mike now lives in northern lower Michigan where he enjoys hiking, kayaking, photography, gardening, and cooking; but his real passion is his horses. He also loves spending time with his children Dawn and Mac and his grandchildren Jonah, Kieley, and Scarlet.

Mike Culbreath-Special Acknowledgments

I would like to thank Eric Stromberg, an electrical engineer and super geek (and I mean that in the most complimentary manner, this guy is brilliant), for helping me keep our graphics as technically correct as possible. I would also like to thank all our students for the wonderful feedback to help improve our graphics.

A special thank you goes to Cathleen Kwas for making me look good with her outstanding layout design and typesetting skills; to Toni Culbreath who proofreads all of my material; and to Dawn Babbitt who has assisted me in the production and editing of our graphics. I would also like to acknowledge Belynda Holt Pinto, our Executive Vice-President, Brian House for his input (another really brilliant guy), and the rest of the outstanding staff at Mike Holt Enterprises, for all the hard work they do to help produce and distribute these outstanding products.

And last but not least, I need to give a special thank you to Mike Holt for not firing me over 30 years ago when I "borrowed" one of his computers and took it home to begin the process of learning how to do computer illustrations. He gave me the opportunity and time needed to develop my computer graphics skills. He's been an amazing friend and mentor since I met him as a student many years ago. Thanks for believing in me and allowing me to be part of the Mike Holt Enterprises family.

ABOUT THE MIKE HOLT TEAM

There are many people who played a role in the production of this textbook. Their efforts are reflected in the quality and organization of the information contained in this textbook, and in its technical accuracy, completeness, and usability.

Technical Writing

Daniel Brian House
Master Electrician, Instructor, Vice President,
 Mike Holt Enterprises
Ocala, Florida

Brian House is Vice President of Digital and Technical Training at Mike Holt Enterprises, and a Certified Mike Holt Instructor. Starting in the 1990s Brian owned and ran a contracting firm that did everything from service work to designing energy-efficient lighting retrofits, exploring "green" biomass generators, and partnering with residential PV companies. He began teaching seminars in 2000 after joining the elite group of instructors who attended Mike Holt's Train the Trainer boot camp. Brian was personally selected for development by Mike Holt after being named as one of the top presenters in that class. He now travels around the country to teach Mike Holt seminars to groups that include electricians, instructors, the military, and engineers. His first-hand experience as an electrical contractor, along with Mike Holt's instructor training, gave him a teaching style that is practical, straightforward, and refreshing.

Brian is high-energy, with a passion for doing business the right way. He expresses his commitment to the industry and his love for its people whether he's teaching, working on books, or developing instructional programs. Brian also leads the Mike Holt Enterprises apprenticeship and digital products teams. They're creating cutting-edge training tools and partnering with apprenticeship programs nation-wide to help them take their curriculum to the next level.

Brian and his wife Carissa have shared the joy of their four children and many foster children during 22 years of marriage. When not mentoring youth at work or church, he can be found racing mountain bikes with his kids or fly fishing on Florida's Intracoastal Waterway. He's passionate about helping others and regularly engages with the youth of his community to motivate them into exploring their future.

Editorial and Production

A special thanks goes to **Toni Culbreath** for her outstanding contribution to this project. She worked tirelessly to proofread and edit this publication. Her attention to detail and her dedication is irreplaceable.

Dan Haruch is the newest member of our technical team. His skillset and general knowledge of the *NEC*, combined with his work ethic and ability to work with other members of the production team, were a major part of the successful publication of this textbook.

Many thanks to **Cathleen Kwas** who did the design, layout, and production of this textbook. Her desire to create the best possible product for our customers is greatly appreciated.

Also, thanks to **Paula Birchfield** who was the Production Coordinator for this product. She helped keep everything flowing and tied up all the loose ends. She and **Jeff Crandall** did a great job proofing the final files prior to printing.